"There are books that nimbly widen our perspective and well-being. This is one of them. Read it in the bathtub and praise God for the solace of good writing."
 —SUZANNE FINNAMORE, author of *Otherwise Engaged* and *The Zygote Chronicles*

"I started *The May Queen* and couldn't stop. This book is wonderful—deeply felt, sometimes hilarious, unflinchingly true."
 —PATRICIA VOLK, author of *Stuffed*

"Finally an anthology for people who don't like lousy anthologies. In Richesin's smart collection, a witty and charming cadre of women write about relationships, motherhood, daughterhood, work, terrible breakups, epic romances, the minutiae of everyday life, and wrangling it all while trying to live a creative life. They tackle it all, with cheek and wisdom and every essay is a winner. At turns romantic and heartbreaking, hysterical and sweet, these rants and testimonials will resonate with anyone who's ever faced a Chardonnay-fueled middle-of-the-night bout of age-induced self-reflection."
 —CHELSEA CAIN, author of *Dharma Girl* and *Confessions of a Teen Sleuth*

"The pleasure of this book is the pleasure of voyeurism. Here is a collection of choices that you did not make, or choices that you did make, neatly spread out side by side so that you can compare and contrast. In that way it's irresistible and somehow compulsively fun to read."
 —ALIX SPIEGEL, creator of The America Project
  and contributing editor to NPR's *This American Life*

"*The May Queen* is a smart, provocative exploration of women's lives in their thirties: the responsibilities, the agonies, and the joys of coming into adulthood. Whether you've reached the big 3-0 or not, the book is a great primer for the decade's dramas to come, and an extremely pleasurable substitute for *thirtysomething* reruns on TV."
 —AMY SOHN, author of *My Old Man* and *Run Catch Kiss: A Gratifying Novel*

"*The May Queen* offers fiercely emotional yet mostly upbeat chronicles of young women finding their way into lives they love, sometimes to their own real surprise. All the writers here share an unmistakable passion for creating—whether it be new art, new babies, or new selves."
 —MARGARET TALBOT, senior fellow at The New America Foundation
  and staff writer at *The New Yorker*

"This varied and thought-provoking collection asks all the right questions about what it means to be female and 'all grown-up.' If there's a common theme to *The May Queen* it's the desire for a meaningful life in a world of seemingly infinite choices."

—LUCINDA ROSENFELD, author of *What She Saw . . .* and *Why She Went Home*

"Reading *May Queen* is like being welcomed to the party you always wanted to go to. The room is filled with beautiful, smart, funny women who will tell you in sparkling, insightful prose how they've reckoned with their thirties: Children or not? How to balance family and career, dreams and realities? By the end of the evening, you'll have coaxed your own fears and regrets to sit side by side on the couch with theirs, and you'll tuck them in with tea before you turn to go out smiling into the rest of your life."

—QUINN DALTON, author of *High Strung* and *Bulletproof Girl*

"A powerful collection—by digging deep into their own life stories, these writers reach the universal stream of experience, capturing the thirties completely."

—ARIEL GORE, editor of *Hip Mama* and author of *The Traveling Death and Resurrection Show*

"Talk about engrossing. The amazingly intimate and forthright essays in *The May Queen* had me nodding my head in recognition—over and over again. Confidence and confusion, love and despair, artistic achievement and the dilemma about babies. It's all in this magnificent collection."

—MARCY DERMANSKY, author of *Twins*

The May Queen

Women on Life, Love, Work, and
Pulling It All Together in Your 30s

EDITED BY

Andrea N. Richesin

JEREMY P. TARCHER/PENGUIN

A MEMBER OF PENGUIN GROUP (USA) INC.

NEW YORK

JEREMY P. TARCHER/PENGUIN
Published by the Penguin Group
Penguin Group (USA) Inc., 375 Hudson Street, New York, New York 10014, USA • Penguin
Group (Canada), 90 Eglinton Avenue East, Suite 700, Toronto, Ontario M4P 2Y3, Canada
(a division of Pearson Penguin Canada Inc.) • Penguin Books Ltd, 80 Strand, London WC2R 0RL,
England • Penguin Ireland, 25 St Stephen's Green, Dublin 2, Ireland (a division of Penguin
Books Ltd) • Penguin Group (Australia), 250 Camberwell Road, Camberwell, Victoria 3124,
Australia (a division of Pearson Australia Group Pty Ltd) • Penguin Books India Pvt Ltd,
11 Community Centre, Panchsheel Park, New Delhi–110 017, India • Penguin Group (NZ),
Cnr Airborne and Rosedale Roads, Albany, Auckland 1310, New Zealand (a division of
Pearson New Zealand Ltd) • Penguin Books (South Africa) (Pty) Ltd,
24 Sturdee Avenue, Rosebank, Johannesburg 2196, South Africa

Penguin Books Ltd, Registered Offices: 80 Strand, London WC2R 0RL, England

Most Tarcher/Penguin books are available at special quantity discounts for bulk purchase
for sales promotions, premiums, fund-raising, and educational needs. Special books or book
excerpts also can be created to fit specific needs. For details, write Penguin Group (USA) Inc.
Special Markets, 375 Hudson Street, New York, NY 10014.

Library of Congress Cataloging-in-Publication Data

The May queen : women on life, love, work, and pulling it all together
in your 30s / edited by Andrea N. Richesin.
p. cm.
ISBN 1-58542-467-6
1. Women—Social conditions—21st century—Case studies. 2. Women—Psychology—
Case studies. 3. Women—Biography. I. Richesin, Andrea N.
HQ1111.M39   2006   2005052917
305.242'20973090511—dc22
[B]

Printed in the United States of America
1 3 5 7 9 10 8 6 4 2

BOOK DESIGN BY AMANDA DEWEY

For the most important women in my life,
who taught me what it means to be a woman:

YVONNE LINE BURLINGAME

RUTH CANTRELL RICHESIN

DEBORAH BURLINGAME RICHESIN

WENDY RICHESIN-DODD

AVA ROAN RICHESIN-DODD

OLIVIA ROSE WARWICK

So now I think my time is near. I trust it is——I know.

ALFRED, LORD TENNYSON,
"The May Queen"
The Lady of Shalott, and Other Poems

CONTENTS

INTRODUCTION   1
Andrea N. Richesin

THE DIFFERENCE BETWEEN THREE AND THIRTY   10
Ashley Warlick

35   17
Jennifer Weiner

FULL CIRCLE IN TIMES SQUARE   24
Lily Burana

A HUNGRY BALANCE   33
Julianna Baggott

CONSIDERING THE ALTERNATIVES   41
Sara Woster

MY MISSING BIOLOGICAL CLOCK   49
  Meghan Daum

BEDSORES AND COCKTAILS   58
  Heather Juergensen

SCHEHERAZADE HAS LEFT THE BUILDING   66
  Laila Lalami

WIDE AWAKE   75
  Marisa de los Santos

A RANDOM SAMPLING AGE THIRTY TO FORTY   83
  Ayun Halliday

I'M THE ONE   91
  Erin Ergenbright

RIVER LOVE SONG   103
  Tanya Donelly

WHEN HE'S JUST THAT INTO YOU   114
  Veronica Chambers

THE LATE BLOOMER   121
  Carla Kihlstedt

OF SWEETHEARTS AND SPERM BANKS   127
  Tanya Shaffer

GETTING READY   136
  Michelle Richmond

WHEN FALLING IS FLYING   147
  Deb Norton

CROSSING THE BORDER   159
   Flor Morales

HOLD YOUR APPLAUSE, PLEASE   167
   Kimberley Askew

THE ONE AND ONLY BUDDHA   175
   Samina Ali

HOW TO BE A SEDUCTRESS WITHOUT EVEN KNOWING IT   187
   Heather Chaplin

SIDE OF THE ROAD   196
   Dao Strom

HOW I SEE IT   208
   Ivy Meeropol

MILK DRESS: A NURSING SONG   217
   Erin Cressida Wilson

TO ALL THE MEN I'VE LOVED BEFORE   225
   Amanda Eyre Ward

SINGLE, MOTHER   235
   Jennifer Baumgardner

PLUS ONE, PLUS TWO, PLUS THREE   244
   Louise Jarvis Flynn

ABOUT THE CONTRIBUTORS   255

ACKNOWLEDGMENTS   265

CREDITS AND PERMISSIONS   267

The May Queen

INTRODUCTION

In the autumn of 2001, I was spending a happy afternoon exploring an exhibit in the luminous galleries of San Francisco's Legion of Honor when I came across a painting of a medieval maiden. Although to this day I have no memory of the artist, I clearly recall the inscription underneath the portrait. It was taken from Alfred Lord Tennyson's famous poem "The May Queen." As I gazed up at this golden damsel, I remembered the ancient legend of the Queen of the May—the young maiden chosen by her village to bestow blessings for an abundant harvest. It was the eve of my thirtieth birthday, and something about this image of a young woman so full of youth and vitality spoke to me. Here I was, a woman on the threshold—no longer young, but not quite old either: I was feeling that the time had come to grow up once and for all yet I still wanted to hold on to my youth for all it was worth. Thus, the ethereal May Queen, so full of purpose—she was chosen after all— became my talisman for this collection.

Facing what might ostensibly be viewed as the end of my youth, I longed for someone to offer me a glimpse of what I might expect to transpire in the decade to come. Now, at thirty-three, I see that my twenty-nine-year-old self thought the time had come to say her farewells—farewell to my younger, invincible, devil-may-care self, farewell to that endless sense of possibility. After all, it was all supposed to come together in your thirties—the relationship, the career, the family, all of it. In the end, however, I learned that while there simply wouldn't be room for all of my dreams, all was not lost, and richer and greener pastures lay ahead for me than I might ever have imagined.

So far for me, and many other women in their thirties to whom I've spoken, this time in our lives isn't nearly as scary as we feared it would be. In the end, the pieces *do* begin to fall into place, but not always at our conjuring and often not in the way we expect them to. And, despite the humorous depictions of desperate and frazzled women in their thirties on television or the silver screen of late (you'll recall our blubbering Ms. Bridget Jones, Ally McBeal, and even the femmes fatales from *Sex and the City*), the women with whom I spoke felt optimistic about this decade in their lives. As our conversations intensified, the idea for this book began to take shape: a collection of writings by women who are not just surviving but thriving in this much hyped stressfully jam-packed period in their lives. And as I began work on this book, I was literally stunned by how many women craved the opportunity to hash out their perspectives on aging now that they had finally reached their ripe old thirties. I was humbled by their passionate response. Hopefully, this collection of women's voices will be for some women nervously facing this milestone the "someone" I had been looking for as I stood on the precipice of this significant decade.

After nearly five years of compiling the essays that appear in this book, I've discovered that women of my generation have grown weary of embracing the modern-day myth of "having it all" and the reality of what this means for most women. It seems that, just as so many generations before us, we are plagued by society's often unrealistic expectations of what womanhood should be, and yet, as the beautifully written pieces in this collection attest, there is no single image of womanhood that we're striving toward—no Queen-of-the-May ideal. We are just, quite doggedly, forging our own way, creating our own new traditions. The women in this book prove that one's thirties can be a powerful time of self-discovery, of learning to trust oneself, and of realizing dreams in meaningful, sometimes surprising ways.

For many women approaching thirty, and for those well into this decade, there is the pull to reevaluate the choices they've made so far. Their priorities are beginning to change, and some find themselves coming to grips with unfulfilled expectations and grandiose childhood dreams. The desire to "pull it all together" once and for all can take on a certain urgency. All of the women in this book describe this sometimes tiring and sad, sometimes comical self-exploration as part and parcel of life in your thirties. And yet all of them have found that there is so much more to this time. In our thirties we are presented with the opportunity to take all that we have learned in our lives and dive deep into our selves to discover who we really are—and who we want to be. After all, we are still young. We can still take huge risks and make big mistakes.

This time of self-searching is also reflected in the changing demographics: women in their thirties today are waiting longer to marry and, if they so choose, have children. And, let the record stand corrected: many of us are quite happy not to date, don't want to get married, and have not even begun to think about children.

Born in the summery love days of the late sixties and early seventies and reared in the greedy eighties, we are now grown women in a new millennium. The leaders of the women's movement created a whole new world and pried it wide open for us—one rich with opportunity and myriad choices. Advertising, the media, and our parents told us we could be anyone we wanted. Yet as their daughters, we have often been—unfairly, in my opinion—considered ungrateful heirs of a generation of women who fought for our freedoms. To the contrary, the women in this book acknowledge this great debt. We were handed a multitude of choices, and with that privilege comes great responsibility, and also great personal strain. After all, we must decide what to choose, how much, and in what capacity or combination. Each contributor to this book bravely articulates her struggle to marry disparate aspects of her ever-complicated life. Their insightful observations lend their work an authority that is hard to ignore.

In these original essays, the contributors sift through their own personal notions of womanhood in their thirties and consider what they have lost, what they have gained, and what they still need to learn. Their stories are confessions from the nursery, the stripper's pole, the university enclave, the carpool lane, the movie set, the office window, the sound-check, small-town America, and Brooklyn Heights. A few of the contributors are not writers, first and foremost, by calling. Tanya Donelly, Carla Kihlstedt, and Dao Strom are also musicians and performers. Heather Juergensen, Deb Norton, and Tanya Shaffer are actors and writers. Sara Woster is a painter/writer, Ivy Meeropol is a filmmaker/writer, and Erin Cressida Wilson is a playwright and screenwriter. Despite their vast range of backgrounds and experiences, a number of common themes have emerged: a questioning of how certain decisions can affect one's path in life, the complicated legacy of seventies and eighties feminism, the often uneasy quest for romantic partnership, and confronting motherhood with all its trappings.

Many of the contributors' stories are about finding a chosen path. Sara Woster's essay is funny, perceptive, and endearing—much like her. Her sarcastic jabs at life in the Midwest barely conceal her indignation and desire to fulfill her own little-town dreams and become what she once feared most—her mother. Of course, she now recognizes and admires her mother as the strong and vital woman she has always been. Lily Burana writes brilliantly about her long-anticipated departure from the world of stripping and what it cost her in the end. In "Bedsores and Cocktails," Heather Juergensen demands that filmgoers look beyond the vapid allure of youth and follow an infinitely more old-world sensibility that defies greedy producers pandering to a teen audience. The ever-clever Jennifer Weiner offers a hilarious overview of the female plight in the nineties when women were expected to follow a man-trapping manual like *The Rules*. She wittily satirizes the notion that women need a man to make their lives complete.

Deb Norton followed her own path to self-discovery; she learned how to tap dance and swim in her quest to parody her own thirties soul-searching. Yet she finally learned how to negotiate with her guardian of Goodyville. Erin Ergenbright echoes many of the contributors' revelations when she notes, "It's frustrating to see that what I've learned in my thirties is what I've had repeated opportunity to learn in my twenties." After a torturous breakup with her boyfriend, she eschewed codependency and confronted the challenge of extricating herself from a tangled relationship—even though she had become accustomed to defining herself by her relationships with men. Kimberley Askew and Veronica Chambers are grateful for their early failed relationships, as they taught them to no longer compromise their dreams. The "journey proud" Louise Jarvis Flynn faced her fears and established roots in North Carolina with her charmed, bearded iris of a husband. In short, she planted her roots, blossomed with her son, and finally grew up. But that's her story to tell.

We tend to define power for women as admittance to a career or position that men once dominated. This also allows us to overlook the power in some traditionally feminine attributes and roles—motherhood, for instance. As Julianna Baggott explains, this is not a cultural moment when we look on mothers as particularly powerful figures. As a young mother of three, her anger grew from the perception that she was somehow less influential than her single, childless counterparts.

Motherhood emerges in varying forms as a theme in many of these essays. It is particularly moving how the contributors view their relationships with their mothers, and the compassion and insight they share about contemplating, and for some finally embracing, motherhood. "Charles breaks with day into our room," begins Marisa de los Santos's "Wide Awake," as if her son were a song for a new day, and what follows is an impassioned plea to fathom the immensity of motherhood. She chooses to become a mother, despite her depiction of the cult of motherhood or, more accurately, "how our culture tends to turn motherhood into a kind of cult, the mother-child connection into a bond of mythic proportions." Her decision to finally have children and share the mystery of owning a body that could create two "miracles" emboldens women confused by the contrast between their biological duty and preserving their creative freedoms.

The road to motherhood wasn't a smooth one for a few of the contributors. Erin Cressida Wilson's "Milk Dress: A Nursing Song," is a story of coming to motherhood just in the nick of time and discovering what being a woman means in a completely new way. After facing a miscarriage, she fully illumes the tenderness and beauty of finally sharing her life with her son. In "Of Sweethearts and Sperm Banks," Tanya Shaffer considers sperm donation as a last resort to motherhood, but in the end is surprised to discover her son's future father at the last possible moment. Samina Ali ("The One and Only Buddha") miraculously endured two brain hemorrhages during her son's birth and then conquered her dismal prognosis with a complete recovery, and now finds an even deeper appreciation for her role as a single mother. After years of working as a pro-choice activist, Jennifer Baumgardner suddenly found herself confronting the same scenario so common to the women she counseled. As a single mother, she has successfully learned how to negotiate coparenting her son with her ex.

A few of the essays also reflect the inner world and pain of motherhood, but ultimately reach a deeper understanding of loss—consider

Ashley Warlick's "The Difference Between Three and Thirty" and Dao Strom's "Side of the Road." Although Warlick discovered what we've learned, we keep learning, and "there is no finish, no pile of things we know growing taller in the corner." In her story's subtle exploration of motherhood, she delicately yet humorously unfolds a tale about her daughter and her stuffed animal, Sally the dalmatian, to illustrate the nature of loss. Like Baggott, Strom also had to deal with prejudice against young mothers, but she notes the isolation motherhood encompasses as well. As she writes, "The outside world pretty much disregards her (a mother), in fact, wanting only to view her as inexhaustibly good-natured and desireless, self-sacrificing and tireless."

Finally, Meghan Daum in her "My Missing Biological Clock" explains her choice to remain childless (a choice Peggy Orenstein termed "the last social taboo") and the stigma that society places on women for whom motherhood is not the ultimate goal. She dispels the pressure society places on women to procreate and the cruel labels ("selfish," "shallow") they apply to those who choose to forgo that particular path.

I have been consumed with the idea for this anthology from the very beginning. I was delighted to review so many compelling essays by women from various walks of life. All are passionate about their lives, and their writings are stimulating, surprising, and full of purpose. In this collection, each of the contributors reveals her secret thoughts, desires, and fears. It is this nuanced vulnerability, this ability to bare their souls that offers a refreshingly honest and insightful perspective. They form a group portrait of women in their thirties that may serve as a road map for traversing that decade and, of course, beyond.

What do I struggle with as a woman in my early thirties? The lull, the calm, the hush, the hum. I am torn between the plans I've made as a young adult and the realities of my current life. I have made my home in the San Francisco Bay Area—this land of golden live oaks that seem lit from within; steep, crumbling cliffs; dusty beaches; and blue. My childhood home is a sleepy southern town nestled in the foothills of mountains teeming with fireflies, waterfalls, and a cool, smoky haze. I've spent most of my postcollege years in Europe and San Francisco, but I remain somewhat painfully aware of an internal struggle between the urban setting I've chosen as an adult and the lush, rural landscape and impossibly beautiful family I had to leave behind. The first lines of Richard Llewellyn's *Green, Green My Valley Now* perfectly capture how I feel about leaving my childhood home: "I suppose if something big is to be felt when you leave a place you love, then something bigger it should be when you go back."

In the calm hours of early morning, before the birds begin their chittering, before my daughter, husband, and dog have risen from the dead (none of them whom you might call "morning people"), I often think about the choices I've made that have led me to this life. Unlike my husband, who likes to spend the end of his evenings in the moonlight of our backyard, reflecting on his day, I much prefer the wee morning hours for contemplation. These days have been rich with blessings. My daughter fills my days with a joy I have never known. Although many women in this collection espouse the same love for their children, I, too, am grateful for the birth of my daughter. She has released me from my vanity, my self-obsession, my fear of growing old, and, most important, she has given my life yet another purpose and passion. As she curiously and proudly waddles about our home, I follow her with the firm determination that she will grow confident and strong. She's my bunny, my goober, my baby girl, and stinker—all rolled up into this beloved child.

Yet I still wonder how my choices led to this moment, this life. In her essay, Ashley Warlick considers how we come to the place where our decisions reach a culmination of sorts. For me, that is what this collection has meant. Suddenly, somewhere in your thirties, all of the quick, sometimes hard decisions fall into place and the life you've been rehearsing for becomes the life you are living. The question then becomes: How do I learn to stop striving—learn to invoke a love of that which seems given, necessary, those things I have come to take for granted as the very air I breathe? Like the contributors, who have all struggled to arrive at this moment of acceptance, I savor these days of my life because, ultimately, our time here is precious and short. So I spend these mornings, solitary, but surrounded by my family and thankful and hopeful for the day. To borrow the poetic words of the gifted photographer Sally Mann, "I struggle with enormous discrepancies: between the reality of motherhood and the image of it, between my love for my home and the need to travel, between the varied and seductive paths of the heart. The lessons of impermanence, the occasional despair and the muse, so tenuously moored, all visit their needs upon me and I dig deeply for the spiritual utilities that restore me: my love for the place, for the one man left, for my children and friends, and the great green pulse of spring."

When I gaze devotedly at my determined one-year-old daughter, I wonder what challenges and decisions she will face in twenty-nine years. Would that she have the spunk and bravery of the women in this book as she pursues her dreams in a new world.

Andrea N. Richesin
Mill Valley, California
April 2005

The Difference Between Three and Thirty

ASHLEY WARLICK

This world is not conclusion.

EMILY DICKINSON,
No. 501

We are sitting in the doctor's office and it is time for shots. My daughter is brave but anxious. The doctor says these are the last shots she will have to have before she goes to school and something snaps in my brain like thin ice. I remember hearing that myself, remember the relief of how endlessly far away starting school seemed when I was four, how old those kids were who went to school. Now, at thirty, time folds, rushes, like I have just slipped over the edge of something and am now heading fast in the way things fall, fast through what I've been through before, only a step removed. I remember hearing what my daughter is hearing, thinking what she's thinking. I should know better now, have had all this life between then and now, have gone to school and written novels, have gotten married and had a daughter. But what goes through my head is how far off first grade is.

There is nothing to say for it except before you turn around, she will be in college. I go home, call my mom, and this is what she tells me. Her birthday, my daughter gets toys, many many toys, and a few she already has. We go to the toy store to exchange. Right as we walk in the door, she sees a ten-foot-high display of stuffed dogs. She wants one. "No," I say, and I'm distracted. They have glow-in-the-dark beetles, and henna tattoo kits, and vacuum cleaners that blow bubbles. "You have so many stuffed animals at home. Let's find something else."

And we do. We find an Eloise puzzle, a book of ballet stickers, Silly Putty, modeling clay. She picks out a game of jacks she's very excited about, which I think is awfully cool. We are reading books together these days, and I select *Charlie and the Chocolate Factory* and *The Indian in the Cupboard*. We've spent a little more than we've returned, but that's part of returning things. I'm ready to go.

She still wants the dog. A stuffed dalmatian. She's asking nicely. I take it from her hands. It has a cute face, something my mother always used to say, like that was how you judged the quality of a stuffed animal. I check the price tag, which is high. We have a garbage bag of stuffed animals in the attic that I took upstairs before a Christmas party last year and she hasn't once missed any of them.

Here is where I make my mistake: I sit down next to the ten-foot-high pile of dogs. I begin to talk about it. I am generally very good about such things. No is no, and if she wants my reasons I will give them to her, but I am the mother. She is the kid. I get to say no, and someday she will get to say no, but right now, it's my call. Vaguely, in the back of my mind, I realize the easy thing would be to stick to what I said walking in the door, but I am already sitting down. I've already started. "You know," I say, "you could get this, this, this, and this." I make a small pile of things on the floor: the puzzle, the Silly Putty, the books. "Or you could get the dalmatian."

"The dalmatian," she says.

"Look. All these things or just that one."

She is beyond this reasoning already, which is interesting. I am not always beyond this reasoning myself. She squeezes the dog next to her face like an advertisement for how stuffed dogs can change your life.

"The dalmatian," she says.

I begin, unwisely, to deal. The permutations are endless.

"This, this, this, and this," I say. "Or this, and this, and this."

"The dalmatian."

There is no whining. I am struck by the fact that she is simply being firm, being persistent, that she knows what she wants. I try sweetening the pot.

"How about this. We get all these things, and then we'll go next door to Target and you can pick out any stuffed animal you want."

"Will they have dalmatians?" she asks.

"Sure."

"Like this one?"

"Close. Yes. Sure."

She shakes her head. What she says, she says with the grace and clear logic of a woman resolved to marrying her high school sweetheart.

"Mommy, I think I'll just take this one."

"Okay. How about we get these things, we go next door, and if you don't find a stuffed animal you like, we can come back and get the dalmatian."

I am still sure I know the landscape here, that acquisition still rules the wants of a five-year-old, that she will be happy with any stuffed dog. She just needs to be presented with another option. But I feel myself slipping toward ridiculous. It's a physical thing, like blushing.

"Okay," she says. She says it brightly, puts the dog back in the pile herself, follows me to the register, and we talk about the game of jacks, the Silly Putty. It's only once we go next door that I realize she is humoring me. She goes to the stuffed animal aisle and finds a unicorn with a pink curly mane, pure five-year-old girl. She shows it to me, saying how cute, how cute, gives it a squeeze and puts it back on the shelf. I find a dalmatian, bigger than the one next door but half the price. She takes it in her arms, cooing and how soft, but then she tells me he's too big and puts him back. I show her little dogs and soft dogs and spotted dogs and then move to horses, cows, cats, jungle animals.

She compliments them all, pats their heads, but then she wants to go back and get the dalmatian.

"Are you serious?" I sound harsh. "You want to take back your ballet sticker book, your Silly Putty, your puzzle, just to get the dog."

"Yes." She is calm. I am not.

"Fine." I spin on my heel, tossing the handful of stuffed chicks back in their nest. I am angry, but mostly at myself. It comes out badly.

"Mommy," she says. "Mommy, it's okay. We can take your decision. It's okay."

But this is a worse option. I feel horrible. I feel absolutely bested by a child far more intuitive than me, and the thing of it is, I want her to make her own choices and stick with them. I want her to have exactly what she wants in life, whether it pleases the people around her or not. And it's just a dog, a stuffed dog, and I'm the one who has made this whole thing such a production, the one who has given her a decision to make. But it's like I can't stop myself. I have the realization she has played fairly, and I have lost.

We go back to the toy store and return three things for the dalmatian. I am not proud of how long it takes me to cool off. Later that night, we work a puzzle together. She tells my mother all about her new dalmatian, and says how Mommy had wanted her to get other things instead, and how I pouted when I didn't get my way. She is right, of course, and I wish I could take it all away, that it just hadn't gotten to be so important to me. And I don't know why it was important to me.

There are lots of things I want that I am beginning to realize I will never have—a clean, uncomplicated conscience, a watertight marriage. I have come to be fascinated with the messiness of desire, of mitigating circumstance, with the ways people fit themselves together, take themselves apart for each other, for want of each other, for want of some parts of each other, be it companionship, be it great sex, be it brilliant insight or common sense. A little bit is often enough, a surprisingly little bit in some cases, and I take comfort in that, that want is so adaptable, so flexible. But I am thirty. To a child, want is another thing, should be another thing, and I don't know why I've fought this fight so hard.

A week later, we take the dalmatian to the mall for dinner. Sally sits on a chair next to us while we eat and discuss the possibilities of cookies afterward. We are full, and decide to shop before dessert and it's three dressing rooms later when my daughter remembers Sally. She looks into her hands, like she has just dropped something. Why do we do that when we've forgotten something, like we carry reminders on our hands, a string around our fingers, even children? She becomes worried, a little frantic.

"We'll go back," I say. "Maybe she's waiting for us right where we left her." She's not. We go to the lost-and-found desk, where my daughter begins to cry. The woman behind the desk smiles at me, hands me a form to fill out. "I've been through that," she says, and of course she has, we all have. She means the crying child, the lost toy, but I am thinking of what my daughter is feeling, the creep of hope being dashed, the realization that somebody else has her dog, and might not give it back. I leave our name and address, and we go home.

My daughter worries about Sally in the mall, alone, at night. She scowls up her face and calls the people who took her mean, and bad. "Maybe someone will call," I say, although I doubt it. If they do, she wants me to call her at her nursery school, so she can know Sally the dalmatian is safe. I think of the ten-foot pile of Sallys at the toy store. I spend a couple of days with this one. Do I go and buy a new dalmatian, tell her the people at the mall called, that they found Sally, and everyone can be reunited? Or do I let her learn to be responsible for her things, and that there are consequences when she's not? I thought one dalmatian cost too much, and now I am thinking of buying another. But she is a child. There are only so many opportunities left in her life for me to work such magic. I don't know if it is possible to learn what it is to lose something from losing a toy, at any rate.

It has only been a few months since I stood out in the driveway with her father while he smoked a pack of cigarettes in the space of an hour. We both had the numbers of lawyers in our daybooks. It was a small thing that saved us then: we had recently met a man who shuffled his fatherhood between two separate custody situations. He lived with his son, but saw his daughter every other weekend. One week she was crawling, the next she was walking, and how do you reconcile losing that? By making someone else lose it? Neither of us could find an answer, and so we began to climb the steep ladder of compromise, the pulling of a marriage back together, not as difficult a daily process as it might seem. In fact, there were a stretch of days where we both felt strangely light, unencumbered by our time in the driveway and what might have led us there, a time where it seemed such magic as a fresh start was possible.

And so that is the thing I am struggling with these days: how what I've learned, I keep learning; how there is no finish, no pile of things I know growing taller in the corner. And time is not cumulative either, but sort of spiraling inward and outward, fast and slow. I don't know when it holds still and lets us take a look at it for what it truly is, but I suspect it's only passing. I know one thing: my mother, at my age, would have bought me the damn dalmatian.

We are at the bookstore in the evening. I have coffee, and my daughter has a tiny chocolate bundt cake she is sawing with a fork. She speaks idly, expectantly about our progress in finding Sally. It has been ten days now, but she has faith. Not once has she mentioned the prospect of a new Sally from the pile at the toy store, just hers, the original, the one. I am reading a travel guidebook, a dangerous pastime. She pulls a silver lapel pin out of her jacket pocket, a rectangular thing with horses on it, holds it in her fist up to her ear, a phone. I eavesdrop. "Yes," she says. "Yes, yes, yes." She's got her drama queen on, studying herself in the plate-glass window by our table. She rolls her eyes. She sighs heavily. "Yes."

"Who are you talking to?" I ask.

She puts the phone to her shoulder. "My boyfriend."

"Oh."

"We always talk about the same thing. Over and over. I get sick of it."

"Oh," I say. "Sure."

She puts the phone back up to her ear. "Yes, yes." She sounds, for all the world, like there is an exasperating man on the other line. She sounds, a bit, like me. I let the travel guide fall closed. I see us, weeks from now, on a plane that will cross the ocean to where her father has been living. There has been the fluster of packing, of rushing to the airport, and we will be tired, a little anxious. It has seemed so far off for so long, the way a big trip looms in the distance, a step outside your real life. She will miss school, her friends, her room, her toys, but there will be other things, for both of us.

We take off. I tell her the people from the mall called, and that they were sorry it had taken so long, and I reach into my bag at our feet and pull out Sally the dalmatian. I can see her cradling it to her face again, and I will never remember how much it cost to replace, how much it cost to buy the first time. And maybe she will lose this other Sally, on a bus, in the metro, left on a chair in a cafe halfway across the world. Maybe not, and maybe Sally will come home with us to grow grimy and old and well loved, or shuttled away in a garbage bag to the attic the next time we have a party. Maybe, years from now, my daughter will have forgotten how we were just about to leave the country and somebody found her dalmation, somebody returned her dalmation, and she was happy. But maybe she will remember.

35

JENNIFER WEINER

There is no such thing as inner peace. There is only
nervousness or death. Any attempt to prove otherwise
constitutes unacceptable behavior.

FRAN LEBOWITZ

"W hat are you working on?" my mother asks me, as I sit in my
bedroom, frowning at my laptop.

"It's an essay about turning thirty, and what I've learned as I've
gotten older," I tell her.

"Oh," she says, and thinks about it. "So, a very short piece, then."

I wish I could have told her that she was wrong. I wish that, at the
grand age of thirty-four, I could look back over my journey to thirty
and retrieve all sorts of wise lessons and memorable, pithy pieces of
advice about how best to navigate the journey into womanhood.

The regrettable truth, as my mother knows, is this: I handled my
approach to thirty with all the gravity and aplomb of a hyperactive
chipmunk on uppers. Basically, I bought every piece of propaganda,
every panic-inducing headline, every magazine article that said if you
weren't mated for life by your thirtieth birthday you were screwed,

and swallowed them down as gospel truth. I read *The Rules,* and laughed at it in public, but privately wondered if maybe the authors weren't on to something. I read Danielle Crittenden's *What Our Mothers Never Taught Us,* a conservative treatise about how marrying at twenty-three is the ideal for women's bodies and their careers, and called my then-boyfriend, Mr. Not Quite Right, and told him we were going to the chapel. The synagogue. Whatever.

I wasn't pulling my fears and rash actions out of thin air. Someday, anthropologists will look back on the literature of the 1980s and 1990s and conclude that, in a time of preterrorist peace and prosperity, American culture had nothing better to do with its time than scare its young women to death.

My generation came of age with "Free to Be . . . You and Me" playing on our Fisher-Price cassette recorders. Our moms were liberated ladies. We grew up with the drumbeat of equality throbbing in our ears. You can be anything you want! You can be an astronaut or a lawyer, our mothers told us. You can be president!

Gloria Steinem once said that the women of her generation were becoming the men their mothers had wanted to marry. Rather than yoking their fortunes to those of a doctor, a lawyer, a labor chief, feminists of the seventies were claiming these lives as their own.

This meant that women of my generation were supposed to become the men our grandmothers had wanted to marry . . . and then marry them, too.

This would not prove an easy task. Sure, we could have any job we wanted, murmured the books and the movies and the women's magazines, but getting a man would not be as simple. The statistics have long since been debunked, but I'll bet any woman born after 1962 knows it by heart: a woman over thirty-five has a greater chance of being kidnapped by terrorists than she does of getting married. Books like *The Rules, Getting to "I Do," The Care and Feeding of Husbands,* and *Women Who Love Too Much* suggested that men were a difficult breed, in need of special handling, coaxing, and ruses and camouflage. Don't tell jokes! *The Rules* warned. If he wanted humor, he'd stay home and watch Letterman! Don't call him first! Don't kiss him first! Let him pay! Giggle! Hang up the phone before he does! All of this made a certain crude kind of sense, but it flew in the face of everything our mothers, Marlo Thomas, and years and years of politically correct *Sesame Street* had taught us—that a good man will love us just for being the smart, confident creatures that we are.

The Rules was just one of a cacophony of voices telling us the secret to the great goal of the 1990s—catching and keeping a man.

Writers like Camille Paglia and Katie Roiphe said that young women had become hysterical about sex, that we'd created a contentious, politically correct culture where any contact was leached of passion and spontaneity and as stiff and mannered as a minuet: "May I touch your breast? Does your sigh signal consent?" The answer, they suggested, was to acknowledge that sex and passion were raw and animalistic and could not be contained by feminist codes of conduct. In other words, lighten up.

At the same time, books like Wendy Shalit's *A Return to Modesty,* and Crittenden's work, told us that we'd cheapened sex, that by fooling around as teenagers and by sharing confidences and college bathrooms with the boys, we'd robbed sex of its mystery. The answer, they suggested, was to forgo sex and passion until marriage (early marriage, if you believed Crittenden), to swap our flirting and miniskirts for modest dress and modest ways. In other words, cover up.

What was a girl to do? If our mothers raised us to be smart, assertive, outspoken, athletic, and ambitious, and men like women who are shy, retiring, giggly, and helpless, well . . . well, then what? Were we supposed to wear long skirts, short skirts, or maybe just a nice pantsuit? Should we shun makeup as a tool of the patriarchal oppressor (Naomi Wolf, *The Beauty Myth,* 1991), or wear makeup as a tool of feminist empowerment (Naomi Wolf, *Fire with Fire,* 1993)? Did watching pornography mean that we were embracing our sexuality or that we'd fallen victim to what male consumer culture had determined our sexuality should be?

These were confusing times, and the only message that was absolutely clear, that all the books and magazines and manuals seemed to agree on, was that you needed a man—no, not just a man, a husband—to make your life complete. You had to find love, and if you didn't find love by thirty-five, you were basically doomed to a life of dating losers and divorcés (lots of overlap there, the popular literature warned). By the time you'd landed a man your fertility would be shot, and you'd wind up a lonely, bitter, Clomid-gulping wreck with resentful stepchildren and a once-bitten, twice-shy husband, clinging to the corner office as a symbol of all you'd missed.

Plus, in my own life, I was also feeling literary pressure, the strain of trying to make it in a field that values youth and precocity more than any other line of work, except possibly competitive gymnastics (and I had breasts at eleven, so gymnastics was out). Publishers like their writers young—while they're still pretty, or at least reasonably photogenic, while the bookers at *Oprah* and the *Today Show* might conceivably be interested. There's something marvelous (or a little freaky, depending on how you look at it), about an author who's barely cleared the hurdles of adolescence putting pen to paper for four hundred pages, and youth becomes the hook upon which to hang the reviews, the newspaper interviews, the morning chat-show visits. An early success can pave the way for a long and rewarding career. But you had to strike while the iron was hot.

Publishers like their authors young, and authors, historically, have indulged them. Bret Easton Ellis and Jay McInerney had published their first books at twenty-one. Donna Tartt, Ethan Canin, and Jonathan Ames—twenties. Stephen King published *Carrie* when he was twenty-five. Erica Jong had delivered *Fear of Flying* to a breathless world at thirty-one (just over the wire, but close enough), and Philip Roth won the National Book Award for *Goodbye, Columbus* when he was all of twenty-six. In my capacity as a reporter for the *Philadelphia Inquirer,* I interviewed a young writer named Jenn Crowell, who'd turned in a remarkably polished first novel at the age of seventeen. The bar kept going higher, and I was getting older, and my twenties were starting to feel like a desperate dash, a mad sprint toward an invisible finish line. My twenties were not much fun. I spent a lot of time constructing to-do lists for my life and worrying about not making my own deadlines. By the time I was thirty, I decided, I wanted to have sold a book or a screenplay (either one would do, really). I wanted to be married, or at the very least engaged, or, barring that, in a serious relationship with an appropriate guy.

No pressure, right? Just the twin monsters of books and biology bearing down until sometimes it felt like I couldn't think, couldn't breathe, and couldn't so much as have a drink with a likely fellow without evaluating whether our future offspring would inherit his hair or mine, couldn't spend a Saturday morning relaxing with the newspaper without hopping over to my computer and putting in an hour or three on the novel I'd been laboring over since college.

In journalism, "thirty" means "the end"—a relic, historians think, of the days when news stories were sent by teletype, or maybe a vestige of the day when Associated Press reporters were expected to churn out thirty stories before their shifts were through. And my life was starting to feel much the same way. If I didn't reach the finish line by March 28, 2000, with a manuscript in one hand and an engagement ring on the other, it was all over. I might as well resign myself to a life of lonely mediocrity, and start investigating online vanity presses and travel to China.

At twenty-eight, I took stock. The situation was not promising. I had a novel reposing in a shoe box in my closet. I had a three-year relationship with a guy who lived in New Jersey that I strongly sensed was not heading toward the altar in my present lifetime. I had a family that was growing less nuclear by the day. My parents had split when I was sixteen. My father had met a woman twenty years his junior, married her when she was three months pregnant, and left her before the baby was born. Two years after that, my mother announced that she'd fallen in love with a swimming instructor named Caren. Suddenly there were dolphin figurines frolicking on the living room mantel, and a Maxwell House coffee can full of cigarette butts on the deck.

Desperate times called for desperate action. I would love to tell you that I achieved success and happiness after I'd jettisoned the myriad messages of the books, the pundits and pundettes, the magazines and talking heads, and my recurring dream of Tama Janowitz taunting me from the top of a bookshelf in the Library of Congress.

Instead, I will tell you the truth, which is this: in a moment of birthday-fueled desperation, I dumped Mr. Not Quite Right, and then, very shortly thereafter, decided that he was Mr. Absolutely Right, Mr. I Can't Live Without Him, and that I'd been a fool to let him go. I tried to undo the breakup. He, quite understandably, was not interested. Plus, he was seeing a social worker, which I took as an especial betrayal. If he wanted sweetness and empathy, I wondered, what had he been doing with me in the first place?

I was miserable in that completely clichéd way that only the victims of romantic mishaps can be miserable. Not only was I bereft, alone, loveless, forlorn, and extremely unhappy, but I couldn't even manage to be bereft, alone, et cetera, in an original fashion. Instead, I sounded like a bad Celine Dion song. At one point in the depths of my misery, I think I even began sounding slightly French Canadian. I could have been bold, I could have been coy, or vague, or direct, or shown up at his door in a French maid's costume, and it wouldn't have mattered. He didn't love me anymore. It was terrible.

I put away the manuscript I'd been laboring over for years and started to write a different story, the story of a girl who was a lot like me. And I did something important—I wrote honestly. I didn't pretty things up, or straighten out the edges. I gave my heroine a plus-size body and a messed-up family, and I gave her every doubt and insecurity that had ever plagued me. I gave her an untrustworthy fink of a boyfriend and a father who'd decided he didn't want to be a father anymore. Finally, I gave her a happy ending, even though I wasn't sure that life had one in store for me.

And then things started to fall into place. My book took me on a journey, introducing me to the most wonderful people, taking me to places I've never been. I met my fabulous agent and my wonderful editor, who are both smart and funny and absolutely passionate about words and books and writing. I met the man who would become my husband, and courted him with the manuscript (he would call to tell me how much he liked it, and I would always ask him what page he was on, because I wanted to be able to pinpoint the exact instant when he decided I was too much of a freak to keep dating). The reviews were good, the money was great, my engagement ring was stunning, and my family was stunned. I had everything I ever wanted by my thirty-first birthday . . . and all because I'd listened to *Cosmopolitan!*

In books, there can be tidy, happy endings, where all the loose ends get bundled neatly together, the good are rewarded, the wicked are punished, and everyone lives happily ever after. Real life, of course, is never that neat or simple. There are always loose ends and disappointments. Getting a book published didn't erase every trace of self-doubt that ever plagued me. Getting married didn't guarantee a happily-ever-after future. It didn't fix my family. And marriage came with its own obstacle course, not to mention the in-laws. Crashing through the finish line of thirty did not, does not, cannot guarantee a happy ending. Because no matter what thirty stands for in journalism, it isn't an ending at all.

"So what did turning thirty teach you?" my mother asks on the phone a few nights later. I thought about how I could answer. I could tell her that in a way, the pressure's off, and that there's a new set of challenges ahead. I could tell her that I feel like my twenties were a battleground I navigated, and now I've come to a clearing, and that I'm excited about what lies ahead.

Full Circle in Times Square

LILY BURANA

I love my past. I love my present. I'm not ashamed
of what I've had, and I'm not sad
because I have it no longer.

COLETTE, *The Last of Cheri*

New York City can affirm you as handily as it can erase you, and that's the blessing and curse of this town. Standing in the middle of Times Square surrounded by hysterical neon, pulsing traffic, and the crush of people is like looking into a starry night sky: you feel your significance and insignificance all at once; you're emboldened by possibility and humbled by life's grand scale. I'm in my thirties now—a sentence I thought I'd never type, at least not willingly—and long ago Times Square represented more to me than just the center of New York. It was the center of my world.

The area was a cesspool then, Times Square and all of midtown, with rows of porno theaters and trash in the streets. The air smelled of bus exhaust and burnt honey-roasted peanuts, and on summer days the spiky aroma of dried urine wafted up from the sidewalks. If you made it from the gum-and-graffiti-pocked subway platform to the street without a creep in a leather bomber jacket hissing as you ducked past, you were having a lucky day. On Forty-second Street, right between Seventh and Eighth Avenues on the south side, stood Peepland, the sleazy little peep show where, at eighteen, I made my inauspicious debut in the sex industry.

When I saw Peepland, with its glittering eye-in-the-keyhole sign staring down on Forty-second Street, I couldn't connect it to *me*. I never thought I'd work in the adult entertainment business—does anyone?—but my friend, an art student from the Midwest and peep-show veteran, dragged me in the door. An eerie Alice-through-the-looking-glass feeling reverberated throughout my entire body. I remember so much obscene neon, alarmingly hard women in cheap lingerie watching me through narrowed eyes, shuffling masses of men, gazes always cast down, popping into booths with fistfuls of tokens. I was too nice a girl to work in the porn biz, but I was also on my own in a big, costly city with no job, no money, and no particular reverence for social convention. So a peep show—with fast money, no set schedule, and no looks or fitness requirement—had its appeal. I could keep my nose ring and punky hair, and keep my own hours. Okay, I thought, I'll take it.

Was I scared? Hell, yes. Was I worried that I might be found out? Oh, sure, even though I swore my friend to secrecy. Was I wondering how this might affect me ten, twenty years later? Not really. This job, I told myself, was *temporary*. Every single hoochie-for-hire says that at the beginning, and every single one of us really, really means it.

What's it like, working in a tiny, screaming yellow booth with nothing but a pane of Plexiglas between you and a man who masturbates as you pose for five, ten, maybe twenty dollars every three minutes? Women tell me they simply can't imagine it, that stripping naked in a room with a stranger would be like entering another dimension. I tell them that that's the perfect description. And entering that strange dimension altered me in some ways. The very first day, my soul shot right out of my body, and any vulnerability was supplanted by that preexam, pre–roller coaster feeling. The minute I ducked into Peepland, I started buzzing, adrenalized and numb. The fear flew away and an overwhelming competence set in. I can do this, I said to myself. I can handle it. I can beat the system. I willed myself to become an approximation of that can-do, badass icon. I became a tough chick.

I thought I was a real New Yorker then, one of those resourceful people who do what they have to do to get ahead, no matter how unseemly. But you know what? I didn't totally hate it, the peep show. I liked the gutter glamour. I liked the other girls. And to my surprise, a cockeyed self-esteem emerged in that sweaty, lurid porn palace, and I almost liked my tough-chick self. As a young girl, I never saw myself as pretty or sexy, and certainly never thought I could make a living marketing myself as either. But at Peepland, I found that being sexy for money was easy, like resorting to a language I had studied all my life but had never dared to speak. My persona was as predictable as it was automatic: streetwise teen; cheap wig; high heels; blood red lips. My expression accommodating but hard, with breasts high and butt pushed out. Every feminine wile was at my disposal. I didn't have to be the prettiest girl or the nastiest or have the best body; I didn't even have to be nice. I could just be the punk rocker in the bargain basement lingerie who stopped in now and again to hustle for her rent money. Duke 'em in, take the cash, whip 'em out, watch him wank, feign patience while he zips up, and send him on his way. Next and over and around again. If I snapped into the role for a couple of hours, I'd have all the money I needed, like this fakey-fake hard-ass sexual image was an ATM card I could pop into the machine whenever I needed funds. Sex wasn't always power, I was discovering, but it was certainly handy currency.

I realized that everyone's got some aspect of themselves that can be sexualized and commodified—not just your genitals or your breasts, but your feet, hands, legs, hair, voice, race, class, age, intellect, imagination, kindness, anger, even your piss and shit and, by God, your spit, too. I've seen it—a man peeling off bills to have a young girl spit all over his exposed chest (I think a loogie went for about five bucks). Peepland proved that if the sex business can be degrading, it can also be oddly democratic. Whatever you're willing to sell, someone's got a wallet open, willing to buy.

Within a few years, I cleaned up and left Forty-second Street behind. I moved to San Francisco and moved up the sex industry ladder. First was a woman-owned and -operated peep show, The Lusty Lady. I got paid an hourly wage with a fringe benefit of sex-positive feminist rhetoric from the other dancers. (Hey, we fashion whatever polemic we can to justify what we do. "My body, my business" is as good as any.) Then I signed on at the notorious Mitchell Brothers O'Farrell Theater, where I learned to lap dance, groom myself to a Barbie ideal, and make fistfuls of cash. Those Peepland fives and tens sure looked paltry the night at Mitchell Brothers when one guy tipped me $2,500 in three hours. I wasn't entirely proud of being a lap dancer, but I was at least handsomely compensated. Five years after I had first crossed the threshold of a triple-X venue (wait, wasn't this job *temporary?*), I had transformed from punky New York scuzz to California corporate stripper.

Meanwhile, back East, Times Square was undergoing a metamorphosis of its own. The entire region upgraded from down-at-the-heels to Disneyfied, and the sleaze went *poof* with a touch of the fairy godmother's wand. Virtually every sex shop and porn theater and peep show shut down. Peepland was an early casualty; it disappeared in the dawning days of the 1990s. Was it voluntary closure? By mandate? A fire? I never knew. During a visit to the city, I walked down Forty-second Street one deep gray winter evening, and the facade was papered over, the eye in the keyhole plucked out. It was the first time I'd witnessed the city dramatically turning itself over, as well as a bit of my own history disappearing, and it struck me in ways I didn't expect.

My early twenties ticked past, and by twenty-five I wanted to quit working in the sex industry, even though it had provided me with the means to pay rent, travel, start a fanzine, and buy cars, jewelry, shoes, and more clothes than I could ever dream of wearing. Lap dancing was lucrative, but I was feeling over the hill. I'd already learned everything there was to learn—how to hustle tips, what to wear, which music attracted the most interest, how to flirt, flatter, and tease. Being a Live! Nude! Girl! was an act of nonstop fakery, and as much as I bought into the alterna-feminist belief that stripping was a legitimate form of self-expression, the amateur theatrics got old. Still, quitting was difficult; it took several exhausting attempts. What managed to get lost in the sexual empowerment chorus was a hard truth about the adult business: people get hooked. I'd get a straight job and quit shortly thereafter, lured back to the strip club by the temptation of "easy" money. I'd panic, imagine myself as unable to excel in the straight world, and find myself back in the club grinding against some guy's crotch in the dark (temporarily, of course!). Suddenly that can-do, get 'er done tough chick wasn't so tough. I'd found my first real vulnerability—my lack of belief in myself as something other than a cog in the porno machine. On the surface, I was a bohemian go-getter with bylines and goals and friends and connections. But deep down, I couldn't imagine a substantial livelihood that involved keeping my clothes on.

If there's a parallel to stripping addiction, it's an addiction to gambling—that need to put yourself at risk, that hunger for the big payoff that defies the odds. This will be the night when I make five grand, you say to yourself as you paint your face in the dressing room mirror. This will be the night that I finally grab that elusive erotic power bolt and hold on to it for good. You really convince yourself that you can do it when other people can't. You'll beat the odds—make the big money, put it toward something sensible, feel good about yourself, feel you're made bigger by this job, not smaller. But strippers are just like gamblers—so few actually walk away from the game better off.

The losses aren't usually material. You don't lose money so much as you lose hope. In a business where your career is so short (I wasn't just feeling over the hill at twenty-five, I was!), your time-horizon gets warped. When you think about it, years-long career or education goals that other people take for granted seem impossible. It would take *how long*? You need things to happen now now now now now, dammit. Before you're too old old old old old. Around about the time you figure out how long it would take to reach your straight career goal, you start missing the immediacy of the strip club, the quick cash, the smoke and lights and drama between the dancers and the men, the adrenaline pumping you up. You aren't addicted to the rush so much as you're addicted to Now.

All my young life, I expected to flame out like a rock 'n' roller at twenty-seven. Morrison, Cobain, Hendrix, Burana. I didn't sweat the travails of adulthood because I was confident they wouldn't happen to me. I sure as hell didn't bother to plan for a life after thirty. Thirty?! Ewwwwwwwww. That's old. I could scarcely picture it. I envisioned a face full of cronelike wrinkles, boobs that hung so low I could tuck them into my socks, and a realm of social interaction entirely composed of people humoring "the old lady." Every adult gets anxious about the passage of time, and every woman has anxiety about aging, but strippers feel it earlier and more acutely. Time makes a hell of an enemy, I'll tell ya, because you can't win. You lie there on your bed, second-guessing every life decision you've made. Or you sit there looking in the mirror, fixating on a fine line forming at the corner of your eye. This is the start of your unraveling, isn't it? Once you're in that mind-set, once you believe that everything is conditional and that it's all over for you, my dear, we call that Cynicism. Something in your heart dies, and you feel like you're at the top of a long, downward slide. Given that the average lifespan of an American female is eighty-two years, you're talking about a fifty-two-year-long off-ramp.

But as fate had it, I did turn thirty, and I wasn't working as a stripper when I did. I was a working writer, with decent skin and boobs that were pretty much where they were when I was twenty-seven, twenty-eight, and twenty-nine. The cosmetic realities of thirty were less significant, on balance, than the internal changes. And things did change, a lot. With every day past thirty, my life became less about what I thought might impress people (Look at that smart, funny strip-perchick! Look at that ballsy writer! And she has such nice *skin*!) and more about what I valued for myself. I became less invested in perform-ing the identity burlesque—parading around various caricaturized versions of strong, determined, self-reliant women who are deathly afraid of living outside that bubble of fascination and a fast buck. Since then, I've kinda developed a rule that I pass on to other women anxious about starting their fourth decade. After thirty, I tell them, nobody gets a vote. So much of being a woman is courting the approval of others, being admired, being chosen, wooed. You can go through your whole life building an identity based on everyone else's response, all the while ignoring what's important to you. Identity is dynamic, of course, and lots of things inform it, but letting the outside forces overrule the inner forces leaves you as half a person, a 24/7 one-woman show. It's a rip-off, really, because when it comes down to it, a spectacle is not a self.

That's not always an easy point to drive home with a woman who is still stripping. I hear from them, from time to time, when they're desperate to leave the business themselves, or just at the start of their turn around the go-go pole, and anxious to do it the smartest way possible. What do I tell them, these fatigued veterans and questing newbies? I say the same two things regarding their work habits: don't commit anything to film or video that you wouldn't want to see in ten or fifteen or thirty years. Images are forever. And save your money. Did I say save your money? Okay, good. Oh, and by the way, save your money.

How do I quit, well, that question is more difficult. When I first started getting these imploring e-mails, I would soft-pedal: ease up on your schedule; make an exit plan and stick to it; get a lot of massages. But somewhere along the away, the old tough chick who was born in Times Square got reincarnated as Little Ms. Tough Love, and now I draw a much harder line. I tell women who want to quit stripping that the choice they have to make is between peace of mind and the bottom line. They can give up the inner turmoil and get on the path to fulfillment, but they have to go cold turkey and be prepared to be poor and confused for a while, just like any other young woman trying to find her way. There's no shortcut if you take that route. Or, I tell them, they can keep stripping and make the fast money and stay in the realm of the familiar—the dressing room camaraderie, the ego boost that all those lusting eyes can bring, the "flake if you want to" flexible schedule. But you'll still be stripping, moving through your life without the confidence that comes from knowing you duked it out in the real world and triumphed. There are plenty of thankless jobs out there. Stripping is just one of many. But not all jobs are thankless. There are exceedingly rewarding careers, but the catch is that few of them are easy. So, which do you want? Fast and easy and ultimately empty, or slower and tougher but ultimately fulfilling? What do you want to have done with your life? Giving men hard-ons and ego-boosts is not nothing, but there is much, much more you could be doing. You just have to stick it out.

I suppose when I was in my teens and early twenties, full of my own competence and daring as a stripper, I would not have been open to advice from an elder. I'd probably have thought she was some bitter, used-up old broad—criticizing the game after she'd been benched. But you know what? They say that wisdom comes with age for a reason. Sometimes it turns out to be true.

A chill went through me that night during my New York visit when I saw that Peepland was gone. To see that dark bit of my personal history vanish was a relief, but it was humbling, too. It was the first tangible proof that time, like it or not, does go on. It's kind of like turning thirty. The milestone birthday can mean different things to different people. I had to make a choice to view it as a beginning, rather than the beginning of the end.

Dancing girls make good friends, and I collected them as I moved along: go-go girls, strippers, lap dancers, bachelor party acts, girls who specialize in "privates." Sometimes, now, we find ourselves in a store that sells trampy clothes, or walking by a club, and the conversation turns to our dancing days. We drift back five, ten, twenty years to reminisce. Nostalgia is an interesting state that simultaneously references both sickness and cure—we're enchanted by the memory of how much fun stripping could be, what an adventure. And how gutsy we were back then, how oblivious. But within minutes, we shake our heads and move on to another topic. Those issues are not germane anymore, that life no longer ours. After that spark of the "good old, bad old days," we grow tired of the subject and lay it down for now. The concentric circles of drama around the fixed center of the strip club that once were so exciting seem dull, and tiring, and woefully static. Somehow, in this moving on to other things, we acknowledge that the past wasn't really all that romantic, and that the best may lie ahead. It looks like optimism. Surprise, surprise, it looks a lot like faith.

Times Square is the blinking, glimmering heart of New York, and there are thousands of us tough chicks in the city's orbit—from Tribeca to the South Bronx, from the East Village to Westchester—and we change as the city changes. Over time, we change like New York itself—we're improved, degraded, evolved, and back again. Our souls are streets peopled with the women we used to be, women we have, in time, come to reluctantly admire. Admiration for your former self, however costly her decisions may have been, is one of the gifts that thirty-something tough girls share. With our common past and singular resilience, we look back and laugh. We look ahead and smile. We do what we have to do: we snap back and step forward.

A Hungry Balance

JULIANNA BAGGOTT

Reeds, caves, shoulders of cypress,
the woman who at this moment
does not need the world.

JOY KATZ,
"Women Must Put Off Their Rich Apparel"

Twenty-one days before I turned thirty, I sold my first novel, *Girl Talk*. I was living with my husband, our two young children, and a pair of Korean boarders who rented bedrooms upstairs. I was pregnant with our third child. It was my fourth pregnancy in five years, since I'd had a twelfth-week miscarriage while writing the novel. My office was in the living room, and I worked late at night, still nauseous, after the children had fallen asleep, after the boarders had wobbled in on their secondhand bikes and eaten the meals I left for them. I was still incognito.

No one really knew how much I was writing and I didn't tell them. I taught a small women's writing workshop at my dining room table, but mainly I was a mother in a small college-town neighborhood. Younger than the other mothers in the neighborhood, yes. A little odd with foreigners living in my home, yes. But rather ordinary. Despite the fact that I had published short stories and poetry in dozens of literary magazines and had an agent for my novel, I kept my writing to myself.

I had tried, at various points, to admit that I was a writer. But I always felt that people were largely disbelieving. I would always tense for the inevitable follow-up question: Do you have a book?

Turning thirty had, for me, an adolescent painfulness. My twenties were marked by a private doggedness, a stubborn, hidden drive. I was a mother, and motherhood freed me. It set me adrift, untethered me from the career concerns of my friends—the desire for promotions and bonuses. It stripped me and made me hungrier in my art. The pregnancy, labor, nursing, this lion's share of instinctive overwhelming love—all of it reminded me that I was an animal in my skin. Motherhood made me fierce.

Here is a short chronology. Note that the professional achievements are parenthetical because they aren't as important to me as the personal. I (published my first short story at twenty-two) got married at twenty-three to a poet, David Scott, finished graduate school at twenty-four, was pregnant at twenty-five, had the baby at twenty-six, was pregnant at twenty-seven (by now had published about ten short stories), had the baby at twenty-eight (by now had published about thirty poems), had a miscarriage at twenty-nine (wrote a novel), was pregnant again at twenty-nine (sold the novel), had the baby at thirty (sold a book of poems and wrote a second novel, which I sold at thirty-one, and then wrote the third, which I sold at thirty-two, and—hopefully—so on . . .).

I was therefore unprepared for the reality that motherhood isn't something you juggle. It consumes you and quite passionately—and surprisingly—I found myself wanting to be consumed by it. Being pregnant, the fetus rolling inside of me, more like an ocean, a shifting landscape than a baby, going through labor (thirty-six hours of it), pushing, then being cut open, a baby lifted from my body, the infant, wrapped, warming under a bulb, was the most transforming, transcending experience of my life. I realized that I'd been living in my head. It was traumatic. Milk-sour and completely in love with my daughter, stunned by nature, the endlessness of my capacity to love, I didn't write for thirteen months.

Honestly, I felt betrayed. I felt that everything I'd been taught about being a woman was heady bullshit. No one had explained this. How could they have? I would think of my daughter and my breasts tinged with pain and soaked my shirtfront. I was in awe.

For the first time, my writing became more personal. I finally felt like I had something to say. But I couldn't do it at home. I had to get away to do it. I went to a writers' colony, the Virginia Center for the Creative Arts and Ragdale Foundation. And when my second child, my son Finneas, was six months old I started writing poetry. First of all, it was something that I could write, given the fact that I had so little time. And second, it suited the way I felt. It was true, essential. I read ten books of poems a week, because that was the limit for a public borrower at the University of Delaware library. I wrote maniacally, reading my poems to my husband at night, often shouting them over the noisy din of the clamoring kids. I wrote wild poems that eventually found their way to literary magazines and that would eventually become *This Country of Mothers*, poems that married feminism and motherhood and religion in disturbing ways.

I wanted to have a family and write. I refused to sacrifice one for the other. I knew that if I didn't have children so I could devote myself to writing, I would resent my career. And if I didn't continue to write while raising my family, I would resent my children. Neither was acceptable to me, and so I did both. I know that this may sound like common sense. It certainly was in keeping with what I'd been raised to believe was not only possible but sensible. In the seventies, during a glowing rush of optimism, the idea that the fully actualized woman could have it all emerged. And I guess I took some of it to heart. Of course, historically speaking, the idea of a woman having to work and raise a family was not a new one. But the idea that a woman would choose to work and raise a family was.

I was a young mother, one who stayed at home with her children despite the first two being born under the poverty level. I felt judged, regarded alternately as a loser and a saint *because of* these wildly varying interpretations of my situation, which I gradually came to see as being generation-based—the former judgment coming from my peers, the latter from their parents. In the movie *Nurse Betty*, Chris Rock's character says, "She's a housewife. You don't get no lower than that!" And although actually he was wrong—she was in fact a waitress—my immediate reaction was "Finally! Finally someone has come out and said it." It was the hushed or carefully worded opinion that I'd felt from society for years. I would love for a sociologist to do a research study on perceived IQs, lining up myriad races, ages, genders, including the pregnant and unpregnant, and asking people to guess at IQs. I know that a young pregnant woman's perceived IQ would be found at the bottom. People looked at me as if I weren't smart enough to unwrap a foil-wrapped condom. It didn't help that a college freshman in town had recently hidden a pregnancy and given birth in a motel room, after which her boyfriend killed the newborn. I was eyed with nervousness, a kind of we-know-you're-pregnant, get-help pleading. I was asked again and again, in so many ways, if the pregnancies were planned. People would congratulate me with "I'm happy if you are!"

The country's opinion on marriage and family had shifted while I wasn't paying attention. My mother married at twenty-three, a surprise to her Southern relatives since she'd already been labeled an old maid. She had four children, which was considered a nice-size family, but not overly large compared with those on our street. But now, with three children, I'm stopped in stores and asked if they're all mine. My twenties were spent sorting through all of these unexpected reactions, trying to understand my own culture and my place in it.

The decision to start a family was also a defining rupture between me and my closest friends. It was as if we had all been standing on a dock and I jumped and they watched, promising to follow me—into marriage and family—but then either the weather or their moods turned. By the end of my twenties, I was still alone in the water. Although I made friends by way of mothers' groups and preschools and parks, it was a loneliness that seemed like it would persist forever.

Only a few of my oldest, dearest friends are married, and out of them, fewer have kids. My closest friends live in New York and are still single or married without children. When they come to our house, they often bring with them a mixture of a *National Geographic* reporter's curiosity and a sideshow-freak visitor's horror. I can't help but feel that there was some sort of manifesto written for my generation and that it must have had a section devoted to the benefits of postponement of marriage, of children. I didn't receive my copy.

I don't mean to be flip, because the struggle with these relationships has been very difficult. Not only has it been hard for us to have common ground for simple conversation, there have been deeper divisions. For some reason, the paths that each of us were choosing in our twenties seemed to be comments on the other's choices. It seemed that because our lives were so different, we were judging each other, instead of, perhaps, just trying to comprehend each other. And because we were so young and still trying to define ourselves in our twenties, it seemed that part of these self-definitions were being reached in defining ourselves by who we weren't, which is to say at each other's expense. And at a time when many of my friends found themselves with more and more in common, I did not.

When people asked me what I did for a living in my twenties before I'd sold my first novel, I didn't tell them I was a writer. Mainly out of a kind of angry loyalty, I told people I was a stay-at-home mother. I found myself in the middle of a generation that believed and preached in postponement of family, which was becoming more and more achievable with medicine. I believe that feminism is about choice, and I felt that my choice to stay at home with my kids, in what looked to many as forgoing my writing career—something I allowed them to believe—was thought by feminists to be the wrong choice. And so I also felt alienated by a group of women from whom I'd expected support.

And yet I used motherhood, too. I wore it like a floppy hat and sunglasses. It was the perfect cover. No one expected anything of me aside from exhaustion. I often felt like a prisoner—not that the children imprisoned me, but because I'd heard stories of prisoners stealing spoons from cafeterias to dig passageways. My writing was clandestine. While no one was looking, I scraped away. If I had an hour, I wrote for an hour. If I had ten minutes, I wrote for ten minutes—late at night, during the kids' delicate naps. Dave would let me disappear as soon as he got home from work. And I would take every minute given. The house was covered with slips of scribbled-on bank receipts and bub-blegum wrappers. If you lifted up my daughter's artwork on the fridge, you would find its backside covered with notes. Dave has since tied small notebooks to drawer knobs and the drink tray in the car, but it doesn't help contain the profusion of paper. My children learned early how to stamp letters, and the people at the post office know my kids by name. And when I think of those years of solitary urgency, I remember that breathlessness, that desperate need. But my cover was about to be blown.

An agent found me and I started to work on a novel. I became pregnant with my third child and sent the agent the first fifty pages. He wanted to see the rest, but I was too nauseous to write, and then, at week twelve, I had a miscarriage. I had been hoarding love for this child and the child didn't arrive. I wrote again, scores of heartbroken poems and my first novel, *Girl Talk*. I lavished all of my characters with this unfinished love. Writing the novel became an act of love for the poems and story collection, coattails on which they could ride. The agent sold my novel twenty-one days before I turned thirty. I was pregnant again, and this baby would make it full-term, healthy. And this marked my thirties, the official turn of the decade, but I don't think I understood the change that I was in for. The private self, the writer, hidden and passionate, was going public, and although I had desired it, I didn't know what it would entail, this coming clean, this 'fessing up.

At the time, I didn't know why I was so restless, why I had anxiety attacks in the middle of the night, sleeplessness. Now I can most easily liken it to being a teenager, but instead of a change from a girl to a woman, it was a change from the me I knew—the private writer whose characters' lives were kept in the safety of my desk drawers—to a writer with my work as public property. I wasn't just going public for the hell of it, either. It was now my job.

At first it was difficult to explain to friends and neighbors that I had a book coming out. I hadn't prepared anyone. They had trouble understanding. And I felt that there was a general resistance to changing their definitions of me. They seemed to think that I was stapling it together in my basement. I'd tell them it was being published by Pocket Books. And I would go on because they seemed confused, a division of Simon and Schuster, a Viacom company. But they didn't understand. They wanted to know if it was a children's book.

That would make sense. That would fit in with their picture of me. No, it's a novel. A romance? No, it's a literary novel. I'll go on a book tour. I'll sign books in bookstores, I said, hoping to give them a clearer picture. They were often still confused.

"How did you sell it?"

"I didn't. My agent did."

"You have an agent?" Agent was something of which they all had some sort of concept. "Yes," I said, relieved by the glimmer of recognition. "Yes, I have an agent." But then there was the question that always came up; I don't know how many times I've been asked, "Where will I be able to buy it?" The idea that I would have a book on the shelves of bookstores was too daunting an idea. And again and again I answered, "It will be available wherever books are sold."

This was difficult, but it doesn't truly describe the awkwardness, the inner anxiety of being public, the pressure on everyone who knew me to comment or not to comment on my work. These small one-on-one interactions loomed larger than the more important words from critics. The writer/critic relationship was defined. The writer/father-in-law relationship was rough, undiscovered terrain that I found perilous. The people at the post office insist that we'll be moving to New York City. Of course not, I tell them. But they don't believe me.

It's been hard to understand the notion of this other persona who has emerged, this woman who shows up at colleges and readings, who is the writer. For a long time it seemed like I was faking it, although I wasn't ever lying. I never affected eccentricities. I just didn't recognize this other self. It has been a slow mending of this public and this private self.

As for my relationship with my generation of women, perhaps that rupture is mending, too. Most of all, I can say that my life seems my own, and the idea of a generation doesn't suit my purposes as much as it once did in defining myself. In fact, I have little interest in defining myself at all. When I look back on my twenties, I'm already nostalgic, although I'm quick to add that I don't desire to return to those years. I remember them in a haze, my babies mining my soul, this swayback fatigue, a beautiful hive of work, and always words.

Considering the Alternatives

SARA WOSTER

Time still, as he flies, brings increase to her truth,
And gives to her mind what he steals from her youth.

EDWARD MOORE,

The Happy Marriage

On a tipsy national holiday when I sit and consider all the things I'm grateful for, just below long legs and just above high pain threshold sits my mother's genetic code. My mother is an uncommonly pretty woman. She has the type of rosy farm skin and amazing figure that are molded out of homemade desserts and brisk winds. She's healthy and high-cheekboned and although those around her talk about her intellect more than her looks, she is a beauty. She's the kind of woman who inspired a former high school admirer of hers to approach my father recently and inform him, "If it weren't for you, I'd be married to your wife."

This, however, is not a woman clinging to her looks. She does not own any product stronger than a facial cleanser, and unless Botox is a character on my nieces' Barney videos, she does not know him. I've never once heard her say she is getting fat, or looking old, or getting saggy. Yes, she is oddly particular about her hair, and she would never go out in public without a matching belt, but to my knowledge she doesn't obsess about her age. Possibly because she's thin and she looks fifteen years younger than she should, due to a life of moderation. But even if she didn't look great, I would guess her Midwestern practicality would find age obsession a vulgar waste of time.

That Midwestern practicality scares me. I think it keeps people down and forces them to eat fruit floating in Jell-O just because they did it last year and they cataloged the recipe. It's the same mind-set that frowns upon dining alfresco, sexuality, and impractical shoes. Sure, it's fine to enjoy the blossom of your youth and wear makeup and good clothes, but this is expected to end after the babies are made. This Calvinist dictate that things of pleasure have no place in a simple life was one of the reasons I left there. This Protestant theme represses everything about the Midwest, including that point in the lives of a lot of Midwestern women where practicality seems to overcome vanity. Hair is shortened, waistbands become elastic, and shoes are suddenly flat. A lot of them understandably gain weight from the lack of available fresh foods and time and the abundance of fast food and microwaves. There is little option but to join this sorority of aging women, but be forewarned that they will like you only if you don't try to keep your weight down or update your eyeglass frames. And if you don't follow the rules, they will revert to junior high tactics and push you out of their circle, where standing out is the loneliest existence.

So you see why I had to leave South Dakota and move to New York City. I was terrified for my future. I was terrified for my waistline. I would not pretend that I didn't want to stay pretty and I didn't want to age at all. The people out west were too rational and serene about things like aging or dying; they lived too close to the cycles of nature and God to delve into the blasphemy of trying to control them. They have churches to worry about, and crop disasters. They weren't making neurotic grasps to try to cling to firm skin or love or pipe dreams. I had to find my own little nirvana where people were standing knee deep in hope and opportunism. If I had to pack up and move across the country to find desperation like mine, I would. And I did.

But it's never what you think. The first six months after I moved to New York were spent in a clinical depression. The type of depression that is so bad that, as a friend described it, you stop eating with utensils. I arrived in a cold December filled with wild dogs and serial rapists, if my memory is correct. I had no job, one friend, no good shoes, and a small bonus check from the college I had worked for in Minneapolis. I spent the check in a week. People had justly warned me of high rents and the cost of taxis. Nobody had prepared me for the irrational spending on something called threading, where Russian women rip out your eyebrow hair with a piece of string. Or drinks made out of something called armagnac, its cost suggesting it must be milked out of a unicorn's tit.

The first couple of weeks I just walked the streets, staring in disbelief at the women. Their beauty and youth and style. They all smelled of lemons and Istanbul. The girls were all petite-figured with petite features. Their teeny little noses could not possibly breathe. Their gazelle legs could barely walk. I felt grotesque and functional, like a Clydesdale huffing down the sidewalk. My clothes hung like costumes from *Fiddler on the Roof*. I felt very old and washed up at twenty-seven. I wanted to be as young and impractical as they were. And the envy grew and grew in me like one of those really aggressive tumors, eating away at what little dollop had been my soul.

As much as I envied their money and little Gallic body frames, at twenty-seven I envied their youth more. I envied all their time. As Joan Didion says in an essay: "It is less often said that New York is also, at least for those of us who came there from somewhere else, a city only for the very young." Notice she didn't even say young, she said very young. Nobody warned me that everyone you meet here would not only look young and beautiful, they would be savvy beyond their years and have three degrees from Brown by the time they were twenty-one. And it is a young city in that you must be able to stay up drinking and dancing on a Monday night until three-thirty and be prepared to give a PowerPoint lecture at eight the next morning. That is just the way it is. You must be fresh-faced and living on ambition and egg sandwiches. And when you can't learn the new moves, you are politely asked to step aside because you clog up the dance of the city.

This creates two ages here, young and eccentric. You don't really see that many normal, middle-aged people. Their age makes people uncomfortable so the sensible ones stay home. The older people you see out and about all look too trendy in some horrible African cape, or terribly awkward in the smoky faux *tabacs.* Age gives them a campy, theatrical air. You see these New York women spending their whole life looking older than they are by attempting to look younger. Like someone Saran-Wrapped their face.

The other night, some friends (from Minnesota) and I were talking about how living in New York had ruined watching *Seinfeld* or Woody Allen films. It used to be funny to watch the comic whining of George and Woody and all these Upper Manhattanites as they obsessed on age and vitamins and restaurants. In Minnesota, the premise that adults behaved like that seemed as plausible as Mr. Ed, the horse that can talk. Then you move here and you realize it's real. You realize that there are millions of Woody Allens whining their way through the workday. That the financial foundation of this city is the circuitry of insecure people hating themselves so much that they will pay anything to fix it. These people do not merely exist among you and I, they are making the rules that we must live by. These are the people working in media, advertising, and fashion. They have lifted the bar of appropriate aging with their bionic laser-burning procedures and golden elixirs. Now, even when we look naturally good for our ages, in comparison to these statuettes, we look like Keith Richards.

And I bought into a lot of this my first couple of years, so eager to be savvy and to scrub off all the prairie dirt. My timing in this endeavor was fortunate. It was the peak of the dot-com era, I was in my late twenties, and I worked in advertising. It was greedy and reckless and fun and everyone I knew had a corporate credit card. My friendships were based around drinking and the only books we read were about loving men too much. My brain ballooned up with knowledge of vintage furniture and protein diets and society It Girls. It was fun and vacuous and we still had Bill Clinton. The only problem was, I was supposed to be painting.

I had moved to New York to become an artist. A famous artist. I spent my early twenties in Minneapolis in a myopic, ruthless pursuit of success, which I had been slowly achieving. I was winning grants and residencies and being asked to curate shows. I had occasional newspaper clippings to send my parents and people would occasionally say they were "familiar with" my work. The cost of living was low and everything was cheap.

In Minneapolis it was easy to pay for my studio and rent and car by working menial day jobs, mind-silencing data-entry jobs. For three years I processed psychiatric records for a huge chain of private hospitals, a chain that was later closed down for fraud. My task was to enter the number of depressives versus manics, suicidals versus anorexics. For extra money I could do follow-up calls to their home to see if they were still alive six months later. At night I worked at a Borders bookstore in a strip mall, then went to my studio for a few hours of painting. On a good night I followed all that by watching rock shows until two in the morning. I never stopped. The reason I could live this way for years in my twenties is that I had endless energy and little financial ambition, my personal favorite traits of youth. And I thought I would move to New York and continue this life while I waited to be discovered.

It didn't exactly happen that way. For one thing, New York takes your endless energy and exhausts it in the subway and at the post office and tussling for bar stools, and for another it does not allow for no financial ambition.

I did manage to maintain my discipline about painting, but I didn't get discovered and I didn't seek discovery. So if you get to twenty-nine and realize you won't be in any big shows the next year, and more important, you don't care, you need to take time to be considerate and pragmatic and . . . Midwestern. Out of all this new practical consideration began to emerge an idea of what I wanted. I wanted to keep painting but I also wanted to eventually make money and eventually make babies. And to do that I had to grow up, throw out all my fantasy scenarios, and alter my vision of what kind of art career I might have. So having committed to that, I had to figure out how to fix ten years of yawning and dancing, and basically begin again. That is the part that sucks.

Maybe it would help if I started acting a little more Midwestern, a little more like my mother. Maybe practical isn't as repressive as it had seemed. Maybe practical gets you the good credit that gets you a nice apartment. You realize with great practicality that it isn't just more economically sound to learn how to cook, it feels nurturing and sweet. Maybe losing a little vanity can't hurt either, and maybe good judgment could be used less frugally. Maybe a few practical pounds on my ass aren't as horrible as boring people to tears by telling them about the last time I ate rice. Is that maturity? It is in my circles.

So I adopted some practical habits, learned a little bit about judgment, and by the time I hit thirty I had kind of figured out that I wouldn't collapse into my perceived Midwestern complacency. And even though I was already thinking of getting Botox and one of those really dramatic capes, I certainly wasn't going to age like a New Yorker. While I may have become a woman without a region, I wasn't a woman without a role model. I had a mother who has figured this all out.

She would appreciate this irony. Part of what has propelled me all the way from South Dakota was a fear of becoming my mother. During my twenties I acted out the worst traits of my dad's side of the family—a family so crisscrossed with alcoholism and bizarre behaviors and loud voices that it was like *Dynasty* without the dynasty. I thought they were interesting and my mother was boring. And they are interesting, and funny and smart. But my mother isn't boring. Since I always had an affinity for my dad and his charm and energy, I had mistaken my mother's composure for conservatism, her pride for being judgmental. I overlooked her sarcastic wit and overwhelming good nature.

For a woman from a corn farm in South Dakota and a Norwegian father, my mother is pretty cool. Growing up, my mother refused to let us watch *Love Boat* or *Three's Company* on the basis that they were "insipid." She stopped an argument with my father over gun control when she volleyed back at him, "I refuse to acquiesce to those punks!" I didn't know what acquiesce meant, but I knew she won the argument. She has a near-photographic memory, especially concerning poetry. My high school English teacher would leave the classroom to call my mother if she couldn't remember who wrote a specific poem. Given the first line, my mother could not only tell her who the author was off the cuff, but also recite the entire thing. She had no time for women's auxiliary groups, but she was the president of the League of Women Voters and was in charge of the televised candidate debates. This is a librarian who told me not to sweat disliking *Atlas Shrugged* because Ayn Rand was "dogmatic and repetitive." At my age she not only had three kids under six, she had been a high school English teacher, an accomplished quiltmaker, could do stained glass, was an amazing cook, had a garden, sewed much of our clothes—I could go on ad nauseam. She did all of this while always looking amazing and being well dressed. She lived gracefully. This is a daunting mother to have. As a girl, it was okay for me to have my equally impressive father because I wasn't supposed to turn into him. But a mother like this is trouble. This is a mother you may have to rebel against just to act like you don't care if you don't live up to her precedent, this is a mother from whom you may even have to move across the country and act like an adolescent for a few years just to appreciate.

In most ways, leaving my twenties was wonderful. There are many things that improved with age. My taste in men has matured into an amazing boyfriend with a bright future, who is more like my father than I would care to acknowledge. The friends I have are better for me. They read and exercise and have great senses of humor. They show up to help me move. They are friends who have stuck around since I was five and friends who I was smart enough to spot when I was older. But thankfully, their imperfections mirror mine. They drink too much, they whisper about each other to me, work out sporadically, switch video rental stores rather than pay late fees.

Some things about aging aren't so good. My hair looks like packaging material, my wrinkles are carving me into something canine. Weight stays and energy leaves. But what I most despise about getting older is my newfound wisdom. It makes me cautious. I used to be beautifully unaffected by fear. I used to ride on the back of fast Japanese motorcycles, ride the empty subway at two in the morning, had no knowledge of folic acid intake and bike helmets. Now everyone is armed and every story is a conspiracy. I had always thought that aging would be more reductive and kind of defining, like sculpting a stream-lined version of me. Instead it's as if all these things have piled up like a turban on my head. If I wake up in the middle of the night, I may not go back to sleep. I may sit up for hours with these fantasies keeping me company: it may be the terrorists blowing me up, it may be a neon topographical map of cancer in my body, it may be cartoon anvils falling from skyscrapers onto my head. But it will keep me up.

So you see, I will never entirely be my mother. If she sits up, she is probably worrying about me or someone else, not about herself. And I think if I were to ask her about my life, while she would have no envy over my late nights or parties or celebrity sightings, she would envy the freedom I enjoy at my age. While I don't envy her early marriage and early children, I do envy her contentment. I envy that she doesn't feel this need for "more" and "new" and "youth." And once in a rare while I envy her Midwestern practicality. I expect that as I get older, my emulation of her will increase appropriately, and if you see me in ten years, I'm sure I'll be wearing a matching belt.

My Missing Biological Clock

MEGHAN DAUM

*The management of fertility is one of the most
important functions of adulthood.*

GERMAINE GREER

When you don't want the things most people want, the world
begins not to apply to you. Even today, nearly four decades
after feminism began, the woman for whom marriage and children is
not the ultimate goal will see the cultural conversation drift slowly
away from her table. The quizzes in women's magazines will have no
relevance, the lifestyle section in the newspaper will leave her orbit,
the radio psychiatrists will dish out advice she is hard-pressed to take.
When the prevailing discourse of contemporary womanhood centers
around the notion of "balance," of how to combine one's career, creative pursuits, exercise program, or sex life with one's family, the
woman for whom balance is not the central issue seems hardly a
woman at all. In the last half century, the catchphrases of female fulfillment have evolved from "keeping your man happy" to "having it all"
to "balancing your life." But there is still no catchphrase for the childless life, particularly when that life is chosen. In the judgment of the

popular culture and, by extension, the judgment of the American imagination, the woman who is not interested in motherhood is still a child herself. She is a possibly spoiled, possibly militant naïf for whom a change of heart is a matter of "the right time" or "the right man." She doesn't yet "get it." She does not know "what it means to really love someone." She is literally unbalanced.

Ask me about my lack of interest in motherhood and my immediate answers range from the typical to the trivial. I will say the usual things about not playing with dolls as a little girl, about not cooing at babies as an adult, about the inexpressible joy I take in being able to pack one suitcase and leave town on a day's notice, and the reduced insurance rate I pay because I don't have maternity coverage. I could go on the usual tear about population growth and remind you that by 2025 the earth will have reached a head count of ten billion. But while that statistic alarms me, it's not the primary reason I don't want kids, nor do I give much credence to most of the childless people who cite overpopulation as the crucial factor. When I'm feeling bold I can say, with some degree of guilt, that the world of childhood simply doesn't interest me. Though I can't say I had an unhappy childhood, I disliked being a child and don't really care to revisit the playgrounds and cubbyholes that I was so eager to trade for adulthood. But as true as these statements may be, they are rarely useful in getting anyone to believe me. Even though no one would dispute the sixteen-year-old, or even the eight-year-old, who expresses her desire to be a mother someday, the thirty-four-year-old who says she doesn't want children is equivalent to the high school sophomore who vows to marry her prom date. She will receive a pat on the head and a knowing, condescending smile. These are words that will be eaten. This is a phase that will be outgrown.

Strangely, though, not wanting children is a phase I've grown into. With every year there has been more clarity, less shame, even a little pride. Like the realization that it is not, after all, necessary to know a great deal of algebra to be a functioning person in society, the idea of motherhood as an option rather than a requirement has been creeping toward me for years. Though it took a long time to realize it, I spent my twenties planning children like I was planning my death. It was as if I had to seal my accomplishments inside a single decade, as if I was being allowed to live in my own skin until my time was up and I was forced, against my wishes, to become another kind of person. Still, I paid lip service to the idea of motherhood. Of course I wanted children someday. Just not for a long time. Not until everything else was in place. Not until I'd seen everything and done everything and gone everywhere and known everyone and turned over every leaf. Boyfriend after boyfriend, the issue will arise, get dropped, then rise again. Breakup after breakup, the subject maintains its ranking in the top five reasons for splitting, and today, happily single and decidedly nondesperate thanks to my silent biological clock, it occasionally spills out on dates like a knocked-over water glass. With rare exception, the adjectives, spoken or not, are always the same: shallow, stubborn, shortsighted. It is, I've heard again and again, "such a shame."

But where exactly does the shame lie? It is, I suppose, a shame that I will not bestow my parents with grandchildren. Though they haven't yet said it out loud, I can't imagine they won't be disappointed when I fail to change my mind on this issue. As their friends' children marry appropriately, hold on to their jobs, and start families, I have drifted farther and farther away from a position that might be conducive to parenthood. I persist with a career whose only financial guarantee is unsteady paychecks. When sizing up possible romantic partners I've all but eliminated "would make a good father" from the criteria. It's not that I see children as enslavers of women, nor do I feel that remaining childless is an instant ticket to the kind of life that is frequently described as "unconventional" or "groundbreaking" (Jane Addams and Georgia O'Keeffe were childless, but so was Eva Braun). The bottom line is that none of my plans, hopes, or fantasies involves being a mother. Just as some people don't wish to own dogs, I don't wish to have children and I feel extraordinarily privileged to live in a time and place where children are afforded the same benefits as dogs, which is to say they don't necessarily have to land in the hands of those whose nurturing inclinations run toward other outlets.

The dog analogy can be problematic, particularly for those who argue that a biological child transforms the values, sensibilities, and, indeed, the entire center of gravity of its parents on such a primitive level that the parents actually become entirely different people from who they were when they were not parents. According to this logic, which is frequently expressed in the form of "you'll understand when you have your own," the nonparent who doesn't want a child doesn't really know what she is talking about, because, after all, she's not yet a parent. But the reason people like me tend to make the dog comparison, facile as it may be, is that the impulse not to have a child, like the desire not to have a dog, can be just as organic as the impulse to have one. I happen to have a dog, and while my connection to him will never be as intense and life-altering as the connection between parent and child, I chose to adopt him as a puppy because I love dogs and have always wanted one. That's not to say that I have framed pictures of him on my desk or even that he fills the emotional gap that would otherwise be filled by a child if I wished to have one. I know that not being a parent means forgoing the experience of a very particular kind of love. If I had a child I'm sure I would love it more than I can currently comprehend. But I'm not sure how much I'd love my life. And I'm not particularly game to find out.

Is loving your life more important than loving a child? Is the inability to combine these loves, to let them feed off each other and fuse them into a single, thriving source of fulfillment a sign of high-grade dysfunction? To be a person who doesn't want children is to be engaged in an endless volley with the word *selfish*. We are forever deflecting it and hurling it back at others, forever tweaking its definitions, considering its contexts, moving it like a chess piece between the macro and the micro, the population growth versus the personal growth, the inevitable consumerism of baby-making versus the utter naturalism of reproducing ourselves. "Selfish" is the Möbius strip that keeps either argument from ever being won. On the one hand, how can it be selfish to remain childless when what you're actually doing is withholding the self, reining it in, making room for that many more school lunches, limited-edition Christmas toys, and places in the Harvard class of 2026? On the other hand, what could possibly be more selfish than this refusal to give, this lack of participation, this disregard for the favorite recitation of all parents: I realize that someone else's needs are more important than mine. What could be more disrespectful to one's own parents than not giving as good as you got?

From what I can see, the problem lies not in the selfishness of parents or nonparents but in the fact that parents are masterminds of public relations while nonparents haven't yet learned the art of image control. Whereas parents hold a place in the culture as nurturers, providers, and people with "concerns," the more visible members of voluntarily childless community—or the "child-free" as they call themselves—have managed to undermine their position by appearing intolerant, even snide. Snippy monikers to describe parents, like "breeders," once an in-joke of the gay community, are now widely used by all kinds of child-free people, many of whom refer to themselves as DINKs (Double Income, No Kids) or THINKERs (Two Healthy Incomes, No Kids, Early Retirement). The result is that the choice to remain childless is commonly associated with a desire to remain affluent rather than taking the time to weigh the moral implications of accepting a job for which one may be unsuited. Too often, the rhetoric of the child-free is reduced to money, the surplus or lack of it, the vacations that can be afforded or the tax deductions that do not apply. The result is that money, with all the attendant images of expensive vacations, sports cars, and luxury condos, remains at the center of the debate. The message is that parents care about kids. Nonparents care about stuff and the money that buys it.

There are a lot of reasons that I don't want to have children and almost none of them have to do with taking expensive vacations or driving a fancy, not entirely safe car. And unlike the members of the countless child-free Internet communities like the Childfree Network (whose slogan is a baby's face with a line through it) and No Kidding!, which facilitate group rants, both in person and online, about toddlers in restaurants and friends who can't talk on the telephone without interruptions from their kids, I am not on a crusade to rid my life of children. I do not regard children as brats (at least not most of them), nor do I resent paying school taxes, struggling with childproof caps on prescription drugs, or the sounds of neighborhood children playing in their yards. I just don't want to be a parent. And I don't want to be one in the same way that I don't want to be a doctor, because there are other things that I can do better, and plenty of other people who make good doctors.

But that argument tends to be met with about as much enthusiasm as the dog argument. And the rebuttal isn't always pretty. As many self-professed liberals and nonracists like to point out, at least in private, "the wrong people are having children." The "wrong" people, in this case, are teenagers, poor people, and, though we hate to say it out loud, certain ethnic groups that have traditionally put a premium on large families. As a "right" kind of person, the common logic goes, it is incumbent upon me to help reverse the trend. I would be a "good" parent in that I would be a white, educated parent who probably wouldn't have more than two children and would not likely be caught leaving toddlers alone in a beat-up Buick while she dashed into a 7-Eleven for smokes. As a product of middle-class America, I've been told that it's my duty to replenish the middle-class (or at least what's left of it), to continue the legacy of parenting that encourages *Sesame Street* over violent cartoons and granola bars over Fritos, and maintains a two-income household that socks away money for university tuition, plus a little extra for family excursions to historical sites. I seem like the kind of person who would take my children to visit Colonial Williamsburg. I might even drive them there in a Volvo. Therefore, I would be a good parent.

The catch is that being a good parent, at least in my book, requires not only doing these things but also enjoying these things, and while I have nothing against Volvos, I can no more pretend to enjoy visiting Colonial Williamsburg than I could, for instance, pretend to be interested in astrology or car repair or the painting of ceramic pots. And while society (with the possible exception of Southern California) tends not to punish us for being uninterested in astrology, a lack of interest in procreation is often associated with a larger existential failing, a rejection of not only one's own genetic legacy but of, I daresay, some kind of answer to life's big question, namely, what is its meaning?

The link between procreation and insight, however illusory, into "why we're here" is fundamental to our very existence. It is the connection that causes parents to say things like "now I see what life is all about" and incites would-be parents to surmise that the spinning particles of the world—the encroaching lines on the face, the lackluster marriage bed, the treadmill of earning and spending and earning more and spending even more than that—will somehow assume a tangible, comprehendible form, will take on a *purpose*, when a child is introduced into the mix. I am not, of course, in a position to judge the validity of this position. The "meaning of life" is as subjective as a person's definition of beauty or his taste for wine or preference for rare steak versus well-done steak versus poached tofu. That is to say, it is in the eye of the beholder. And while some people may find a piece (or several pieces) of life's meaning via a child's arrival and subsequent journey through the world, I continue to suspect that my own existential quandaries are far too cumbersome to try to work out through a child. That's certainly not to say that my big questions are any bigger than most people's (most days, they have to do with where I put my sunglasses). But for some reason—genetic wiring, social influence, my own personality quirks—I have yet to be convinced that having a kid will help me figure things out.

And so I go on, in the shadow of my thirty-fifth year, with burning desires for a great many things—a beautiful home, an exciting career, a safer planet—that don't happen to include children. As single women go, I realize I am, if not a total anomaly, noticeably out of the norm. At times, the silence of my biological clock has the effect of a bodily sensation I simply don't have. As if I can't feel hunger and don't understand why others are compelled to eat, I find myself distanced from the concerns of many of my friends, some of whom, in the quest to find husbands, have made a second career of online dating and others of whom have entered the physically and emotionally ravaging arena of fertility treatment. In both cases, my interest is more anthropological than personal. It is in a largely journalistic spirit that I listen, occasionally in fascination, often in horror, to my friends' stories from the trenches of Match.com and the Yahoo personals. *Scott was nice but he's not Jewish. Steve was tall and cute but he mispronounced gnocchi. I cannot seriously picture myself with someone who cannot pronounce common Italian foods. Brad was perfect but he never called again.*

Relieved of the hope or expectation of someday raising tall children with good pronunciation, I am exempt from these humiliations. Knowing full well what happens when you search these Internet sites for single men who don't want children ("your search found no results") I am free to go out with platonic friends rather than attend a giant meat market of a party, free to spend Saturday evenings lying in the yard with my dog, free to forgo the whole online dating scene (indeed, it's now the *only* dating scene) in favor of a "more organic" way of meeting someone. What "organic" means exactly is something I wrestle with daily (it's one of my Big Questions). Would I like to find someone to share my life with? Sure. Do I need to? That requires a longer answer, though it should be said that lack of need could be far scarier than complete helplessness. But for all my uncertainty about the world, I am certain that what is best about my life is intrinsically linked to the good fortune I've had not to be racing a time clock. While my life may not include the particular joy of holding an infant to my chest, it has always granted me the pleasure of experiencing each day and night as a wide expanse of possibility. There is no mountain in front of me to obstruct my view or divert my course. There is no lying about my age, no dashed hopes when there aren't any eligible men at the party, no time wasted talking with the stockbroker who "might be interesting after you get to know him." There is nothing to wait for and, therefore, no reason to wait. When the womb becomes a receptacle of neither compromise nor guilt nor failure, its very barrenness bears the fruit of a certain ecstasy. It is a joy born of the balance of one's own two feet. It is the morning that breaks through your windows and hands you the keys to the entire day.

Bedsores and Cocktails

HEATHER JUERGENSEN

There are only three ages for women in Hollywood—
Babe, District Attorney, and Driving Miss Daisy.

GOLDIE HAWN

The day I turned thirty I stayed in bed all day. I never in a million years imagined that's what I would end up doing, but that's what I did. While still safely ensconced in my twenties, I loved spouting wise, pithy aphorisms like, "All good things happen in your thirties," or "Youth is wasted on the young," or worst of all, "I can't *wait* to turn thirty!" Flash forward to the day itself and there I was, lying catatonic in bed like some hideously trite *Cathy* cartoon. Staying in bed all day— that is, alone, with no gorgeous guy licking my toes to make it more interesting—is a lot more painful than I would have thought. As some- one who has suffered from depression, I thought I understood the general *motif* of being involuntarily prostrate. But depression, I real- ized, is actually a bit more varied. When depressed, I curl up into the fetal position in whatever room I happen to be in when the darkness overtakes. The corner nook of the kitchen, the tiled bathroom floor, the living room rug . . . depression actually offers good opportunities for discovering that crack in the dining room floorboard that needs mending, the missed grease stain at the base of the stove, the broken tile on the fireplace. But staying in bed, not leaving the bed . . . that's a whole other form of torture, when all you can really contemplate is the same ugly floral pattern on the duvet over and over. There's a relentlessness to whatever the malaise is that doesn't want you to venture forth into the world. At one point I actually pulled the blanket over my head. What the hell was going on? Other chicks got freaked out about turning thirty . . . not *this* fiercely independent, do-my-own-thing, turn-my-back-on-traditional-mores kinda gal. But the fact was, I was indisputably hiding under the covers at the prospect of becoming a Woman in Her Thirties.

A friend happened to be having a cocktail party that night under completely other auspices and she phoned me up, thank God, saying, "Come over, let us toast you." I was mortally grateful for the invitation—it meant that I was finally forced to leave the 320-thread-count safety zone of the bed and venture out into the world. I don't think I was actually worried about wrinkles or gray hair or sagging skin around my neck. It was like I was troubled by the word itself: *thirty*. "Twenty" was light, carefree, capricious. Twenty had a twinkle in its eye. Thirty was rounder, slower, more circuitous. Thirty had the beginnings of saddlebags.

After graduating from McGill University in 1991, I promptly set about realizing my dream of becoming an advertising copywriter, a dream I had nurtured, incomprehensibly, since high school. I took a job at J. Walter Thompson (the "Harvard of Advertising," as they liked to remind us), but soon came to my senses, realizing that if my livelihood depended on coming up with catchy slogans for Cool Mint Listerine or Halls Mentholyptus, I'd kill myself. I tried my luck at a smaller boutique agency that handled sexier, softer accounts in categories like fashion and stemware, but I still got to work every day feeling suicidal. At one point, as if in desperate protest of my stultifyingly repetitive nine-to-five existence, I dyed my hair platinum blond. The agency president, a conservative Christian from Ohio, stopped at my desk and looked at me the way one might examine a prehistoric insect at the natural history museum—repulsed, but interested.

One afternoon I was hanging out next to Bill the Copywriter, on my third hazelnut coffee of the day, gesticulating my way through some animated anecdote to avoid the numbingly mindless work at my desk. Jacquie from Casting looked up and drily asked if I'd ever considered a career in the theater. I couldn't quite tell if she was joking, but it did put me in mind of my first week at J. Walter Thompson, when my boss marched up to my desk and said declaratively, "You should be an actress," before marching back to his office to finish the weekly status report.

The caveat was I *had* acted once. At the tender age of seventeen, I had been cast in a Columbia grad student's thesis film, which was a brilliant, fun, romantic, life-changing experience. But it also felt like it would never add up, practically speaking, to anything more than a lark. It prompted me to spend a couple of summer breaks during college flipping through *Backstage* and responding to the occasional cattle call—the pinnacle of which came when I landed a job playing a battered wife in a Blue Cross/Blue Shield of New Jersey corporate video. Despite being paid a whopping $50 for the day's work, I wasn't convinced I was ready to pursue an actual *career* as an actor. The idea of spending my life struggling with no money and multiple jobs and constant rejection in the hopes of beating out thousands of competitors for scant jobs and even scanter chances at "stardom" seemed unthinkable. Until I got a taste of the corporate grind. Then it didn't seem so crazy.

Having finally made up my mind that I was going to take the leap, I quit my job, got headshots, enrolled in an acting class, and broke the news to my parents that from then on they should refer to me as an "actor." I was twenty-three years old. Even though I'd heard it took a solid three years to launch a career (assuming you had a manager and agent plugging for you, which I didn't) and that once "launched" it took a good ten years for the public at large to really know or care who you were, I figured I had plenty of time. At the dewy age of twenty-three and sporting a dazzlingly naïve optimism (and a much classier mane of honey blond), I knew these statistics didn't apply to me. I gave myself six months for the "launch," and figured the public-recognition part couldn't be too far behind. I estimated I'd be enjoying a modest amount of success in, say, two years or so.

Four years later, I was still toiling away in acting class, working in a night-shift typing pool, and staying up till four in the morning sending out flyers to shows that no one ever saw. I knew something had to change. And that was when I started writing. To fully understand what would possess someone to willingly tangle with the terror of a blank sheet of paper, you have to understand the hopelessness of the Endless Acting Class.

The first Endless Acting Class I found myself in was conducted by a former protégé of Lee Strasberg. As I navigated my way through the convoluted cottage industry in New York designed to lighten the wallets of hungry young actors, and read the many teacher ads in the back pages of *Backstage,* I discovered that Strasberg had a hell of a lot of protégés back in the day—more than one would have thought humanly possible! The way it worked was, some association—however obtuse—with the great Method teachers of the fifties (Strasberg, Adler, Meisner) was invoked and acted as the hook, and then once they had them hooked, the ex-protégés busily went to work making their young charges feel perpetually insecure, and therefore perpetually in need of their guidance and training. I noticed that there were some students, particularly women, who had been in class forever. Because the business was so hard, class became a kind of cocoon, and the longer these students remained in the cocoon, the colder and harsher the world beyond it appeared. There are some good acting teachers in New York who willingly and forcefully push the student out of the nest when it is time. But many don't—motivated not only by the need to maintain their income but by a warped psychological compulsion to "mentor" people with weak egos and hazy game plans.

So, as if the universe wanted to make sure I understood just what kind of a jungle of an industry I was leaping into, my first teacher was one of these teachers. She used to talk about what "Lee" would say as she critiqued some hapless student's work. I think wistfully recalling the scene work of guys like Paul Newman and Rod Steiger made her feel justified as she sadistically told students how much more "work" they had to do.

One night after another meaningless showcase the class had produced that nobody attended, she joined some of us who were going out for drinks. We were all swapping war stories and one lively girl with an innocent air was outlining her upcoming plans—agent meetings, auditions, obscure plays—the usual depressing agenda of the struggling actor. When the subject of her suitability for a certain role came up, we asked her how old she was and she breezily told us: twenty-six. All the color drained out of our teacher's face. She picked up the student's hand, looked her very seriously in the eye, and said, "Sweetie, I had no idea." And then, as if the girl had just been diagnosed with cancer, but had not yet decided on a course of treatment, our teacher solemnly said, "You have to get on with it."

I cannot imagine any other field, with the notable exception of professional athletics, where an authority figure—a mentor, no less—would baldly tell someone she's over the hill at twenty-six. Especially given the fact that women in their thirties invariably become smarter, sexier, and more accomplished than women in their twenties, this admonishment feels even more intuitively demeaning and illogical.

At the time of this exchange, I was twenty-four and, not really believing deep down that a whole lot was going to change for me over the next two years, save taking more classes and performing in more showcases, I had no choice but to take the breathless admonition as meant for me as well. *You have to get on with it.* Why? Why should a twenty-six-year-old actress feel this fear and loathing in her heart? Why should her teacher be worried for her? *Why this response?* Because, went the unspoken postscript, before you know it, you'll be thirty. And if you don't have some kind of decent career going by the time you're thirty, then you should probably just pack it in altogether.

I think it's safe to say that most women in our society are driven quietly mad by the blatant double standard that exists with regard to aging. Men are allowed, and have always been allowed, to age, and age sexily. Deep substantial lines around a man's face only show how rugged he is, what a robust Hemingwayesque existence he has led—if not actually killing wild animals, at least bagging a decent 401k. On the other hand, women whose faces sport the lines of their many and varied (and courageous and vital and generous and brilliant) experiences are considered less attractive for it. I myself hope I can welcome the battle scars, not be ashamed of them. I want to be one of those women who wear the lines around her face proudly, badges of my own many and varied experiences, fondly remembered laughing fits and crying jags. But the fact is I am, deep down, petrified of wrinkles.

The irony is that my face is still smooth. Sometimes I think fear of lines to come is worse than for those we already have. My nightly routine in front of the bathroom mirror is comical. I peer invasively at every teeny line, God help it, to assess the likelihood that it might become a Serious Wrinkle. I tug and pull at my skin with a morbid curiosity, imagining what the plastic surgery that I am not planning to have might look like. I, like many thirty-something women, find myself in a perpetual purgatory of the face: the fear of aging that is to come.

My feeling is that, as more and more women flock to the surgeon's knife and the Botox needle, there is no way for us as a society to ever move to a more enlightened place, to ever even *see* enough attractive older faces to be able to decide, "That's for me." Most successful older actresses in Hollywood have had work done, so we don't have any idea of what an attractive older woman's face really looks like—not in the public sphere, anyway. I remember a few years ago I saw a magazine profile of Diane Keaton. I stared at the photo and exclaimed "Oh my god, she hasn't had surgery!" It seemed that strange.

I hope I have the courage to follow in Keaton's footsteps—to allow myself to age naturally. It's my job as an actress to reflect what's real, what's out there in the world, and the vast majority of women do show their true age as the years tick by. Sometimes I wish more audiences, particularly female audiences, would go out in bigger numbers to films that celebrate older or middle-aged women, films like *Iris* and *Tumbleweeds*. If the box office numbers for movies like this were stronger, it would ensure more of them got made in the future. I dream of an entertainment industry that increasingly respects and profits from the rich, infinitely complex beauty of women thirty and beyond.

I have an actress friend in Los Angeles who assiduously lies about her age by precisely one year and has done so for ages. I asked her about it once—could a mere 365 days really boost one's career by that much?—and she always says she does it because when she first got to town, her manager and agents "accidentally" understood that she was one year younger than she was, and, not wanting to jeopardize these relationships, she has never 'fessed up to the real deal. To me, this epitomizes the age panic that women in Hollywood feel. She's got one year on the rest of us—better not lose it.

But that brings us to the other nasty truth about ageism in Hollywood. Because it exists, most actresses lie about their real age by anywhere from two to five years. That means that those of us who are *not* lying are automatically aged up, and end up at a competitive disadvantage by adding years to our perceived age. The only real solution is for *all* actresses to stop lying about their age, an extraordinarily difficult thing to ask of them given the current industry (and societal) obsession with youth. And so the cycle perpetuates itself.

When I first got to Hollywood, I usually lopped a few years off my age if it came up, but I found it too exhausting trying to remember how old I was. I think Malcolm X had it right: If you're not part of the solution, you're part of the problem. So I've stopped lying. Like most other actresses, my default position on the subject is just to say nothing. I'm aware that this solution is less than ideal, a separate peace, if you will. Ignoring the subject always reminds me of how Victorians pretended women didn't sweat or excrete waste. But keeping mum still seems more dignified than nervously clinging to a lie.

Ralph Waldo Emerson once said, "To be yourself in a world that is constantly trying to make you something else is the greatest accomplishment." I've found this to be true, and one of the guiding touchstones of my life. Now that I'm in my thirties, I feel a growing confidence, power, and intelligence, a deeply rooted emerging strength. But it's testament to the volatility of the subject of age that I often feel my strength countered by a quiet, forceful dread lurking stubbornly behind. It's stoked when I pick up a women's magazine, when I see the airbrushed photo spreads of famous movie stars, and when I see the plethora of newspaper ads for facial surgery and Botox. Will I be one of those women—in addition to Keaton, Meryl Streep and Susan Sarandon come to mind—who takes the risk of aging authentically? So many women over forty are put out to pasture and told to go away. This is what an actress's fear of aging really reflects. But I don't think the answer to the dilemma necessarily lies at the end of a surgeon's knife. I think when you radiate something real and something true, people are interested in it, whether you're twenty or eighty. So I know the answer lies with me. It's *my* will, *my* spirit and *my* creativity that will keep me prominent in my field, not the agility of my dermatologist. And if my honesty—combined with the honesty of a growing number of women—can help dismantle a status quo that equates beauty with the antiseptic blank slate of youth, that would be great. I hope I can follow in the footsteps of the strong, dynamic women who have come before me and grow more courageous—not more fearful—as I get older.

Scheherazade Has Left the Building

Laila Lalami

The Moving Finger writes; and, having writ,
Moves on: nor all your Piety nor Wit
Shall lure it back to cancel half a Line
Nor all your Tears wash out a Word of it.

Omar Khayyam

My mother always says I'm just like my father, and for quite some time now I've suspected she doesn't mean this in a good way. I try to point out that my father is quiet while I'm talkative, that he rarely leaves home whereas I travel all the time, that he tends to be a loner while I have many friends. "It doesn't matter," she says. "You're just like your father."

I was born in Rabat, Morocco. My father, a mechanical engineer by trade, wanted his children, my sister and me especially, to have a career and be independent. He was the kind of man who was as likely to buy me a doll as a truck for my birthday. In addition, he was a fiercely uncompromising man, so much so that it cost him more than one promotion at work. He preferred to design his projects in the right way rather than just follow his bosses' orders. My mother complained about his stubbornness constantly. My father was also a huge fan of comic books and spy novels, and my childhood memories of him nearly always feature him with a cigarette in one hand and a book in the other. I, too, loved books, devouring anything from Driss Chraïbi to *Spider-Man* to Alexandre Dumas. When, at the age of ten, I started writing poetry, my father said it was "cute," the way one might praise a child who can throw four coins up in the air and catch them before they fall. He and my mother sat on a divan in the living room, under a framed photograph of a younger version of themselves, watching me recite my verse. My father clapped enthusiastically. "Lovely, isn't it?" he'd say, turning to my mother, who smiled proudly and asked to have the poem so she could read it again later. Sometimes my sister, my brother, and I would stage plays after dinner, making capes out of our sheets and using the broom as a sword. My parents thought our plays were great fun.

But when I announced, at the age of fifteen, that I wanted to be a writer, my father's reaction was no different than if I had told him I was planning on selling chickpeas in paper cones at street corners. "A writer? You can't be serious," he said. "That's not a job," he sniffed, pushing his plastic-frame glasses farther up on his nose. He wanted me to pick a sensible career, like law or engineering, something that would earn me a living when I grew up. We ended up arguing heatedly, and I ran up to my room, sobbing, slamming the door behind me. "He says I can't be a writer," I wailed, and threw myself facedown on my bed. My sister, who was working on her science homework, looked up from her notebook and watched me in dismay. She got up from the desk and came to sit next to me. "You could be a journalist," she offered, diplomatically, as she stroked my hair. My father and I went back and forth over this for a few weeks. "How about a teacher?" my father suggested at last. "You could always write," he said, "as a hobby." He meant well, of course, but after stubbornly asserting and reasserting this mantra, he eventually convinced me that writing was just not something people did for a living.

Fast forward fifteen years. I had just finished a Ph.D. in linguistics at the University of Southern California and I was working for a start-up company in Los Angeles, developing language processing software. I loved my job and spent long hours there on weekdays, sometimes weekends. My father was quite pleased with the way things had turned out. He and my mother flew from Morocco regularly to visit me or my sister, a neuroscientist who worked for a medical device company in northern California. On one of their visits I took them to see my office. My father picked up one of my business cards and slipped it into his wallet, a big grin on his face.

There was only one problem with this picture. After work, instead of watching TV or going out to dinner or the movies, I'd sit at my laptop, writing stories I saved in a file that, perhaps tellingly, was labeled "Personal." I had become a closeted writer. Writing is a solitary activity to begin with, but, in my case, it was also a silent one. I never talked about it to my friends or colleagues. Given my upbringing, my image of the writer bore quite a bit of resemblance to that of the starving artist in a Paris garret. Like a drug addict, I would not admit that I partook in writing every day.

With my thirtieth birthday looming, I began to wonder why I still felt unfulfilled. I went into a depression that lasted for several weeks. It wasn't the prospect of added wrinkles around my eyes or the appearance of cellulite on my thighs that made me feel this way, nor was it the sound of a biological clock ticking somewhere. I just had a niggling feeling that I wanted more from life, and I knew that the void wasn't something that could be filled by having a more youthful body, or a bigger bank account, or even a baby. I wondered if maybe I had been right all along, if there was more to writing than just a hobby. I'd written poems, short stories, and even seventy pages of a thinly disguised roman à clef, but I'd never taken any of them past the stage of early drafts. The only significant goal I could think of for my thirties was to try my hand at writing.

Shortly after my birthday, I announced that I was leaving my job to write full-time. Needless to say, my father was not pleased. Every time I called, he asked me why I wanted to do it. Our phone conversations at the time went something like this:

"But why do you want to write?"

"Because I want to."

"But can't you write and work at the same time?"

"Writing *is* work, Baba."

"How about you work part-time?"

"No."

"How about you work from home?"

"No."

And the next time we spoke on the phone, the conversation would start all over again. I suspect that a big part of his resistance to the idea was that, despite having a good relationship with my husband, my father didn't want me to be financially dependent on a man. I don't think he believed I would do it until he and my mother visited again, and he saw me at home on a weekday, sitting at my desk, writing. My mother was supportive during this time. I think she was quite proud that I had gone through with my decision, because standing up to others wasn't something I had done much of when I was still a teenager living at home.

Eventually, my father resigned himself to the reality of my new life. He even wanted to help, in his own way. Sometimes, when he told me a particularly juicy anecdote about his past, he would end it by saying, "You should use this in one of your stories." However tempting it was, I never did. Writing was a refuge, a place where I could let my imagination and my vision come alive. I didn't want to be telling *his* stories; I wanted to tell mine. But I often talked to him about my work, asking him to confirm the name of a street in our hometown, or to elucidate a confusing detail of history.

Then I decided to take a writing course at the extension program of a local university. When I arrived for the first day of classes, I discovered, much to my horror, that students were to bring copies of their stories and offer them up for critique by their peers, a process known as the "workshop." I'm not sure what I had expected, but it wasn't having my work publicly dissected, which seemed to me to be only slightly worse than having to strip off your clothes in front of strangers. I signed up for the last available slot. Each week, I watched my classmates make polite starts on what they liked in a story, and then settle into the part that occupied the greater portion of their time—telling the writer what was wrong, what they disliked, and what they would change. Finally my turn came. My story was about a woman who was visiting a friend of hers in Fez to ask for money owed her, but was so shy she couldn't quite bring herself to come out and demand it.

Instead of the outbursts that other stories usually engendered, mine was met with a long silence that stretched for an interminable minute. I shifted uneasily in my seat. Luckily, a man in a white button-down shirt, who kept capping and uncapping his pen, smiled at me. "I liked your story," he said, "but, well, I thought it didn't have enough detail. For example, you mention in passing a rug under the table. But Morocco has such beautiful rugs. And you don't describe this one!" A woman sitting at the other end of the table nodded her head vigorously. "You have to make the most of your exotic setting," she chimed in. I dutifully wrote down their comments, even as I wondered what they thought about the characters, their relationships, their longings, and their failures.

I went home and wrote another story, this time adding as many details about the rug as I could. To be safe, I even described the clothes, the furniture, and the dishes. I felt like I was writing something for an anthropology paper—this is the Moroccan in his native habitat; his house features hand-woven wool rugs in warm colors and geometric motifs; he wears a long-sleeved robe with a hood thrown over the shoulders; he has a wife and 2.8 kids. I registered for another class, thinking I had it "right." This time, I thought, with the scenery out of the way, I might finally hear something about the story, in which a young girl, faced with an abusive teacher, resorts to manipulation in order to get him caught. I signed up for the first available slot.

A week later, I waited eagerly as one of my classmates leafed through my story again, slipped the manuscript on the table, and heaved a sigh. "There's something missing here," she said. "Morocco is a Muslim country and yet I don't get the sense that the girl in your story is Muslim. There's no mention of her being covered." I would have reminded her that the story was set five thousand miles away from Afghanistan, in the urban jungle of Casablanca, where women are as likely to wear jeans as they are jellabas, but one of the rules of the workshop was that attendees could not respond or defend their stories. A friendly guy in our class, a musician by day, added, "I think you're right. I mean, I didn't understand why the father here drinks whiskey with his friends, alcohol being forbidden and all." If I wasn't told that my women characters ought to spend their time like Scheherazade, reclining on harem sofas and smoking cigarettes while being waited on by eunuchs, it's probably because I had stopped listening. My thoughts had drifted to another period of my life, when I had been confronted with similarly narrow-minded views about my culture.

I was in college in London when the Gulf War erupted in 1991. Newspaper headlines in big, block letters used words like *evil* and *Satanic* to describe the land and the people. Television reports constantly told of the cowardice and atrocities committed by the Iraqis, and the courage and generosity of "our boys." I remember sitting in an underground train on my way to Euston station, the seats around me remaining empty even as the car filled, passengers preferring to stand by the doors rather than sit next to an Arab. I remember putting my purse down at Marks & Spencer to try on a wool coat, and seeing the saleswoman run toward me. "Ma'am, please keep your bag with you at all times!" she cried, a look of concern on her face. Everywhere I went, I made myself small because I was so afraid. Mostly, though, I felt ashamed, as though I had done something wrong.

But instead of voicing my objections, or at the very least ignoring people's comments, I listened. I tried to blend in. I started to blow-dry my curly hair straight, even though it took me forty-five minutes every morning. I wore cream foundation two shades too light and plucked my eyebrows. I watched BBC News every day, trying to perfect the *r*s and the *o*s that would make my English accent flawless. If I saw other Arabs at a grocery store, I did not say hello or make eye contact. On Sundays, I would gather five one-pound coins and walk to the phone booth down the street from my apartment to call my parents. If someone walked by while I was talking to them in Arabic, I switched to French. I would have done anything to hide my Arabness, to be indistinguishable, invisible even. I felt alone.

Whatever I did, though, I still couldn't change the way some people acted. They still said the same bigoted things, no matter how much makeup I wore or how straight my hair was. It was worse, in a way, because when my disguise was successful, they felt even freer to voice their hostile opinions. I was in line at a bookstore once, and a woman who was buying a newspaper pointed to the picture on the front and told the clerk the appropriate thing to do about the "people in those Arab countries" was just to bomb them all "and start from scratch." One day, on a double-decker bus, I sat next to a charming old lady in a red cashmere coat, with whom I had a pleasant conversation on our way to the mall until a Bengali woman came on with her three children. The lady shook her head, turned to me and whispered that this country was being overrun with immigrants.

What saved me were books. I was reading as voraciously as ever, and, by then, I'd come across the novels of Mohammed Choukri, Tahar Ben Jelloun, and Ahdaf Soueif, the memoirs of Leila Ahmed and Leila Abouzeid, the scholarship of Noam Chomsky and Edward Said. I read about people who sounded like my family, dilemmas I recognized, experiences I'd had. It wasn't the first time that I'd read books like these, but it was only then, after I'd been taken out of the comfort of my home and transplanted in another country, that their meaning took on a personal resonance. I thought about the narrator in Soueif's story "1964," and how she got through school abroad, and I didn't feel so alone anymore.

Instead of wanting to change, I learned to rejoice in my traditions, in my corkscrew curls and the color of my skin. I learned that being an outsider wasn't a bad thing, whether I was in school in England or back home in Morocco. It gave me a vantage point from which I could observe, and it taught me never to take things at face value, a useful lesson for a writer, I think. I tried to remember that lesson while I sat in class and I wondered whose story I was trying to tell. I knew I didn't want to fall into the trap of recounting titillating incidents straight out of the five o'clock news, devoid of relationships or nuances, and which, rather than challenge Western readers, tend to merely comfort them that they are lucky to live in a free country. I wanted to build a complete, complex picture, in which the people, not the exotic scenery, are in focus, and to engage the readers in the characters' relationships with one another. I stopped taking notes and politely waited for the foolish comments to stop.

I used to worry about having started writing seriously on my thirtieth birthday. Most writers I admired had published their first books before the age of thirty, people like Chinua Achebe or Flannery O'Connor or Salman Rushdie. These days, one often hears about twenty-year-old prodigies who land big advances, publish their books, and are hailed as the next big thing until they fall into oblivion. Looking back, though, I'm quite content with the way things turned out. If my early workshop experiences had happened in my early twenties, I fear I may well have listened to the feedback and churned out one of those short stories or novels that services the Orientalist imagination but has no basis in reality, or at least in *my* reality or that of people I know. I realize that this means I probably won't have a bestseller like the *Princess* series or be selected for the next TV book club. But now that I'm in the third decade of my life, I'm either too old or too stubborn to change my writing to fit whatever agenda a reader brings to the story. Or maybe I'm just committed to seeing my own vision, instead of someone else's, come alive in a story. And to anyone who asks me about rugs, I don't mind going on the record as saying I don't care about the rug. If you want rugs, I suggest the Pottery Barn catalog. But if you want to hear about the kid who wove the rug, then maybe I've got a story for you.

My father's belief that writing wasn't a serious job changed the course of my twenties, and there were times when I resented him bitterly for it. But, having waited so long to make the leap into the writing life, I knew I would have the strength to write exactly what I wanted, how I wanted. So my mother may be right after all: I am stubborn, just like my father.

Wide Awake

Marisa de los Santos

*The child's round head pushes its one, one, one
into the world and then the lament begins
about being set apart, about being next in line.*

Michelle Boisseau,
from "Cardinality"

Charles breaks with day into our room, his clear voice, black eyes, and small square shoulders registering as radiance, even to my half-awake, half-reluctant senses, even in the early dawn dark. In the crib next to our bed, Annabel stirs in her delicate, animal sleep. I am waking, and my waking is—or wants to be—an easing into morning, stretching, groaning, relearning the joints of my body, testing the climate of wakefulness. But Charles is newly three, an age when moving from one state of being to another is as effortless as stepping through a doorway, or running through it full tilt, yelping about pancakes. The kid is loud. The baby is asleep. She's five months old; her sleep time is something we feel we've worked for, earned in some hardscrabble way, scratched from the earth like coal or diamonds. No way she's waking up.

It's my turn, so I'm up and downstairs with Charles, who's started a conversation with someone, possibly me, possibly not, about the pachycephalosaurus, the hardness of its head. He's breaking the word into its roots—pachy means thick, like pachyderm, Mama, thick skin, elephants are pachyderms; the mouse in *Dumbo* says it like packee-doym, remember, Mama, and cephalo means head. And as only the world's worst parent would ignore something like this, I start to talk to him, point out the bigness and hardness of his own head, groggily coin the word *megapachycephalocharlesaurus*. I lay a hand on the top of that warm, round head, and—boom—here I am, wide awake in the middle of my life; there's no going back.

I'm thirty-six, just turned. I've been married ten years. I have two children, although it might be more accurate to say they have me, because it's a clear certainty that in both the most basic and most complex ways, I belong to them, as they will never belong to me. I have had two pregnancies, two births. Because of my circumstances (amazing husband, financial stability, planned pregnancies), I was able to experience both births as miracles. Though it sounds odd, they were miracles I was prepared for, which is not to say they weren't startling. Foreknowledge of one's participation in the divine, the eternal, the cycle of life, biology's best magic trick, however you want to imagine it, doesn't preclude being rocked to the core when the actual baby, screaming and slick, emerges from your actual body.

What I was not prepared for was that as soon as they were born, my children were inevitabilities. Both times, I looked into my new baby's pink face, leaf-shaped eyes, and understood that in a very real way, all the events, not only of my life but of human and prehuman history, had been leading up to this particular grouping of cells, this live, loud, singular organism. In being born, they could never not have been born.

Except. Except that my thirtieth year was the year of profound indecision, of back and forth, the year our children slipped in and out of my imagination like little ghosts. It was the year my children almost didn't happen.

There seemed to be no reason not to go for it. David and I had been married five years, a rock-solid, joyful marriage; we were both finished with school; our writing and teaching careers were doing reasonably well; we were by no means rolling in dough, but could definitely swing one small baby. We lived in a converted sugar factory overlooking the Brandywine River in Wilmington, Delaware. In brave moments, I would imagine standing with my baby on the balcony of our apartment, surrounded by potted plants and dangling wind chimes. She would gaze at the spangled water and laugh; he would clap a furry eggplant leaf between fat palms. But the brave moments never lasted long.

I went off the Pill, back on. Off. On. At some point, I think my hormones stopped seesawing and just buzzed around like angry bees in the locked jar of my body. I remember hitting a particularly low point in bed at a friend's rented house in Amagansett. All night, I lay taut and shivering with panic, while my husband slept beside me. As the morning rippled blue and green outside the sheer curtains, I felt an idea take shape, a word: never. I placed it between us on the bed like something hard and solid, then fell into a calm, decided sleep, a thief's sleep.

What David and I said was that *we* couldn't make up our minds; *we* kept changing them. But even as we presented this unified front—to our friends, to each other—we knew it wasn't quite true. I was the one. I was the problem. David was ready, was gung-ho, but good sport, kind man that he was and is, he said "we" and carefully kept the disappointment out of his eyes. He hoped. He waited. I felt his waiting, felt also the weight and power of the trump card I held: it was my body.

Was this it? The holdup? Body. The body thing. It could have been; it was an excuse I toyed with anyway. At thirty, after years of animosity, I'd established a kind of wary truce with my body. I cheered for the shoulders, loved the neck, accepted the stomach, gave a thumbs-up to the cheekbones, praised the arms, saluted the hands, shrugged at the caboose, and scrupulously ignored the thighs. At thirty, my body was what it was. The idea of it becoming something else for nine months was exciting. The idea of it becoming something else forever was unsettling, but not too unsettling. I'd heard of movie stars who adopted children to avoid the weight gain, the stretching, the maybe-incomplete bouncing back. I was not a movie star. I was not hounded by paparazzi. My body wasn't all that great to begin with. My husband would never stop loving me. These were comforting thoughts.

In fact, I didn't think them very often. More often, I considered the loss of freedom as a possible excuse for not having kids. Freedom to go on spur-of-the-moment trips: a week in Maine, a weekend in New York; freedom to have sex anywhere, anytime; freedom to splurge on cashmere and high-heeled boots; freedom to drink cock-tails out of fragile glasses; freedom to cook elaborate dinners involv-ing black truffle oil or cardamom seeds or morels; freedom to spend the livelong day writing. Et cetera. Et cetera. Again, not the real rea-son for waffling. David and I liked our life; we had fun. But we weren't exactly Scott and Zelda. We didn't work and play at a fever-pitch pace. We had a taste for ordinariness, were full of inner reservoirs of quiet and concentration. And we weren't so absorbed in each other that the two of us were the whole world, binary stars whirling around the galaxy. Our marriage was spacious and abundant, plenty of room to spare.

As I teetered on or stepped back from the edge of motherhood, what I spent a lot of time thinking about was my own mother. Until I was fourteen, I loved my mother and knew everything about her. In the fall of my fourteenth year, I loved my mother and I didn't know her at all.

The day my mother's life slanted off, for me, into mystery, the sky was that single, brutal blue that looks hard enough to smack a hand against. I'd come home from school to find her perched on the edge of the kitchen counter, nervous and too vivid, with a herky-jerky smile lipsticked coral. In the past several months, weight had fallen off her at a remarkable pace. She'd loved being thin, would come home swinging shopping bags full of new, borrowable clothes. As she sat on the counter that bad afternoon, I saw that without my noticing, her slenderness had tipped over into frailty. Her hands looked almost translucent. They fluttered and dropped, fluttered and dropped.

Later, my mother, who should, on that day, have been nowhere near a car, drove to my sister's elementary school to pick her up, and I went with her. My mother laughed and cried, her words jetting off suddenly out of nowhere into nowhere. She told me suddenly, in a high, singing voice, that married women should only ever have sex with their husbands, told me that certain people were stealing dogs from our neighborhood—it was a ring, a dog-ring—and were then bringing them back to collect the advertised rewards. She followed one car a long way down a wrong road because the car was red. She stopped once for a hitchhiker, an unthinkable thing for her to do, and then sped away laughing, bright mouth wide open, when his hand touched the car-door handle. I remember looking out the car window and seeing a world I didn't recognize. Sunlight turned windows of strange houses into mean rectangles of glare; the road we drove on was a twisting, scribbled line. I'd been on those neighborhood roads hundreds of times; they no longer belonged to me because she no longer belonged to me.

Somehow, we got to the school, and I ran in to get Kristina, who was ten, as chubby and smart then as she is lithe and beautiful and smart now. That year, 1981, probably marked a high point in our sister-hood's long fighting era. Until I left for college, our relationship was all extremes. One night we'd sleep in the guest room and talk until morning; the next day, we'd fire insults and harder missiles (books, shoes, once a can of Pledge) at each other. But on the afternoon of my mother's transformation, I felt only immense tenderness for my sister; while she sat in her classroom, our world had slid into chaos. As I walked with her through the halls of the school, hand prints blooming in gar-ish colors on the wall, a large paper train curling back in places to re-veal spent loops of masking tape, I tried to explain the change in our mother. "She's not herself" was what I came up with, which naturally wasn't quite right. I see that now. She was herself and was a person unrecognizable to me, two things I felt could not possibly be true at the same time.

When we got to the sidewalk outside the school, my mother was not waiting in the car, restored to "herself" as I'd hoped she'd be. I had thought, *She will not want to scare Tina. She will repair herself. I will walk into the school and walk out, and she will be herself again.* Instead, she was gone. No green Volvo and no mother, and I stood with my sister and prayed at the brittle blue sky. When the car pulled from around the back of the school and stopped in front of us, I opened the door, and my mother did not say "Get in, girls. I'm fine; everything's fine." She said, "Didn't you get my signal that you should meet me in the back? When you were inside, I sent you both a signal. Why didn't you get it?"

Later that day, my mother and I sat in the basement den, and she looked at me through someone else's eyes, the pupils swallowing all the familiar brown, asking, pleading for a birthday party, a big one, with her brother Charlie there playing his guitar.

The treatment of my mother's manic-depressive illness was eventually as successful as that sort of treatment ever is. The chemicals in her brain were able to pull themselves back into balance (at the time, I was a gymnast and pictured fallen performers climbing wearily back onto beams to complete their routines). It felt like a miracle that soon after she was admitted to a hospital in Washington, D.C.——not the hospital where my father was a surgeon——she was able to call us on the phone, shaky and tearful. Her voice sounded sodden, weighed down with lithium, but she made sense, was lucid, reassuring, *there.*

But sixteen years later, what I remembered most was not the gift of her return, but the hopelessness that preceded it. The evening my father took my mother to the hospital, my sister and I sat together on the back steps dully watching a glassy sky lapse into heaps of color behind the trees in our yard. I was blank, unbelieving, completely unmoored. I thought, *Gone, gone, gone.* I thought, *Everything is over.*

Years later, in graduate school, I would learn how many cultures, ours included, wrongly turn motherhood into a kind of cult, the mother-child connection into a bond of mythic proportions. We talked about the Mother with a capital "M," an exaggeration, a lie, a scam, a construct in desperate need of deconstruction. Because it just wasn't fair: too much weight, too much responsibility, a universe of guilt.

But if my experience as a student of postmodern feminist theory taught me one thing, the experience of being my mother's daughter taught me quite another. What I have known since I was fourteen is that the bond between mother and child is a ruthless one, one that renders concepts like fairness and proportion moot. At thirty, as I considered motherhood, I had to confront my experiential knowledge that when you are a mother, you become a world to your child, or a way of being in the world, whether you like it or not. Also that motherhood means holding a baby in your arms and accepting an essential truth: nothing, not one thing, not me with all my wonders and complexities, matters more than this.

How did I finally get comfortable with the immensity of motherhood? How did I put my fears to rest? I didn't. But one day I was talking to a fellow thirty-year-old, a friend who was terrified of marriage. She said it was the word *forever* that got her; she just didn't see how two people could make a life with something that big, that final hanging over them. I explained to her that once you are married, the idea of marriage doesn't sit in the middle of the room like an elephant while you live your life. Eternity doesn't peer out at you from your morning coffee or down at you from the ceiling as you and your husband laugh your heads off at *The Graduate* for the tenth time; it doesn't poke its head around the corner as you fight. Later, it occurred to me that the same must be true for motherhood. It must be like any other kind of love, figured out minute to minute, achieved in acts and dailiness. And, like any other kind of love, it requires a leap of faith.

My son calls me in the night, and I rush to his room, tripping over noisy toys, a clattering block tower, Rock 'n' Roll Elmo, something that plays, endlessly, "Eine kleine Nachtmusik." In the next room, my daughter babbles in her sleep. I whisper, "Charles?" in the dark, and it all combines to make a fractured song, my nightmusic. My little boy is sound asleep. He is a solid, damp-haired, fragrant fact under his blanket. It always surprises me: another day over, and I have had love enough for everyone—son, daughter, husband. There is even some left over for the thirty-year-old woman I was, the scared one, the one with sense enough to tremble before an absolute, then plunge into her life.

A Random Sampling
Age Thirty to Forty

AYUN HALLIDAY

Every time I recall something I'm not recalling it really,
I'm recalling my last memory of it.

SPALDING GRAY,
quoting Jorge Luis Borges quoting his father in *Swimming to Cambodia*

I'll be turning forty in a few months.

A random sampling of things that happened to me between the
ages of thirty and forty:

Moved to New York City
Got married
Got pregnant
Had a baby
Started a zine
Got pregnant again
Moved to Brooklyn
Had another baby
Wrote a book
Book got published
World Trade Center collapsed

Wrote another book
Book got published
Wrote another book (should be out by the time you read this)

A random sampling of things that happened to me between the ages of twenty and thirty:

Graduated from college
Bummed around world
Got pregnant
Worked in several dozen restaurants
Acted in several low-budget plays
Lived with three men, including the one I would marry

A random sampling of things that happened to me between the ages of ten and twenty:

Played Heidi in *Heidi*
Parents split up while I was at Disneyworld celebrating my
    thirteenth birthday
Got stepfather
Got driver's license
Got drunk
Got stoned
Lost virginity
Graduated from high school
Went to college

A random sampling of things that happened to me between the ages of zero and ten:

Born
Learned to walk, eat solids, talk, use the potty every single time,
    read, write, draw, pledge allegiance to the flag, lie, masturbate,

and regurgitate Bible verses in return for prizes (most notably a lime green polyester pillow with an embroidered cross and a small medallion of Jesus' head with the words *I Am an Episcopalian* stamped on the back)

A random sampling of things that didn't happen to me between the ages of thirty and forty:

Didn't learn to play the accordion
Didn't learn to speak Spanish
Didn't learn to ride a unicycle
Didn't buy an apartment
Didn't get six-pack abs
Didn't get cast in a movie
Didn't even audition
Didn't sell any illustrations to the *New Yorker*
Didn't even try
Didn't mend any of the clothes I refused to throw out because all
     they needed was a minor repair
Didn't look up every unfamiliar word I came upon while reading
     and jot its definition down in a little notebook, even though
     that's been my only New Year's resolution for at least six years
Didn't learn how to make paper

A random sampling of some other things that happened to me between the ages of thirty and forty:

Subscribed to at least four magazines (but didn't always renew
     when the subscriptions lapsed)
Broke down and bought an air conditioner
Asked for and received an accordion
Cut hair really short
Grew it out

Simultaneously lost passport, marriage license, and driver's
   license only to find them several months later
Stopped pretending to like someone who simultaneously stopped
   pretending to like me
Determined that "favorite book" is still "favorite book" after
   rereading it for the first time in fifteen years
Scooped the kitty litter

*A random sampling of some things that happened between
the ages of thirty and forty, but probably only because I had children:*

Exposed breasts in public
Excrement in purse
Started zine
Wound up in hospital
Wound up in hospital again
Book contract #1
Met ninety percent of the people I would consider friends
Lice

Complete listing of stamps in passport, age thirty to forty:

Netherlands (we were supposed to honeymoon in Paris, but
   Pakistan International Airlines changed their flight pattern
   and failed to notify the passengers in advance of takeoff)
UK
Japan
Mexico

(Canada wouldn't stamp my passport. Neither would Germany. Except
for the Canada part, is this some new European Union deal?)

Complete listing of stamps in passport, age twenty to thirty:

UK
France
Spain
Portugal
Italy
Austria
Germany (they stamped it back then, all right)
Belgium
Netherlands
Tanzania
Rwanda
Kenya
Singapore
Malaysia
Thailand
Indonesia
Hong Kong
Japan
Vietnam
India

A random sampling of things that brought me great pleasure, age thirty to forty:

The children
Husband's artistic success
Old boyfriend's artistic success
Okay, I'll admit it, my own artistic success (let it continue)
Running around the circus ring in Vermont, dressed in white,
    waving a hand-printed flag labeled "Sister Frying Pan"

Mexico
The Ramones
Health insurance
The Brooklyn Bridge, especially at night
Eel avocado rolls

Illicit affairs, age twenty to thirty:

Four (if I remember correctly)

Illicit affairs, age thirty to forty:

Zero

New friends, age thirty to forty:

Close: three
Friendly: maybe ten
Friendly acquaintances: innumerable
E-mail friends: I'm suspicious of those
Friends lost: three

A random sampling of things that made my blood boil, age thirty to forty:

The children
Other assorted family members (one day I'll write a book)
The current administration
The Broadway revival of *The Music Man*
The whole circumcision thing
Divine Secrets of the Ya-Ya Sisterhood
When that courtesy call never came

False alarms, age thirty to forty:

Breast cancer

Breast cancer again

Disappearance of cat means death of cat

Loss of passport, marriage license, and driver's license

A random sampling of things that happened to other people but still had a significant impact on my life between the ages of thirty and forty:

Wrote a play that eradicated the need for day jobs (husband)

Started having seizures, which were eventually controlled
through medication (daughter)

Died in the playground (Viola)

Died in World Trade Center attacks on September 11, 2001
(2,630 people)

Enrolled in public school across the street (daughter)

Enrolled in public school across the street (son)

Five world events of the last decade that spring to mind immediately:

1. Itzhak Rabin assassinated (on my wedding day)
2. O. J. Simpson acquitted (shortly after we moved to New York)
3. World Trade Center attacked (saw it out the window)
4. Yassir Arafat died (just a couple of days ago)
5. Bush reelected (that sucks far more forcefully than M. Lewinsky)

A random sampling of things that scared the shit out of me, age thirty to forty:

Being prepped for an emergency C-section

Palpating that "ropelike" mass

The possibility of a dirty bomb being released in the New York
City subway (with me on it)
That one of my children would come down with a septic infection
The President's Christian faith
The two weeks the kids and I spent all alone in the woods of
Cape Cod

A few goals for the time between now and my fortieth birthday:

Find a red leather couch that can fit up the stairway and through
our front door, and buy it without excessive dithering
Paint the office a nice shade of snow pea
Look fit in bathing suit
Read *Don Quixote*
Get to the Dominican Republic
Take accordion lessons
Find a cheap church basement that will rent to an atheist, book a
contra band, send out invitations
Look up every unfamiliar word I come upon while reading and
jot its definition down in a little notebook

I'm the One

ERIN ERGENBRIGHT

"You can't repeat the past."
"Can't repeat the past?" he asked incredulously.
"Why of course you can!"

F. SCOTT FITZGERALD,
The Great Gatsby

At twenty-two, I remember suddenly awakening in the thread-bare sheets and rented room of my then-boyfriend, a thirty-year-old, ADD-afflicted physics Ph.D. candidate. I had just graduated and was leaving both him and the state, and as I looked at my neglected surroundings I thought, *When I'm thirty, I'm going to be married, own a house, and be writing for a living.*

I believed myself to be independent because I spent a lot of time alone in the sunset fields of Findley wildlife refuge, reveling in the shimmer of green-gold grasses and the lonely honking of southward geese. I once lay down for a long time in the giant, frozen imprint of a tractor tire, watching the clouds feather above me, happy that no one knew where I was. But I was far from independent; in fact, the reason I was leaving the state was because I couldn't walk down the street without running into somebody I'd dated. I was headed for Savannah, Georgia, where my best friend was in art school. I wanted to take a year off before graduate school, and also take a year off from men. I wanted to remember who I was, and what I loved, and figure out why I considered the attention and opinions of others the only proof of my worth in the world.

It took me only three and a half weeks to abandon my plans for self-improvement for a guy I worked with at the coffee shop inside Books-A-Million. He was funny, he was nice, and we were sitting in the dark corner of an Irish pub on the riverfront when he told me he knew he could assuage my relationship fears and untangle my issues. "Won't you trust me?" he asked, pushing aside our basket of fries to grab my hands. "Sweetie, I'm the *one*," he said.

He spoke with such authority and tenderness that I assumed he was accessing some deep wisdom I didn't have. The band began "Whiskey in the Jar," which, at that point, I'd heard only twice in my life and still really appreciated. The subsequent clapping muffled the voice in my head that said, "*Him? He's* the one? Shouldn't *I* get to decide?"

Then, at thirty-two, with far too many similar incidents behind me, I was on the flip side of that same crossroads. For the last two years I'd been in a difficult, confusing, all-consuming, on/off relationship that was suddenly, finally, truly over.

Weeks after the breakup, I was still waking at five a.m. with my heart pounding, feeling as if I were dying. I'd pull my knees to my chest and rock myself, trying to summon all the wise and soothing things friends and family had said. There was an ache behind my breastbone, a place I could push on and dull for a moment, though I knew heartbreak didn't really happen in the heart, but in the body and the mind. I remembered how a week before the new girl appeared Henry had said he'd never felt closer to me, that he envisioned a future with me, and I'd fallen asleep with his feet pressing against mine in a Morse code of tenderness. Far too many thoughts and memories of him circled and hovered like the late summer fruit flies that had commandeered my kitchen. I'd almost given up on them; no matter how many I killed, they multiplied, seeming to feed on air.

I likewise fed my sorrow by thinking about the trip Henry and I had recently taken to Lake George for a friend's wedding. A week after his tender words and two weeks before the trip, he'd simultaneously announced that he finally saw all the amazing things in me he'd mostly been blind to before, and that he was seeing someone else. And I didn't cancel our plans because I needed a bookend, a last hurrah, one last high before the requisite low. Or perhaps I wanted to cement an indelible memory, like a song that reminds you viscerally of a time and place and person.

After spending a few hours on the beach, we lay on our motel bed looking at guidebooks. Our bare feet touched. We hadn't slept together since I knew there was someone else, and now, alone with him, the buzzing electricity of proximity was nearly audible. I imagine he'd told the new girl, "Oh, no, we have separate beds, separate rooms; we're separate."

But we weren't, of course, and when he pulled me close and asked, "So what should we do now?" I didn't protest too much.

What about the fact he had a date the night following our return? It didn't matter. Was I sure I wanted to do this? Of course. I would have agreed to anything, and I did. We would be utterly together this weekend, let go of the reins, no holds barred. And when the wheels touched down on the runway of our hometown, we would take some time apart to assess the situation. I still had hope for him, for us, I had always loved a good lost cause. "Are you ready?" he asked, our mouths inches apart.

At the wedding luau on the shores of Lake George, most guests wore grass skirts over their jeans and were happy to let the rented hula girls teach them a few steps. Henry and I had never danced together, I realized, as we were forced onto the carpet of fake grass to be taught the steps and hand gestures, which included a pantomime of fishing—casting off and reeling in, then casting off again. We improvised the best we could, laughing, blushing. He pretended to cast and reel me in, then cast me off, and do it again. We were giddy. We watched the sun glitter and sink over the lake, behind the Adirondacks.

Our weekend together didn't change anything, of course. We came home and he went over to the new girl's house, likely to reassure her. Monday morning I woke early, alone, and in my body was the sensation of being cast off and reeled in. It was like my childhood days at the beach, when the pushing, pulling motion of the waves stayed with me, and lying in bed, rocked me to sleep. But now I was wide awake, and I ached.

I also understood, finally, viscerally, that that very motion is what I had been steeping in, and what I'd come to expect during my two years with Henry. The anticipation of the next go-round kept me there like the forgetful goldfish Ani DiFranco describes, to whom the little plastic castle is a surprise every time. My plastic castle was that I knew well the way the story ended, though each go-round inspired hope. "But this time is different," I'd say, earnestly. "He really wants to try."

"You said that last time," my friends said, tiredly, sadly.

When I first met Henry, I didn't really like him. We were at a local winery, listening to a mutual friend playing guitar and crooning Radiohead covers, and though I thought Henry very handsome and fairly charming, I also thought he was rather vain, elitist, and self-important. He had come on his motorcycle, and carried around his helmet to mark that fact. Talking to him, I had one of those moments where you receive a message from yourself so clear it's as if it's written in chalk on a blackboard inches from your face: *Do not get involved with this guy.*

It wasn't an unfamiliar blackboard or a new message, but, as usual, I ignored it. My historical lack of self-preservation had made me slightly wary of my thoughts, as one eventually becomes wary with a careless, flaky, or untruthful friend.

We hung out for a few months, a few times a week, with frequent e-mails and phone calls. I didn't know how he felt about me, but also thought someone who wasn't interested wouldn't pay me so much attention, or give me so much time. His knowledge and opinions and stories and bright smile literally mesmerized me. He seemed to suck the air out of a room; sometimes, around him, I found I was barely breathing, or rather, breathing shallowly, as if frightened, waiting, always, for the inevitable dropping of the other shoe.

One night Henry dropped me off, and ten minutes later, knocked on my window. He had come back to kiss me good night, our first kiss. Pressed against him, nearly crying for joy and relief, I whispered, "Why did you wait so long?"

He shrugged. "We were grown-up flirting. I'm more cautious these days."

I thought he meant he was making a well-considered, adult choice, and it turns out he was. Over a year later he revealed he'd come back that night not because he felt compelled by love or passion, but because he knew I was getting impatient. He wasn't sure he wanted me, but he also wasn't sure he didn't.

Coming back is one of the oldest tricks in the book, because it illustrates both reserve and passion, and plants the seed of never quite knowing what to expect. And this seed blossomed. Indeed, I never knew what to expect. But with time, our lives became increasingly enmeshed. Though our first few months of dating were not particularly successful, and he broke up with me over the phone on Valentine's Day, we continued a sporadic physical relationship that mostly hinged on him. I was ever attuned to the subtle and regular energetic shifts between us, and knew, within minutes of seeing him, where we were headed that day. But even on the days when it was clear we were headed nowhere, I didn't leave.

Soon, I began freelancing for the magazine he edited. Then, knowing my precarious financial situation, he offered his basement apartment in exchange for thirty hours of work on his house each month.

I knew it was a horrible idea, but I believed then what he much later admitted was actually true: he was scared. He was offering as much as he could give, and I wanted whatever I could get.

And toward that end, when he decided to run for public office, I slipped into the role of campaign manager without quite examining my motivations or the time commitment it would require. His home office, washer, and dryer were in my apartment, so he had constant access to my space; his campaign lawn signs were stacked high on my kitchen table and counters and in the backseat of my car. I spoke his name many, many times, every day.

Many nights, late, we sat on the back porch, debriefing. We'd hug good night, then stand breathing against each other's cheeks and ears, and rub our faces together like animals marking. Slowly, as if not wanting to have to acknowledge what was happening, our mouths would find each other. We'd have weeks of closeness then, but at some point he'd hug me good night, without the nuzzling or kissing, and suddenly we'd gone back to being companions, or housemates. We didn't talk about it. And once we did start talking about it, over a year later, the drama and confusion increased as I tried to connect the dots between his actions and his words. He was in love with me, but didn't know if I was good for him. He thought of me mostly platonically. I was the woman he wanted to come home to. His life was open to me. I was his constant. He'd become interested in someone else, and was pursuing it mostly because it would be simple, and not profound, the way it was with me. He wasn't ready for me. Not yet.

We came together and apart so many times that the pain of each ending was familiar, as was the energy and hope of beginning again. Sometimes I understood that had we been on smooth waters for more than five minutes, and I'd had the chance to examine the relationship without the distraction of trying to keep my balance, I might not have wanted it. There were a few times when I woke next to him, slightly panicked, and looked around the room, thinking, *Him? He's the one? Shouldn't I get to choose?*

. . .

My gentle therapist finally gave me an ultimatum: cease contact with Henry or she wouldn't continue to see me. So, since I couldn't see him, I looked at the Lake George pictures taken on a disposable camera. I was strangely surprised and hurt to see that they were nearly all of Henry—clowning, smiling, and showing off, the sun glinting brightly off his golden head. The few pictures he took of me were dark, unfocused; in one my head has blended with the background as if I were in the initial stages of vanishing. Unbidden, a Mariah Carey song I'd long and secretly loved came to me, crooning, "You're vanishing; drifting away." It was a song I'd always associated with strength, an anthem to leaving someone and having his memory fade, but suddenly it felt as if *I* was disappearing, vanishing because I cared more about this man than I cared about myself.

For the first time in two years, I truly, deeply understood there wasn't going to be another beginning, a next go-round. This ending was the real deal, and an old friend said, evenly, "This is the best thing that ever happened to you. Everything else about you is interesting, but *this* is boring. I've heard this story a million times."

I was horrified. Both from hearing such a stark and true view of my sad, fruitless pursuit and from the raw, howling, animal pain I felt, but also because I realized that my friend was right. This relationship was just a new version of the same dance I'd been doing my entire life. Going through the spiral-bound journals I filled through my twenties, I kept finding repeating phrases and epiphanies: *I have learned and forgotten and learned the same simple truths endlessly, like the smooth, mournful cycles of the moon; I want him desperately when I can't have him and when I can, feel disinterested. It's an addiction of sorts, a strange dance, a push and pull.* I found unsent letters that I assumed were to one boyfriend then realized, no, in fact they were to a boyfriend three years later. Same issues, same words.

I don't remember what I felt previously upon discovering that my epiphanies were not really epiphanies, but this time, at thirty-two,

I lost my shit. I cried intermittently for three days, both from the lost possibility of Henry and the yawning, embarrassing realization that I'd spent an inordinate amount of mental and emotional energy plowing hopefully through relationships, having perfected the pattern of running away from men who loved me, and pursuing men who didn't but were happy to keep me around. And despite myself, I'd managed to work and obtain advanced degrees and maintain friendships, but this was despite *myself,* the very "person" who should provide support and self-preservation. This time, I had to change my life, or lose it. Maybe my pain threshold had finally been crossed, and the truths, which had fallen repeatedly on rocky soil and withered, might have a chance to grow.

That day, my day off, I drank too much red wine and had soggy, sad, slightly hysterical phone conversations with seven friends and three ex-boyfriends who concurred with my findings. What a *waste,* I kept thinking. And that night, standing against the bathroom sink, I swirled my toothbrush with blue gel, then looked up into the mirror. I saw my face, and my sad, soft, beautiful eyes, and suddenly felt enormous compassion and tenderness for myself. It was like seeing an old picture of yourself and recognizing how exquisitely perfect you were, though you clearly had no idea.

Then one of the fruit flies from the kitchen zigged in front of my face, having followed the wineglass sitting on the nearby counter, and I remembered the small army massed in the kitchen. "That's *it,*" I said, aloud, using my anger at my lack of self-preservation, a spray bottle of Simple Green, and a sponge to kill each red-eyed fly. I was through being apathetic. I climbed on counters, chased them from refrigerator to cupboard door. I squished them with my sponge and my fingers. It took nearly two hours, but then, they were gone.

The next morning I woke with a throbbing head and the clear remembrance of my month-ago conversation with a lithe clothing designer who said her workout was a dance form called NIA. It incorporates yoga, tai chi, jazz, and aikido with modern dance. She was obsessed with it. She was also dating the instructor, so it was free for her. My memory is like a sieve, but I recalled the class ran every morning at nine-thirty. I knew I had to be there, and pulled on my sweatpants, got in the car, and drove to the downtown dance studio, crying the whole way. The sun broke though the clouds in a jagged golden line over the autumn-hued hills, and it seemed like a sign.

The woman at the desk was a dancer, thin-shouldered and calm, and before buying a monthlong pass I asked her if she thought it was a good workout. "It's simply transformative," she said.

I started to cry again. "I just think I need a month of healing," I whimpered.

She touched my hand, and said "I know what it's like" more sincerely than I knew that line could be said.

I took off my shoes and stepped into the studio to join the circle of dancers. The instructor, Carlos, welcomed me. Small and wiry, with curly, shoulder-length hair, Carlos was wearing gold nail polish and a rhinestone-studded belt. In his gorgeous Mexican accent he talked about moving from the heart, and about the difference between getting lost in the movements and getting *lost*. I gathered that the lost in italics was bad, and was pretty sure that was where I was headed.

We spread out on the smooth wooden floor and started to pulse our hips to the thumping tribal drums—feet wide, bending to scoop the air and then whoosh it over our heads. We moved as if through water, moved as if through clouds. We kicked toward the mirror like warriors; we crouched and twirled and shimmied. I wept. Waves of sorrow came from deep in me, and it was only the loud music that kept my keening from being heard, but I didn't want to leave the room. I wanted to keep feeling, keep moving, and as quickly as the tears came on, I felt rage rising in me, through my stomach and arms and toes. We followed the lead of our instructor, forcefully karate chopping the air, yelling, *"Uhh! Hai!"*

The air from the ceiling fans glanced off my arms and chest, and I moved with an abandon I'd long ago abandoned, or maybe I had never had. We were all sweating and smiling, and I was seriously in love with everyone in the room, including myself, and moved by the bright sheen of the clean wooden floor and the sheer curtains billowing from the tall, east-facing windows, and the nearby clatter of early-morning sidewalks. I was exactly where I was supposed to be at that exact moment, a feeling I don't often have, and I was taking myself back, goddamn it. I was going to heal myself if it killed me.

I left the class sweaty, spent, and without any ability to don my normal-person facade. I cried in the car, thinking about the slaughtered schoolchildren in Russia and the ridiculous, horrible war we'd started. I cried about my mother's sad childhood, and the hurricane victims' terror and the genocide in Sudan. I cried at the vet's and the Verizon cubicle at the mall, and on the street corner while signing up to sponsor a twelve-year-old child, Julie, in the Philippines. While waitressing that night, I tried my best to keep it together but welled up a little talking about a local farmer's heirloom tomatoes and the humane slaughter of grass-fed beef.

But the next day I woke with a floating, calm sensation, and a stillness I'd forgotten existed. I went back to dance class, and only cried a little during the deep-breathing exercise. By the third day of class I wasn't simply walking from place to place, I was swaying. I had music in my head and in my hips. I couldn't stop smiling. I felt as if my body could scarcely contain my hope, or my heart. I thought of how often I'd filled myself with men, literally, and that suddenly I felt full of *myself*.

The next day a few fruit flies came back, but I killed them before leaving for dance class. On the freeway, the golden light illuminated the edges of buildings and trees, and their dimensions were strange and immediate, as if they were cutouts in an enormous pop-up book. *This is where you* live, I thought.

. . .

The gift of yourself sometimes comes at a high price, which is likely why my earnest high school youth pastor campaigned so hard to keep us from "giving it away." But no one takes over your life without your permission, and it's frustrating to see that what I've learned in my thirties is what I've had repeated opportunity to learn in my twenties. Looking through my tattered old journals, in which I've recorded thoughts, in-depth details of boyfriends I can no longer remember, and conversations with wise or intuitive friends, I see I've always had the answers I sought. But perhaps because they were mine, and were in me, I thought they weren't as valid as those found outside, and in others.

I'm still disappointed and sad about Henry. Thoughts of my future used to always include him, and it's hard to witness the fading of the many habits and activities and conversations we shared. It's hard to think about him sharing those things with someone else. But rather than let myself vanish in these feelings, I'm focusing on seeing and doing things differently. My shamelessly silly dance class continues to be the transformative experience I was promised. Yesterday, while we were warming up, Carlos shared some of his own history. "For thirty years I lived in my head, and I was unaware of how much happiness and joy and power I was missing." He changed the steps to a sort of cha cha, and we followed. "You understand, you and your body are co-creators—your body connects you to the world! And you are *creating* your world through your body," he said. His hands reached heavenward, and then out toward us. We mirrored him. "With your hands, you are creating nature! Now big strokes, like a paintbrush! Now little wiggles of your fingers—you're creating trees, and bushes, and all the little creatures."

Someone speaking with a beautiful accent while wearing a rhinestone belt and gold nail polish can get away with saying things that most of us can't, and we were all grinning at him and one another like idiots, but we do create our world, I realized, with our actions and our thoughts. And with Henry, and with a lot of other men, I'd created a lot of unnecessary suffering.

"Now, you can either dance a dance you know, or you can dance a dance you *want* to know," Carlos said. I saw the women around me smile at themselves in the mirror. I looked at myself in the mirror and thought, *Take care of yourself. You get to choose. Be here now. Do something different this time.*

In bed that night, I pictured myself on the sunset shores of Lake George, trying out the unfamiliar, unsteady steps of a dance I didn't yet know, having finally snapped the line that would reel me in but inevitably cast me off again. Dancing alone still felt a little awkward, and trusting myself is hard, as I'm not used to it. But then I hear the strains of Mariah Carey, and see that I'm wearing a rhinestone belt, and I know I'm ready to shake it.

River Love Song

TANYA DONELLY

move the river
so now it goes by my house
so now it flows by my house.

TANYA DONELLY,

from the song "Angel" on the Belly album *Star*

The Berbers of Morocco call the source of creativity *tapregt*, and say it can come to you in the form of a lightning strike or a ghost. *Andagift*, in Icelandic, means "gift from the spirits." In Hebrew, *Hashra'ah*, directly translated as "beyond human power," means both inspiration and the influence of a magnetic field on its environs. The Chinese *qi*, meaning "life-breath," is thought to encompass natural creation as well as the human creative force. I love the Zulu *ugqozi*, where inspiration enters one person and then spreads to the rest of the tribe—a communal event. Shamans believe we draw creative and healing power from the occasional merger of our spirit with the "infinite flow." Painter Paul Klee said: "From the roots the sap flows to the artist, flows through him, flows to his eye. Thus he stands as the trunk of the tree. Battered and stirred by the strength of the flow, he moulds his vision into his work." *Ilham,* in Arabic, was called the Devil of Poetry by Arab poets. I call it the river.

I'm a songwriter and musician, mother and wife. These are my jobs and my joys. If this were a song, I'd end it there. In songs, the tips of mountains will do. You don't have to mention the bulk below; it's implied. Here, when you're writing prose, you often have to clear away the cloud cover to find more mountain. So here goes.

I've been a songwriter and musician since I was fifteen, professionally since twenty-one. This was not an inevitability. I'd made up songs and provided my own soundtrack from the time I could hum, but this might easily have remained a personal quirk. I was seriously shy as a child. When spoken to, I either blushed or blanched, depending. I also had an unfriendly habit of vomiting in crowds. I was the kid whose desk was kept separate. I spent much of my childhood trying to magic myself invisible. I thought this would just be a matter of concentrating my energies on disappearing, but it turned out to be a little more complicated than that.

I finally learned to hide by smiling. This little magic I discovered in the chaos of my parents' social life, which spilled constantly into our house. Born and raised in the artsy-folksy Newport, Rhode Island, of the sixties and seventies, my baby brother and I were surrounded almost constantly by my parents' friends: artists, musicians, actors, activists, feminists, writers. We were treated like peers by many of these people, and were mostly happy for the crowd. And when we needed downtime, we had our tricks. My brother learned to fall instantly asleep anywhere at anytime. I learned that a certain smiling makes you disappear. You're written off and gone, and once you're gone, you can watch and collect. I collected a lot.

There was always music playing at our house, and loud. The Beatles, the Stones, Joni Mitchell, Bob Dylan, Janis Joplin, Woody Guthrie, Hendrix. These people woke me in the morning and sang me to sleep. Even in utero, I listened underwater to the Newport Folk Festival, where my parents worked during the summer I was born. Music was a part of each part of our days. I felt, down deep in me, that I might want to be a part of it, too. I wanted a place to put all the things I was collecting. But that might involve being seen or heard, and this was not for me.

It was my stepsister, Kristin, who became my musical midwife. She had an already demanding, impatient muse by the time we were teenagers, and as a result, couldn't afford to care who could see her or what they thought they saw. She was scared to death and fearless, and she dragged me into view with her. We started playing guitar, we started writing, we started a band, and Kristin started finding places for us to play. By the time we were out of high school, we had label interest and regular gigs. We also had a surprise: as we were getting noticed, the fact of our gender started to become the dominant theme. "What's it like being a woman in rock?" we were asked. I never knew what to say. Had these people never heard of Carole King, or Stevie Nicks, or Chrissie Hynde, or the Runaways, or Carol Bayer Sager for that matter? What did they mean? We weren't giraffes with guitars; we were people. Playing music. Female people playing music. Not circus folk. Our drummer, David, was asked, "What's it like to be in a band with women?" He never knew what to say, either. We were confused that one gender among us would be treated as a strange and unexpected guest. We were coming out of what I now see was a rarefied atmosphere, with plenty of bighearted, mind-speaking women who pretty much did what they wanted. It had never occurred to us that we might be treated as an oddity. It seemed to us that the main difference between men and women in music was that women were asked about being women, and men were asked about their music. Kristin started saying, "Men see boulders; women see the stones." In other words, we are in the details. I came to realize that the subject of Women in Rock is interesting because women in general are interesting.

During these years in Throwing Muses, I continued to think of music as a tangential path that I was temporarily enjoying until I settled down to something I thought would better suit me. Something like beekeeping, or lighthouse keeping, or methodically brushing old dust from some old bone in a comfortably lonely old museum lab. Something that didn't involve rooms filled with people, watching. My shyness had begun to manifest itself as intense stage fright, and more throwing up. In spite of this, I developed as a guitarist, and I developed the strange and fortunate lifestyle of the semi-successful musician. I was able to put an end to my string of jobs by the time I was twenty-two, a string that began at fourteen. This end of day jobs began the cycle that continues to be my job today: writing, rehearsing, recording, and touring. My total immersion in this cycle had two major effects: (1) a growing tendency to define myself by music alone, and (2) the gradual and insidious falling away of my responsibilities as Adult Citizen. I took this as a matter of course, natural to the kind of work we were doing. These effects peaked in my years with Belly, the band I fronted after leaving Throwing Muses, when I decided that I was going to be a songwriter after all and put away the bees and lights and bones.

Here's a sample day from my brief era of fame with Belly, and the few years of aftershock: I am woken up by a phone call from a handler, who makes sure I take a megavitamin prescribed by a doctor because I've been working and playing too hard, drinking too much, and eating too little. I meet the rest on the bus at the designated time, unless I have to be fetched when tardy. Then I'm driven to my destination, where if I have an obligation, I'm again escorted and walked through the situation. Then hopefully I eat something (when coerced) and am taken to a hotel after the sound check. Then I do some interviews and hopefully take a nap, from which I'm woken by a handler who then picks me up and takes me to my show. I sing and play music for a roomful of people, then I go out and drink wine and hang out, then I'm taken back to the hotel, where hopefully I sleep. Now, aside from the wine, this sounds suspiciously like a day in the life of a child. I let this happen. Some do, some don't. (Eventually, a doctor told me that if I didn't start eating and stop drinking, my heart would eat itself. I appreciated the imagery, and started to pull myself together.)

. . .

This lifestyle went on for years. It was simple: my bills were paid through my manager's office, who arranged my finances, arranged my schedule, arranged my life. I wrote, rehearsed, recorded, and toured. I even fell in love with and married a man who joined me in this.

It was during these years that I created a nickname for the spirit of my creativity—I began to think of the source of my songs as a river. I felt that I needed to revere and tend this source, pay it taxes of some kind. I thought of writing as something that required the full energies of my soul, something that wanted rites. I experimented, searching for perfect conditions to "merge with the flow." I tried staying up late, getting up early, listening to music, not listening to music. I tried walking, journaling, meditating, and isolating myself. Belly had broken up, and I took the "solo" position a little too seriously. I took every-thing a little too seriously. I made myself lonely, and held myself hostage to a process that eluded me. (And somehow, in all of this soul-searching, I still managed to write a few songs.)

I was thrown from this microcosmic bubble when I became some-one's mother. This was not an inevitability. I'd always wanted my daughter, but I wasn't sure I was going to have children. I mildly re-sented the implied biological imperative to do so, and I worried about parenting taking me away from work, and not just because I'd lose the time. I suspected that procreating might absorb other creatings, and that the river of songs I had access to would dry up when my water broke. I knew myself; I could only give myself to one thing at a time. I was also nervous about rising to this occasion as Adult Citizen. I wondered if the belated adolescence of my twenties just might have stunted my growth irrevocably.

But then my husband and I made a quick decision and I was preg-nant two weeks later. This was a shock to my system, obviously to my body but also to my spirit, which was used to hovering in the general vicinity of my body and not always fully inhabiting it. I didn't really relate to myself on a visceral level. In the beginning weeks of my pregnancy, I moved into my body, a harrowing process. My daughter and I were like roommates in a house that was new and strange to both of us. We made the adjustment, and were happy. I learned to eat well, and she grew in me. I sang her songs, and she danced under-water. And when she came out, she brought me into the world as surely as I brought her into it. She dragged me into view with her. We were here, finally, together.

And the love took over. I thought love was some bluish, intangible thing that you have some role in creating and defining. I thought it had limits. I thought it was fragile and needed careful care. Then this brute and unwavering love entered me and took over. My suspicions were confirmed. I had less to give. I had less to offer the river, I had less to offer my husband, I had less to offer my friends. In some cases, I even took some back. I hoarded love. I shoved it in my cheeks and held my breath. I'd been in the studio recording in the last months of my pregnancy, and I'd pictured myself touring with my baby strapped to my back. I thought I'd bring her seamlessly into my existing life, but it turned out I was a different kind of mother than I imagined I'd be. I cocooned myself around her, and my focus became almost com-pletely myopic. I stared into her face, and forgot everything else. She came so very first with me that a telescope would have been required to see my other priorities trailing down the road behind her. But there they were, struggling to keep up.

When it came time to work again, I took it slow and tried to write what was happening to me as truly as possible, hoping that the result would be more than some kind of domestic journal. I wondered how Kristin, who has four sons at this point, continued to produce so steadily, both boys and records. She'd had her first child when she was nineteen and had found her balance. I felt like I hadn't caught up with myself yet, and wondered what my river would tell me. Oddly, and in spite of my new perspective shift, I found myself writing on some of the same themes that I had in early years. There was maybe an older edge, a new take, but the old ghosts were all there: death, fear, the moon, and scary love. My daughter's presence had revived my earliest interests, thrown them a line.

When the record came out, it was described as "mature," "adult," and once, "veteran." I was a little concerned about these words, but I was also getting a certain satisfaction from them, the same kind that my daughter now feels when an older kid recognizes an accomplishment of hers. I was also once again surprised at being further marginalized by the music press; moving from the suburb of Women in Rock to its smaller subset, Rock Mamas. "What's it like being a mother in rock?" This time, though, I had answers. But they were still half-formed; I knew that motherhood had obviously changed my life, but I was still too subjective to see how this had really changed me artistically. And while the almost unanimously positive feedback from fans was a huge relief, it was marred by the suspicion that these people weren't getting what was really going on; that I might have less to give them.

It was only when this same possibility was suggested by someone else that I finally started the process of getting over myself. This happened a few months ago, when a smart young man of twenty-seven posted a message on my website that called my artistic and personal evolution into question. He claimed that he couldn't get into my latest album (*Beautysleep*) because it seemed dominated by adolescent themes, themes that he had outgrown. My reaction to this guy's post was initially defensive, because it felt as if someone had called me out. My childishness, my obsessions, my inability to evolve in a timely fashion. This guy could tell. I was embarrassed.

He wrote to me:

John Keats said in a letter to his brother that he was "still in the chamber of maiden-thought" and that he was yet to enter the phase in which "we feel the burden of mystery." I think you're hitting that phase now—the "providential imprudences of youth" have led you onto a strange shore, and the genius girl is now a woman and mother. Your new album though, still has the legacies of adolescence and celebrity clinging to it like barnacles, as if you're afraid to shed them, or don't know how. Sorry to be so personal, but I don't think I'm saying anything you haven't considered already. For me, most of Beautysleep *had a sort of hollow ring to it, as if you really are sleepwalking right now and won't enter the next phase with head held high. Are you just trying to nurse your younger fans into that phase, or are you really sleepwalking?*

I wrote to him:

I'm glad that at one point in your life, my words were in keeping with your experience and meant something to you, and I understand your disappointment in no longer feeling that in my music. I've had similar disappointments myself. But it's rare to impossible that an artist could resonate with anyone for that person's entire life. You don't relate to the record; it doesn't speak to you. That's fine. But you conclude from this that I'm sleepwalking, or that I've beached myself on a "strange shore." I am not, and have not. The providential imprudences of my youth that you mention have led me, albeit circuitously, to my family. You are right in this. But this shore is less strange to me than any that came before. I am gratefully present in my current life, and in this album that expresses it.

I fall into this weird, stilted formality when I'm rattled. It's bad. Obviously, I was trying to seem more calm than I actually was. He'd touched a nerve and I was pissed. I wanted to convey that fact without seeming, well, adolescent about it.

He wrote again:

Adulthood, I think, begins when we start a deliberate process of selection of what we want to keep from all that stuff—we ascribe values to things and (unfortunately) have to clean up and shelve a lot of stuff.

Human nature selects what is most useful and meaningful from experience, and keeps these within the realm of reason, and sifts the rest into the realms of memory/fantasy/nostalgia etc. This is an unfortunate truth, and if we don't allow it to happen, we go nuts! This fantasy stuff is what I insensitively called "barnacles" or remnants or whatever. I don't mean to devalue it—just to put it into context.

At this point I realized that he was unknowingly providing me with a catalyst, one that I used to start this conversation with myself, as well as with him. This exchange brought me back to my record, and I listened until I caught up with it. There wasn't less of me in these new songs at all. I'm right in there, and wide awake. But I had changed, and I could finally hear it, in there among the ghosts and barnacles. And when I did, I remembered: the river doesn't care. The river isn't charting its course by my life's events. It's not my river. I just visit it, like everyone else, and bring my own to it. After a few more back and forth posts to each other, we both started to realize we were more in line than we'd thought. His last words on the subject, writing about a personal epiphany of his, were inspired by his work with children:

For me it was a bit like a wind blew the dust off the tablet of my heart, and I saw words written there that had always been there and always will be there, and it gave me a sense of the interplay between continuity and change. I saw that I had a character and a soul all of my own that were somehow immune to the flux of circumstances.

I wrote:

First of all, that's lovely. And also, I suspect we're describing the same things using very different terms. This is why I sometimes feel uncomfortable with compartmentalizing self-definitions like Inner Child and Adult. I think we are not so tidily arranged. (To quote my daughter: "Sometimes I'm big, and sometimes I'm little.")

So I still write about the moon and ghosts and fear and scary love. And despite the recently acquired (and welcome) knowledge that I come, at best, second in my own life, I'm also still relatively soul-and-self-centered. Immune to the flux. The moon isn't something you grow out of, if you're careful. And if you get good enough at being self-centered, you find all kinds of things in there that have nothing at all to do with you. And maybe you can get away with being preoccupied with the same themes, as long as they're good ones, and as long as you make sure to chart their progress. Leonard Cohen spent twelve years in a Buddhist monastery and he still writes beautiful songs that are basically about women. (And God.) But he's changed, and you can hear it, in there among the girls.

If there is a border between postadolescence and adulthood or whatever, maybe it's when your events and actions stop feeling like symbolic acts of Life, and start feeling more like symptoms of your life, lowercase. Once you represented something; now you are someone. I am a songwriter and musician, mother and wife. These are my joys and jobs. My fears of trading my muse for a child seem silly to me now. My daughter and I are constantly singing and humming our songs. It's a part of each part of our days. She's a great inspiration to me, because I adore her, and because she says the wildest and truest things. She's my bighearted, mind-speaking baby woman. And it turns out that all that early magicking for invisibility apparently did create someone invisible, someone who writes lyrics while I make lunch and build snowmen and dance with my girl. Because now when I do sit down to write, these little songs jump from the river, where they've been waiting for someone to come along and gather them, up from the flow.

> my return to wildlife
> by satellite,
> by beautiful moon-shining girl.
> whether by hard ground

or splashdown,
we're safely back in the world.
　　　—"KEEPING YOU," A LULLABY FOR MY DAUGHTER,
　　　　　　　　　FROM *BEAUTYSLEEP*

time to make sure
the current pauses at your door.
time to seek your own level, baby.
　　　—"ANOTHER MOMENT," FROM *BEAUTYSLEEP*

When He's Just That Into You

VERONICA CHAMBERS

Would you become a pilgrim on the road of love? The first condition
is that you make yourself humble as dust and ashes.

RUMI

I have about three things that I can say with confidence I am really good at: cooking, Monopoly, and training. I have no awards to show for my prowess in the kitchen or the way I kick ass on a Parker Brothers game board or the continental flair with which I navigate the subway in Shanghai or bullet trains in Tokyo or the metro in Paris. But I pull these skills out of my pocket with the same cocky confidence some women display when showing off their killer backhand or their ability to walk in five-inch Manolo Blahniks. These are the things that make me proud.

There are about three hundred things that I am unabashedly mediocre at. They are all the things you might imagine—including a really underwhelming backhand and, despite six seasons of faithful *Sex and the City* viewing, a complete and utter inability to walk around in anything higher than a Sunday-school heel. These are my shortcomings, and the older I get, the more accepting I become that it is my stunning lack of ability in so many things that connects me so strongly to the human race—and keeps me from getting a big head about my cooking, my traveling skills, and my whup-ass Monopoly technique.

There is only one thing at which I can admit to being an unabashed failure, and this thing is dating. I was a big fat loser at dating and, God forbid my marriage ever ends, I am fairly confident that I will be a big fat loser at dating once again. It was like that video game where you try to follow the dance moves and the further you get in the game, the trickier the moves become, until you are just a flailing mess, some graceless, hapless thing like Baryshnikov break dancing. I was clingy and desperate and wore my heart on my sleeve, falling madly in love not once, not twice, but four times. Only to meet with heartbreaking rejection at every turn. Which is why it is nothing short of a miracle that I was, two years ago, swiftly and happily married.

A certain self-help book has topped the bestseller list for weeks on end. The title of it is *He's Just Not That Into You.* I have not read it, only because my friends have assured me that it would not be a pleasant jaunt down memory lane. Apparently, the book is all about women like me. Women who are wearing blinders about the men in their lives. But the reason I am writing this essay is because I wish someone had told me this: it's okay. It's okay to fall head over heels for one loser after another. It's okay to show up at a guy's house with a dozen roses and declare your undying affection. It's okay to have too much to drink and call your ex twenty times and then to be mortally embarrassed when you realize your number must have shown up on his caller ID. It's okay to stand at a phone booth in Times Square on New Year's Eve, drenched like a sewer cat in the pouring rain, crying your eyes out because the man you are infatuated with has decided that he needs some space. It's okay, because I believe that all of these grand gestures and heroic attempts to follow E. M. Forster's simple advice to "only connect" are not really about this guy or that guy. Making a fool of yourself for love (or lust or rebellion or temporary insanity) is ultimately about you, how much you have to give and the distances you will travel to keep your heart wide open when everything around you makes you feel like slamming it shut and soldering it closed like the wiring around a chain-link fence.

Not to digress into too much pop psychology, but I sometimes think that I never really had a chance at being one of those girls who could play it cool. My parents' marriage was a soap opera–worthy saga of dramatic exits and mind games and affairs. When I was little, my father would force me to choose which parent I loved more. If I chose my mother, he would react with fury and rage. If I chose him, he would cover me with hugs and kisses, luxuriating in his victory for all of ten minutes, then promise to come back for me "soon." Soon could mean two days or two weeks or two months. I learned early on that love meant never having to follow through on your promises.

My mother, bless her heart, tried to keep me from becoming a desperate girl with a daddy complex. In seventh grade I got my first boyfriend: one very handsome junior high school star athlete named Chuck Douglas. We went to different schools, so our relationship consisted of long, meandering phone calls—most of which were initiated by me. In those days before call waiting, the hours I spent on the phone were a real issue. One day, when my mother could not reach me after school for three hours straight, she came home early, with the intention of beating some sense into me. When she found me sprawled underneath the dining table, the cord of the phone wrapped like a bracelet, or a handcuff, around my arm, she took sympathy on me. She took me into her bedroom and asked me how often I called Chuck. "All the time," I told her. "And how often does he call you?" she asked. I shrugged. "You can't chase boys," she said. "They don't like it." I was thirteen. Chuck Douglas was dating me, a certified nerd, in a sea of buxom cheerleaders. My mother's words meant nothing to me. I was already lost to the cause.

In college, I discovered women's studies and somehow managed to neatly wrap the words of Gloria Steinem and Angela Davis around my now well-solidified boy craziness. "I'm a feminist," I declared. "I don't need to wait for a man to ask me out." So I asked out guy after guy after guy: the very epitome of he's just not that into you. I dated numerous gay men who were not yet out of the closet. It became a kind of service after awhile, coaching ex-boyfriends out of the closet. I went out with a techno DJ who invited me to go sailing with his parents. It wasn't until we were parking the car at the boat dock, and were a good six-hour drive from our college, that he announced his parents were nudists. I hated his taste in music, he was a terrible kisser, his parents were weird, but I still cried a week later when he dumped me. I went out with a cool art director that every woman at the magazine at which I was interning was head over heels in love with. It took me eight months to realize that he had a long-term, live-in girlfriend. I did the breaking up then, but it hurt all the same.

I didn't date only unavailable men. In my twenties, I had two long-term relationships with men who were all-around great guys: smart, funny, committed men who were "just that into me." The reason I broke it off with those gentlemen is hard to describe. I can only say that in their own ways, they were both very privileged and I couldn't help but feel that if the relationships continued there would come a point when I would feel more like their mother than their girlfriend or their wife. And I knew that eventually that kind of situation would suffocate me.

So I found myself back out in the wilds of the dating world. At this time, the hot self-help dating book was *The Rules*. There were many rules that were supposed to help you lasso a man, but the one I remember said that you should never accept a date for Saturday, after Thursday. *The Rules* reminded me of that conversation I had with my mother about the swoon-worthy Chuck Douglas when I was thirteen. I understood that the rules were good for me, but so is tofu and I just can't stand the stuff.

Desperate for role models, I turned to cinema therapy. I spent long hours watching women like Katharine Hepburn and Audrey Hepburn and Lauren Bacall be smart and sexy and absolutely irresistible. My girlfriend Cassandra insisted that men are like lions; they want to chase their prey. She asked me to show her how I put on my makeup. I tore through the routine in six minutes flat. Your face is like a painter's canvas, she said, trying to get me to blend colors and take the time to be the beauty I wanted to be. She suggested that I smile at a guy I was interested in, instead of barreling him over with conversation. "See what he does," she said. "If you're feeling playful, then maybe give him a little wink."

Soon after, I was invited by a friend to take a trip to South Africa. One enchanted morning my friend and I were having breakfast in the hotel restaurant. Across the room, I saw the most charming man with the kind of friendly face that you feel you have known forever. Leaving the restaurant, I stood up and saw that he was looking my way. I smiled. He smiled back. Feeling bold, I winked, then tripped on a step and fell flat on my face. The next few minutes were dizzying as I was surrounded by hotel staff, offering me ice and bandages and one very irate manager, who insisted that I could not be moved until I signed a waiver releasing the hotel of all responsibility for my fall. Then I heard a voice amid the cacophony. It was the man I had winked at. I turned away, mortified. He said, "You should see a doctor." I insisted that I was fine. He said, "Well, let me be the judge of that, because I happen to be a doctor."

He took me out to dinner that night and every night for the rest of my trip. We exchanged phone numbers and despite the fact that I lived in New York and he lived in Sydney, and my mother had been warning me for close to twenty years about my happy-go-lucky dialing finger, I called him and I called him because I was so sure that what I felt for this man was, if not love, then certainly "magic." It wasn't. To give the guy a little credit, we lived continents away from each other. Even if he was that into me, it would've been a hard row to hoe.

It was about this time, when I was in my late twenties, that I read a nugget of advice, probably in a women's magazine, that I took to heart.

This article suggested that if you knew you were going to meet the love of your life in one year, you would really enjoy this year. This seemed reasonable. So while I still tended to wear my heart on my sleeve and commit too quickly, I also had some really fun one-off dates with guys I knew were never going to call. I went to the theater and to hip-hop shows and tried to relax about the whole dating and mating thing.

About a year later, I met the man who would become my husband. I was introduced to him, three times over the course of eight months, by my very good friend Lise Funderburg. Lise never said that Jason was my soul mate, she simply kept saying that, unlike the vast majority of men I was meeting in New York, he was a guy who could hold his own. He was not a *Sex and the City* Mr. Big, a type I was well acquainted with in New York—the über-successful guy who always keeps you at arm's length. Nor was he a starving artist, who was willing to fall head over heels in love while nursing major commitment issues about things like holding down a job and paying bills. Jason was a regular guy: he had a good job, he owned his own house, he liked his parents. Eight months after our first date, he proposed.

All of a sudden, the role I had been playing my entire dating life was reversed. I did not want to get married. I had never been angling for a ring. What I had wanted all throughout my twenties was a really great boyfriend: someone who called when he said he would call, someone who would get up early and go running with me over the Brooklyn Bridge and who would jump at the chance at weekend getaways in the Berkshires. I wanted simple things like reading the Sunday paper together in bed, someone who would bring me chicken soup when I felt ill. I wanted someone to sit next to me during foreign movies and someone who would send me flowers on Valentine's Day and, sometimes, for no reason at all. Jason, my then boyfriend, said he wanted all the same things, too. But to his mind, the relationship I described was marriage, not dating. And so I said yes.

Which is probably why after two years of holy matrimony, I still make the mistake of calling Jason "my boyfriend" instead of "my husband." He is, in every way, the best boyfriend I've ever had. No one ever told me that a really great marriage can make up for two decades of horrible dating. No one ever said that all those guys who were "just not that into you" can be, for women, the psychological equivalent of notches on a bedpost. I'm so happy, now, that I dated the DJ, the doctor, the candlestick maker. When I look back at those relationships, I can see that, in the midst of all the drama, I managed to have a goodly amount of fun. What would have happened if any of those relationships had lasted, bumbling along in all their glaring wrongness? Instead of just being dumped and consoling myself with pints of Chunky Monkey and multiple viewings of *Breakfast at Tiffany's,* I could've been facing any one of these men in divorce court, or being forced to see them every Saturday afternoon, when we met to swap custody of our children or our cocker spaniel. Thank God all those men were just not that into me. They did me a bigger favor than I could ever have known.

The Late Bloomer

CARLA KIHLSTEDT

Never fear: the world spins nightly toward
its brightness and we are on it.

C. D. WRIGHT,
Crescent

Grandma Carla always said that it would all begin at thirty for me. In her thick Croatian accent, she would say, "I vish zat I vould be alive to see her ven she is sirty. That vill be somsink." From the very start, I did everything late and slow, but with total determination. I took my first steps late, but when I had spent enough time studying the art of pedestrian mobility from afar, I just up and walked with minimal stumbling. I spoke so late that my parents began to worry that perhaps I wouldn't speak at all, but when I finally did, I skipped right to the three-syllable words. One day, after a family trip to the zoo, sitting on the dining-room table, I came out with a very deliberate, albeit awkward, interpretation of the word *elephant*.

My late physical development was something of a minor trauma for me. All of the girls had bras or at least training bras, and I couldn't even justify a couple of Band-Aids, until at the beginning of school one year, I came in with full-fledged boobs that left the double-A-cupped girls in the dust.

My Grandma Carla (for whom I am named) knew by then about the consistent nature of people, and so knew that everything for me would come late, and she was right. My life has always been on a slightly slower train . . . no Swiss precision for this girl. Late, late, late. I was late to be born by many weeks; I was late to get my period, late to experiment with drugs, and extremely late to grow into the clear acne-free skin of adulthood. Yes, and I'm late to act like I'm well into adulthood now. My hair is often blue, or some other-than-what-God-meant color. I only recently grew out of the collegiate futon-on-the-floor situation. I still have trouble keeping my room clean, bills paid on time, receipts filed.

I'm thirty-three. Thirty-three. Yessiree. Whoop-dee-dee. Feels like me. Though the knees are a bit stiff, and the hands are just like my mom's. I remember the day I pinched my knuckle-skin and it stayed where I left it instead of eagerly snapping back to the bone. And I thought, my hands are just like my mom's hands. And my mom, she remembers the day she looked down and pinched her knuckle-skin, and said my hands are just like my mom's. And Grandma Patti, too . . . she remembered the same day when her hands were just like her mom's. Mom hands. And bruises, they happen more easily now . . . a gentle nudge on the coffee table corner, and a small sunset shows itself like a slow French film on my thigh.

Do my cats know how old I am? Does my neighbor know how old I am? You know how old I am. I told you. What *is* there to know about a thirty-three-year-old woman? Some of the usual questions: Is she married, and does she have kids? No, and no. And if she's not and doesn't, does she wish she were and did? No, and not yet. Doesn't she know that she's not getting younger? No, she forgets that sometimes. Maybe we should tell her. Some of the more unusual questions: Does she still have overalls in her closet? Yes, several pairs. And she mentioned cats? Yes, two. One is Milo—for Venus de—and one is Diego.

Who are her friends? They are six and fifty-six and forty and twenty-five. Most of them are musicians . . . not all. A lopsided version of the world, for sure.

I tour a lot. A lot a lot. In buses and cars, in trains and airplanes. I have spent a lot of time hurtling through space in these small metal capsules, and getting out each night for several hours at a time to contribute my noise to the general din of various towns across the United States and Europe. Most of my home-ec skills I've picked up in the service of my bands. I learned how to sew by making costumes for Sleepytime Gorilla Museum, and I've learned how to cook in the kitchen of our tour bus during the two-month-long trips across the middle of the country, where road food usually means brown, fried, and unidentified. Cottage cheese is pretty safe, and if you add enough hot sauce to it, it actually gets really good. There's a certain comfort in constant movement, and in the bizarre juxtaposition of 60 mph with a whole lot of sitting still.

It is an odd life, but I like it for now. Its financial realities are less than encouraging, but it's really built on a leap of faith and reason that is akin to religious fanaticism; the belief that somehow, somewhere, it is important enough to someone or something that we keep making and performing music. Every gig, every song, from one perspective, feels like a matter of life and death, and from another perspective, just shades away, feels like it's only rock and roll.

As a kid, I was always very serious and focused. When I was three, I would examine bugs on the sidewalk with my tiny forehead all crumpled up for hours, and come inside with a list of questions for my parents: "How do they tell each other apart?" and "Do they have names?" By the time I was five, my bug obsession had been supplanted by a violin obsession, or at least a music obsession. I drove and was driven to faraway lessons and farther away summer camps (maybe that's really when the touring seed was planted). But I could never really put my blinders on securely enough to block out as much of the world as the staunch classical music education would like. From the beginning, I was causing my violin teachers grief by exhibiting what they all call "talent," or "promise," or "charisma" (all strangely nebulous, but dramatic terms) and then getting so easily "distracted" by an art project, or a history-class trip, or writing, all of which are deemed secondary to a young classical upstart.

I also had the inherited belief of a younger sibling that somehow, everyone has the answers except me, especially my big sister, Rya. There must have been some great confab that I had missed where everyone was briefed on the rules. I never thought I could learn how to drive, for instance. The fact that billions of people before me had learned without a hitch was not at all convincing. I was sure that there was some reason I alone would not be able to coordinate the eyes, hands, and feet to make the car go (and stop) in the right direction, or at the right time. And in fact, the first day that my father took me out to an empty parking lot for a trial spin, I mistook the accelerator for the brake and drove right into the bike rack, which was the only object in the entire lot. My big sister, on the other hand, seemed to have things all figured out. She had a social ease and an apparent confidence that were utterly baffling to me. I wasn't sure what she had figured out exactly, but I knew that whatever it was, it would always elude me.

Even now, in musical situations, I always re-create that same "little sister" role. I seem to find people whom I believe are more experienced and more knowledgeable than I am, jump in and hang on for dear life. I joined a female-fronted vocal band, Charming Hostess, under totally false pretenses. I hadn't really ever sung before . . . not anywhere but alone, anyway. So there I went. Sink or swim has some merits, if you end up swimming.

I love being in my thirties, except for that one knee thing. I like that forty used to sound close to dead when I was a tyke, and now it seems young. And I think it's funny that college campuses make me feel like a lascivious old lady watching the young colts and bucks romp and shuffle. In many ways, the anticipation of thirty was much worse than its actual arrival, much like the scare that had everybody storing up their canned food and securing small fortresses in their basements on the cusp of Y2K. The day came and went without event. I was, predictably, on tour with Tin Hat Trio, playing in Amsterdam. Mark and Rob got the audience to sing a rousing and cacophonous rendition of "Happy Birthday" that would have made Harry Partch smile. At midnight, I did not turn into a charwoman, and my train out of Amsterdam did not turn into a mouse-drawn pumpkin.

Relief was actually the prevailing sentiment on the first days of my thirties. The worry about where I should be, what I should have accomplished by now, has been replaced by an enjoyment of where I actually am, what I have the opportunities to do, who I get to spend my time with. In a way, turning thirty replaced ambition with a kind of trust. My goals became simpler, based less on proving things to the outside world, and more on exploring parts of the world that are still new and curious to me. I finally began to embrace the quirks and oddities that make up my musical and personal tendencies, without being proud or embarrassed by them.

It seems that as I turned thirty, a whole layer of unnecessary chatter has evaporated from my head. I have come to suspect that perhaps the great confab never happened for anyone, that maybe nobody got the epic tome with all the rules and answers printed small and upside down in the back. That maybe everyone else makes up their own answers, and that these bits of imagination are as real as anything needs to be. The legend of classical music that I grew up believing in finally took its place in my own pantheon of ideas, instead of the other way around. I spent my nights torturing my family with scratchy violin noises, my teens learning the ropes of the classical world, my twenties trying to get untangled from them, and now finally, in my thirties I get to pull at them when I need them. I have much more fun playing music than ever before. It all seems more transparent than I ever understood it to be. Those tortured youthful questions of identity seem not answerable so much as necessarily fluid, and even, at times, irrelevant. And that's when things get really fun. That's when people get really interesting. That's when music is more about experience than it is about me or you or him or her. That's when pride and embarrassment both fall away. These things, I like about being older today than I was yesterday.

Grandma Carla's prediction was a fairly bold statement for a woman who grew up in a time when thirty was considered almost over the hill. I don't know if I am "somsink" yet, but I like this better than any other age I have been, at least out of the ones I can remember. But then my mother says that sixty is better than fifty is better than forty is better than thirty, so maybe this somsink is yet to come.

Of Sweethearts and Sperm Banks

TANYA SHAFFER

I've dreamed you for so long, I can hardly believe you're with me now.
Yet here you are, a tiny human voyager,
sleeping off the shock of migration.

TANYA SHAFFER,
Baby Taj

On May 10, 2001, I sat on a mountaintop near Dharmsala, India, watching the last rosy gleam of the sunset reflect off the snowy peaks of the Himalayas, and made a decision. Throughout my adult life I'd boldly proclaimed to anyone who would listen that if I found myself thirty-five years old and single, I would have a child on my own. Yet for all my bravado, I'd never imagined that day would come. Now my thirty-fifth birthday loomed large, and I was, in fact, unpartnered. Blame it on the writer-slash-actor's peripatetic lifestyle, excessive pickiness, a volatile emotional temperament, or just plain bad luck: my intimate relationships had not panned out as I had hoped.

In the wake of a recent string of disastrous romances, I'd fled to India for some serious soul-searching. After two months of packed trains, magnificent temples, guru-seeking travelers, and sweltering meditation halls, my mind was no closer to finding peace. Then, in a single glorious day, I shook hands with His Holiness the Dalai Lama, climbed six hours up a stony trail, watched the sunset reflected off the Himalayas, and reached a decision. Perhaps it was the simple clarity of His Holiness's gaze that led me to it, or the thin, pure mountain air. Or perhaps it was just my time. Whatever the trigger, as the moon rose cold and bright over the Himalayas, the choice before me became breathtakingly clear. I could continue pining after the life I'd imagined I would have, or I could embrace the life I did have and get on with it. I chose to embrace.

My home base at the time was a close-knit community of three other women and a dog with whom I'd shared a house for the past seven years. One of my roommates was close to my age and longed for a child with as much fervor as I did. She was a lesbian and I was hetero-sexual, but we were both in the same position: single and aching with mama lust. We decided we'd both get pregnant through artificial insem-ination, coordinate our schedules around shared child care, and raise our children in the loving environment of our San Francisco home.

I returned home and shared the news with my friends and family. They urged me to reconsider—after all, women are having first chil-dren well into their forties these days—but the more I thought about it, the more convinced I became that I was making the right choice. I felt as though everything else in my life was filler, using up time until I could move forward with the one thing I really wanted: raising a child. This wasn't a permanent good-bye to romantic life, I assured them. If anything, I'd be able to date in a more relaxed way when the subtext of my every sentence wasn't "want baby now." Rather than act-ing out of desperation, I was taking a powerful step toward defining my own life.

Valentine's Day 2002 was my target date. If my cycle followed its usual course, I would inject myself with the first vial of anonymous donor sperm on the day dedicated to Cupid, the mischievous vixen of love. It seemed a fitting date to begin what I hoped would be a lifelong love affair with my child.

In January, I purchased four vials of sperm belonging to two separate donors. Although choosing a person I'd never met to donate half of my child's genetic material was nerve-racking, the selection process was no shot in the dark. The thick donor catalog provided more information about these men than most people know about their spouse on their wedding night.

My criteria were fairly simple. The first thing I looked for was intelligence. Though I knew it wasn't a foolproof indicator, I looked for a GPA of 3.5 or higher, coupled with good spelling, grammar, and vocabulary throughout the application. Beyond that, I wanted creativity and well-roundedness: foreign languages, musical instruments, and other artistic pursuits were a plus. Things like warmth and compassion were important, too, of course, but those were harder to spot, and who knew if they were genetic anyway? Still, I spent hours poring over the documents, trying to glean personality traits from handwriting, word choice, and the answers to questions like "Why do you want to become a donor?"

My first-choice donor was tall, dark, and—according to the clinician who interviewed him—handsome, the oldest son of a Spanish mother and Italian father. He was a medical internist in his twenties for whom the extra $60 to $120 a week (depending on whether he came in once or twice) was a quick and easy way to help defray the high cost of living in the San Francisco Bay Area. He played piano, guitar, and drums, and spoke fluent Spanish, English, and French. His GPA was 3.8 and his family medical history showed no cause for alarm. He described himself as genial and even-tempered, though slightly shy when getting to know someone. I wished I could get a date with him instead of just a shot of his DNA.

Unfortunately, I wasn't the only would-be mama who'd noticed this guy's assets. When I called to purchase his sperm, only two vials remained. I'd hoped to get four, in case it didn't take right away, but alas, he had left the program and would make no further donations. I snapped up his last two vials and set about finding an alternate candidate.

There was an amiable Portuguese screenwriter whose parents were both dancers. There was an undergraduate Eastern European physicist with a penchant for classical music, whose response to the question of why he became a donor—"I've got nothing better to do with my semen at the moment . . . long-distance relationship"—endeared him to me immediately. And then there was a Korean-American computer programmer whose heart's desire was to travel to Greece, "to follow in the footsteps of Odysseus." This last one stood out for the originality of his responses. In tiny, controlled handwriting, he made his droll, faintly ironic personality felt in every line of the application. I felt I would have had a crush on him had he been sitting next to me in class. I dubbed him Odysseus and ordered two vials of his sperm.

Three weeks before my planned insemination, I received an e-mail from a man named David. David and I had been in sporadic contact for about three years, since he'd attended a performance of mine with a mutual friend. I'd met him for about thirty seconds backstage, and I vaguely remembered a bespectacled intellectual type with a shy, lopsided grin. He'd e-mailed me that same night to tell me how much he enjoyed the show, and as I do whenever I receive correspondence of that kind, I'd promptly placed him on my mailing list for the duration of his (or my) natural life.

Over the next three years, whenever I sent out a performance announcement, I got an e-mail back from David. He lived in Washington, D.C., and traveled constantly, organizing eye-care programs in developing countries and setting up manufacturing to make medical products affordable for developing country economies. His e-mails invariably came from some far-flung corner of the globe and said something to the effect of: "Wish I could see the show, but I'm in Malawi setting up an eye camp to treat 2,000 people with cataracts." I was intrigued, and after a few years of this sporadic correspondence, I suggested to David that the next time he was in California, perhaps we could meet for tea.

I was performing in San Diego when I received his e-mail telling me he was in the state. It turned out he was going to be in San Diego for a single day the following week. Since his daytime schedule was full, we decided to meet for dinner.

Let the record show that I had absolutely no ulterior motive for dining with this man. I could barely remember what he looked like! Furthermore, I was absolutely determined that nothing should stand in the way of my planned insemination. In the eight months since I'd made the decision to have a baby, I'd already been sidetracked by three short-term dalliances with men. In each case I'd plummeted headlong into an apparently promising relationship and postponed my insemination, only to have the relationship crash and burn a few weeks later. I wasn't going to let it happen again.

At seven P.M. I opened the door of my apartment to a disheveled dark-haired man with wire-rimmed glasses and a sweet, self-effacing grin. We walked through the lively downtown streets of San Diego chatting about the joys and challenges of developing-world travel, until our growling bellies propelled us into a dimly lit Italian restaurant with red-and-white-checked tablecloths and Coke-bottle candleholders covered in melted wax. When I suggested wine, he asked me the difference between white wine and chardonnay.

"You're kidding," I said, wondering whether the bumpkin act was intended to charm (or disarm).

"No," said he.

I cocked an eyebrow skeptically.

"It's a *type* of white wine," I explained. "You can share my glass if you're not ready to commit to your own."

But he was serious. And so we each had a glass of chardonnay, split a salad and a couple of dishes of pasta, and followed it up with a whopping slab of tiramisu that we couldn't half finish between the two of us. At some point in our far-ranging conversation, I mentioned that I planned to curtail my travel for the next couple of years because of a personal project I was working on that would keep me close to home. When he asked what the project was, I coyly responded that I wasn't at liberty to say.

My favorite moment of the night occurred while David was removing his sweater—a bulky black wool number with orange snow-flakes, which he'd purchased in Norway. It was half-on half-off, his shirt rising with it and exposing a slice of furry abs, when the waitress came by and asked if we were ready to order. He froze that way, sweater midair, one arm above his head, and gave her that sheepish, caught-in-the-act grin. It was, I'm afraid, almost unbearably cute.

Do you think any carnal activity took place that night? Well, you're wrong. I stuck to my resolve, and we parted without so much as a butterfly kiss. We did, however, hug good-bye and then stand in the lobby of my apartment building gabbing for a while before parting with a second hug. It was the second hug, David says, that gave me away. With that second hug, he says, he *knew*.

The next morning I received an e-mail from David saying that he'd had a great time and I was a wonderful being. I wrote back saying I'd had a good time, too, and too bad he didn't live in San Francisco. The next morning I got another, longer e-mail, saying he loved the Bay Area and had often felt it was the part of the country in which he felt most at home, and by the way he had some vacation time coming up. I wrote back saying, great, you're welcome to visit, but given your transient lifestyle I don't see this turning into a deeper, shall we say, involvement.

The next day I received a long response saying that he knew that his constant travel had contributed to the demise of his marriage the previous year, and that since he deeply desired a committed relation-ship, he was eager to change his lifestyle.

That night I couldn't sleep. I was enough of a veteran of the dating wars to know that the words *I want to change* uttered in the courtship phase of a relationship were the romantic equivalent of a deed to a bridge in Bora-Bora. And yet there was a sincerity to this David that I couldn't ignore. After all, he'd used the "c" word before I had! Fur-thermore, he was just the sort of person I'd always imagined myself with. In addition to being smart, cute, sweetly nerdy, and quirkily funny, David was committed to the world. He had a passion for helping others that manifested in large-scale, meaningful ways. And then there was that sweater moment.

I rolled around in my queen-size bed, flipping the pillows this way and that. *How do I always manage to conjure up this particular brand of self-torture?* I wondered. *I have a plan; why can't I stick to it?*

At five-thirty A.M.—eight-thirty East Coast time—I called. David was in New York City attending the World Economic Forum, and I wanted to reach him before he left for the morning session. I got his voice mail and left a terse message: "We have to talk."

Half an hour later my phone rang. We talked for four hours, while his sessions and meetings slipped by. He confided that he'd thought of me often since the time we'd first met. When his marriage dissolved the previous year, he'd wanted to get in touch, but until this week he hadn't had the nerve. When I told him the nature of my "personal project," his response was immediate. "I'm a walking sperm bank," he said. "I'm practically swimming in sperm." David's ex-wife had been unable to have children, and he had accepted the prospect of a childless life. Since their separation, however, the idea of having children had opened up for him. For the first time, he'd felt a tug, as though somewhere out there a voice was calling.

We determined that day that we would have children together. A week and countless phone hours later, he asked me how I felt about marriage as a general concept. I told him I didn't really care that much one way or the other, and he said he didn't either. Then a few minutes later I said that, if I was honest, I probably would prefer to be married, and he said so would he.

For a while we reminded each other that our plans were only a fantasy until we'd spent more time together. But as the days passed, it became harder and harder to keep that in mind. With each conversation our connection felt more real. Though I wasn't trashing my vials of sperm just yet, I decided to postpone the insemination once again.

When I returned to San Francisco and told my roommates I was engaged, they looked at me as if I'd joined the Moonies. What's amazing to me is not that David and I made these decisions so quickly—God knows I'd made rash pronouncements before while under the narcotic influence of my romantic imagination—but that we actually turned out to have the right combination of chemistry, compatibility, and commitment for the relationship to endure. David explains that he went about our relationship the same way he goes about his work: he began with intuition, created an assumption, then gathered data to test the assumption. On the night of our third meeting, a month after that fateful San Diego dinner, we greeted each other at the airport with an awkward hug and couldn't figure out what to do with our hands. That night, we split the better part of a bottle of merlot ("a type of red wine," I explained), and tested our chemistry on a futon couch of his D.C. apartment. Fortunately, the data was good.

Last month I was walking on the beach in Carmel with David and Tavi, our four-month-old son. David and I walked a few feet apart, absorbed in our thoughts, less like newlyweds than two people who have grown easy with each other. He carried the sleeping baby around his neck in a sling. The pale sun glanced brightly off the corrugated ocean and the flat expanse of near-white sand. My body remembered the countless hours I had walked alone on the beaches, roads, and pathways of this world. For a moment I had the distinct sensation that I had slipped sideways out of my life and into someone else's, that I had somehow eluded the story line that should have been mine. It was a bittersweet sensation, and I took a moment to salute my phantom double: that solo traveler who shadows me still.

Had David not come into my life, I might have become a parent in a less traditional way. Had that come to pass, I'm sure my delight at the miracle of motherhood would have been equally profound. It would have been harder, no question, but I would have made it work. My former roommate has a one-year-old boy, and mother and child move through the world in a bubble of radiant love. Although being a single mother is challenging, she enjoys the strong support of a tight-knit community of friends, of which I am proud to be one.

And so the moral of this story, as I see it, is not so much *buy the sperm, and the man will come* as it is *take a stand for your own happiness, and you can't lose.* As I lie in bed at night, nestled against the warm curve of my husband's back, I marvel at how, once I made my choice, the universe seemed to rise up and support me in mysterious ways. What I feel then is gratitude—tremendous gratitude—that I was able to muster the courage to take a step toward my deepest dream while still staying light enough on my feet to follow the path when it took a most unexpected turn.

Getting Ready

MICHELLE RICHMOND

The past is hidden in some material object . . . which we do not suspect.
And as for that object, it depends on chance
whether we come upon it or not. . . .

MARCEL PROUST,
Remembrance of Things Past

In June, my younger sister and I went home to Alabama. We arrived in Mobile at seven o'clock on a Sunday morning, following a red-eye from San Francisco. Our older sister, who lived in Birmingham, met us at the airport. On the way to our mother's house, we stopped at Krispy Kreme. As we waited in line, watching sheets of golden doughnuts travel by conveyer belt from grease vat to glazing station, I was shuttled back in time to the Sunday mornings of my youth. Back then, Krispy Kreme was a weekly ritual. On our way to church, we always stopped to buy a dozen doughnuts for continental breakfast, which was a fancy word for the array of doughnuts and prepackaged bear claws around which churchgoers gathered before Sunday school.

My mother didn't know we were coming. The trip was a surprise, a gift for her sixtieth birthday. It was hard to believe she was sixty, harder still to believe I was thirty-four and Misty, the baby, was twenty-seven. At thirty-six, our sister, Monica, had long since accepted her lot as a thirty-something: the nine-to-five job, the well-cut suits, the sensible shoes. I, on the other hand, earned my way with pieced-to-gether teaching gigs and the slim proceeds from books and short sto-ries. My closet in San Francisco was filled with Dr. Seuss–inspired Fluevog shoes and baby Ts from Urban Outfitters, and I wasn't averse to wearing pigtails in public. Fashion regression was my way of hold-ing firm to my chosen illusion: that I had only recently left my roaring twenties behind.

Driving home, the car filled with the intoxicating scent of Krispy Kreme. I opened the box—that nostalgic cardboard concoction of white, green, and red—and dipped my fingers into the gooey rows, pulling out a single hot doughnut for the three of us to share. My third of the doughnut melted on my tongue. Although a puff of fried dough topped with a dollop of sugary grease could not compare in elegance to Proust's French confection, the doughnut's ability to conjure the past with dizzying specificity was no less powerful, in my mind, than that of the famous madeleine. Herein lay the sweetness of my youth, the grease and the honey of it. Herein lay the memory of hundreds of Sundays, when the fear-inducing fire and brimstone delivered from the pulpit was somewhat mitigated by the sabbath's culinary delights. After "big church"—the doleful hymns and frightening admonitions, the somber ritual of invitation—there was almost always pot roast and buttery mashed potatoes, or fresh Gulf shrimp dipped in cold ketchup and mayonnaise.

Now, the familiar, flat green landscape spooled out before us. The car's air conditioner was cranked up high, but I could still feel the heat of an Alabama summer bearing down through the windshield. Six months before, I had given birth to my first child, a delightful, en-ergetic boy who still woke several times during the night and could not be persuaded to take naps. Although I had been reluctant to leave him in San Francisco, something magical happened during the long flight home: as the airplane traveled southward, from Silicon Valley to Bible Belt, from Pacific to Central time zone—simultaneously backward and forward in time—I felt myself relaxing for the first time in six months.

Soon we turned into our old neighborhood, where the obligatory brick entryway bearing the subdivision's name had recently been revamped. Hickory Ridge, the enormous sign said, its grandeur silently contested by the seventies-era homes flanking the street. We pulled into the driveway and stepped out of the car into the muggy heat. Azaleas climbed the walls of my mother's house, wisteria hugged the fence. In my ten-year absence from Alabama, broken only by brief annual visits, I'd forgotten how lush the place is; in that climate, everything grows.

We walked through the front door into our own version of the Cleaver household. Family photos crowded the walls, the mantel, even the top of the piano. The bookshelves were stuffed with photo albums. There was the smell of coffee mingled with bacon and a whiff of Windex. From the kitchen, I could hear my mother back in her bedroom, getting ready for church. The blow dryer was going full tilt. By now it was eight A.M., which meant she'd been getting ready for an hour and had another hour to go.

When I think of my teenage years, I think of my mother banging on my bedroom door at seven-fifteen on Sunday morning—every Sunday morning—shouting, "We have to leave for church in two hours, and you haven't even started getting ready." Then she'd go to Monica's room, same routine. She would repeat the offense every ten minutes until the sound of the showers verified that we had extracted ourselves from bed. (Since Misty wasn't yet old enough to wear makeup, she was allowed the luxury of sleeping late.) If Monica or I dared venture into the kitchen for a cup of coffee before wrestling with the blow dryer, our mother would go into panic mode. "We have to leave in an hour and you haven't even dried your hair yet!"

To tell my mother that "getting ready" didn't take more than forty-five minutes was to invite skepticism and ridicule. "It takes me longer than that to do something with *my* hair," she'd say. At this point, she would have already spent an hour with the blow dryer, the "straight" curling iron, the brush curling iron, and a number of products and potions. The closer it came to nine o'clock, the more frantic she became. "You're not even wearing base!" she would cry, as if going out without cosmetic foundation was equal in blasphemy to venturing forth from the house totally nude.

On those endless Sundays, days that stretched out across my childhood like railroad tracks leading to infinity, the preacher exhorted us to put on the full armor of God. Our mother, on the other hand, insisted that we put on the full armor of femininity, which consisted of a half-hour makeup job, a helmet of stiffly coiffed hair, nail polish, jewelry, and waist-to-toe panty hose, preferably control top, even if the temperature topped ninety, which it often did. Looking back, it seems that I spent most of my time from age twelve to seventeen getting ready to meet the world.

My mother's obsession with getting ready extended beyond the cosmetic case. When we went home for her sixtieth birthday, she'd been getting ready to leave Mobile—"too hot," she said, "I don't have any friends here"—for thirty-five years. She had spent about five of those years getting ready to leave our father—putting credit cards in her name, stashing away money in a secret savings account—although in the end he was the one who left, without really getting ready at all.

I remember clearly a cool November morning in Morro Bay, California, during the weekend of my thirtieth birthday. My husband and I were standing in the Aquarium looking at an impressive display of jellyfish. The jellyfish had about them an air of regal patience, their mushroomlike bodies ballooning slowly in vibrant displays of color, their tentacles slithering out gracefully as if to test the width and breadth of the tanks. To my surprise, I was having a wonderful weekend. I had spent so long dreading the day when my clock would click over from twenty-nine to thirty, so many years prematurely lamenting the impending demise of youth, it had never occurred to me that the birthday itself might actually be fun.

As I admired the Zen-like quietude of the elegant jellyfish, I realized that I, like my mother, had spent way too long getting ready. I'd spent my teens getting ready for college, college getting ready for my career, a couple of years after college getting ready to meet the man of my dreams, and the years following graduate school and true love getting ready for my big break. If it is possible for epiphanies to happen in life, not only in the pages of books, I am convinced that I experienced one while standing in the modest aquarium that November day in Morro Bay.

Whereas Chekhov might end a short story with an epiphany perfectly captured in a single sentence, real-life epiphanies tend to be a bit less tidy. Looking back, it seems my own moment of grand realization went something like this: my thirties need not be a terror of pre—middle age into which I would descend kicking and screaming. No, my thirties meant liberation. My thirties meant no more getting ready.

I was thirty years old when I married a man I couldn't have dreamed of in high school, because I didn't know such men existed. Thirty years old when my first book was published. Thirty years old when I got my first gig teaching creative writing at the graduate level, which was the job I'd coveted for a decade. All the years of preparation, all the anxious getting ready, had finally paid off.

A year after the birthday trip to Morro Bay, I spent a summer month at a writers' colony in Costa Rica, where I began writing my third book. One of the other residents, a talented composer from New York named Edward, told the story of a friend of his father who met his end in a very unusual way. The friend, a marine biologist, had been swimming off the coast of northern Australia on a warm spring day. He was in Queensland for a conference, and a number of his colleagues, Edward's father included, were sunbathing on the beach. At one point Edward's father looked up to see his friend running from the water, screaming, his head horrifically encased in what looked like a live, writhing hat. Edward's father immediately recognized the creature that clung to his friend's head as the box jellyfish, whose excruciatingly painful stings can kill a man in sixty seconds flat. Dozens of tentacles draped over the man's face and neck like hair. As he ran screaming from the water, the marine biologist must have known that he was already a dead man. The scientific name for a jellyfish's body form is "free-swimming medusae," a poetic nomenclature for an undeniably poetic creature. In the case of the marine biologist, the name was doubly, unfortunately apt.

When Edward related this story, I thought of the beautiful, deadly jellyfish at the aquarium in Morro Bay, imprisoned in their briny tanks. And I thought about time, how we have a little less of it each day. This sort of morbid thought never occurred to me as a teenager racing toward my twenties, only rarely as a twenty-something racing toward the career and the romance that I envisioned as essential elements of a productive, happy life. For many of us, our thirties are the time when we first confront the specter of the swimming medusa. We do not know what our medusa will be—an illness, a violent crime, a freak accident—but the possibility of it looms large. We may have fifty years left to live, or we may have five, but we no longer subscribe to the illusion of youth, the false notion that we will live forever.

For me, my thirties have meant living more fully, because I am always aware of an invisible clock sounding its inevitable tick, its ominous tock. The moment my son, Oscar, was born, the clock began to speed up. If Oscar follows the traditional route, I will be fifty-six years old when he finishes college—just four years shy of sixty, which once seemed like a very old age to be.

On her sixtieth birthday, a sweltering Sunday in Alabama, my mother emerges from the bedroom with her hair combed and sprayed into submission, her hips trussed in shiny support panty hose, her laugh lines partially hidden by a noticeable layer of foundation. She is wearing a beige slip, and I know the next step of her routine, because it has remained the same all the years of my life; she is on her way to the laundry room to iron her skirt. Despite (rather than because of) all the artificial wrangling to make herself presentable for church, she looks beautiful. This is something my mother has always been good at—looking beautiful—though she would never admit it.

As she emerges from her room, the first person she sees is my younger sister, Misty, the intrepid one who has done lengthy solo stints in Ireland, France, and Ecuador. My mother's face registers shock, elation.

"Misty!" she says, "what—" But she doesn't finish her sentence, because she glances past Misty toward the foyer and sees Monica, then me.

"Surprise!" we say. The word comes out synchronized, as if we'd planned it, which we didn't.

Our mother lets out a little cry, runs toward us, and wraps us up in a hug. Her musky perfume—she seems to wear more of it with each passing year—is layered with the slightly medicinal tinge of hairspray, the waxy scent of lipstick. She's crying, literally speechless for several seconds. She catches her breath, stands back to look at us, to take it all in.

"I can't believe you're home," she says.

Then the tears really start coming. For most of my adult life I've been immune to my mother's emotional outbursts, which seem to be calculated for the greatest dramatic impact. These tears, though, are genuine ("the real McCoy," she would say). Ever since my sisters and I surprised my father for his sixtieth birthday a year and a half ago, our mother has been hinting that she hoped we'd do the same for her. Her hints reached a fever pitch in the weeks leading up to her birthday. Although we fabricated elaborate excuses for why we couldn't make it, I assumed she would have known about our plan, assumed she would have pushed and prodded until her new husband let the cat out of the bag. Apparently, he didn't.

"Happy Birthday," Monica says. Then the three of us launch into a badly off-key version of the song.

"Sorry about our timing," I say. "The only flight we could get from San Francisco was a red-eye. We're going to make you late for church."

"No church today," she says. "I'm just going to sit here and enjoy having all three of my girls home."

She goes back to her room to change into a pair of jeans while Monica makes a fresh pot of coffee. Then we sit around the table eating doughnuts and bacon, talking about the recent developments of our disparate lives: Monica just received a hefty bonus at work and her little girl is about to start second grade; Misty is teaching ESL and trying to get a photography business up and running; I'm slowly adjusting to motherhood and have just sold the book I started writing in Costa Rica. Our mother is one year into her marriage to a quiet man she met three years after my father left, and they're making plans to buy an RV and fulfill her lifelong dream of traveling the country.

I go for the cake doughnuts, Misty for the chocolate-filled, Monica for the glazed. Our mother nibbles at a cruller, staring at us in blissful alarm, as if at any moment we might vanish into thin air. Sitting here, I'm reminded of afternoons after school, when Monica and I would arrive home on the bus to find the kitchen table set for my mother's version of four o'clock tea. There would be tiny teacups filled with milk, and chocolate cake or peanut butter cookies. Our mother would sit us down and ask us about our day. Misty was a toddler then, the center of our attention, and she would play on the floor, beating on pots and pans with a plastic spatula, while we recounted the dramas of elementary school.

Those dramas come to me now in bits and pieces, little flashes of scenes complete with names and vivid colors: the day Boone Scroggins stole my prize-winning potato and smashed it to the ground; the day Billy Grimes kissed Monica on the cheek after chapel and she promised to marry him; the day I got sent to the office for talking in the bathroom (it was Nancy Dees who reported me); the day Ms. Blade, the extraordinarily mean principal, had to chase her wig across the playground, all the way from the merry-go-round to the Love Tree.

For a few minutes, sitting around the familiar table, laughing and telling stories, my sisters and I are kids again, and our mother is young, and there's a whole world out there waiting for us, a world we believe we'll conquer. It was our mother who taught us to believe this, our mother who persisted, day after day, year after year, in getting us ready for the future. She taught us how to play the piano, enrolled us in ballet classes, scraped up money for us to take trips and join clubs and go to expensive private schools. She filled out our loan applications for college, chronicled our small successes in photo albums and scrapbooks—Monica's stint as an Azalea Trail Maid, Misty's trips around the world, my stories and articles (she has a copy of everything I've ever published, starting with my high school yearbook).

Misty is talking about her current boyfriend, a smart, funny guy she met two years ago in Chicago. She can imagine having children with him; she can imagine living with him into old age. My baby sister— the one who exists so clearly in my mind as a toddler beating pots and pans on the floor and sleeping at the foot of my bed, the one whose spunk and spontaneity has always leant an air of youthfulness to our family—is just three years shy of thirty.

As I dust the crumbs off my Oscar the Grouch T-shirt and kick off my Fluevogs, settling into the slow rhythms of home, it occurs to me that there was one thing our mother, for all her careful advising, did not prepare us for, one thing even she must not have seen coming: our thirties. How could she have? We all left home as teenagers, set off to pursue college and careers and love. In her mind we must still be, in some way, those children for whom she arranged afternoon tea parties nearly three decades ago. "As far as I'm concerned," she often reminds us, "you're still my little girls."

On my refrigerator in San Francisco there are two black-and-white photo strips, the kind you get from miniature booths, where you insert a couple of dollars into a slot, close the curtain, and smile four times in rapid succession. The first strip is from 1974, a photo booth in the Rocky Mountains. I am four years old, Monica is five, our mother is knocking on the door of thirty. She bears an alarming resemblance to Jackie O, with her short, dark hair and sultry eyes. In the first frame, her mouth is open and she's leaning forward, looking down, and Monica and I are tottering on the edge of the picture; I can imagine my mother in that moment reaching forward to punch some button in the photo booth, and being caught unaware by the flash of the hidden camera. In the next frame she is smiling, and Monica and I have been righted, although we are looking at each other, not the camera. In the third frame, Monica is fretting, and I'm captured in profile, head tucked down in a way that accentuates my double chin.

I don't know what happens between the third and fourth frames, what soothing or scolding words my mother utters in the brief seconds between flashes. Knowing her, she would have been wary about spending the quarter or two for the photos, would have been determined to get her money's worth. Whatever she said or did, she must have invoked some sort of maternal magic, for in the last frame we have been transformed into the ideal, photogenic threesome—all of us looking directly into the camera, Monica and I smiling angelically, showing teeth and major dimples.

The second photo strip is from the San Francisco Zoo, April 2005. Oscar is five months old, I am thirty-four. In the first frame, he's pulling my hair. In the second, he's still pulling my hair. In the third, his head is turned away from the camera and my eyes are closed. In the fourth frame we're both a mess—my hair is sticking up, his fuzzy hat is askew—but I've somehow managed to focus his attention on the little red light above the blank screen. There we are, frazzled mother and rambunctious son, both of us looking into the camera, grinning. The photo is a bit too close-up to be flattering for *one* of us, and it reveals an unfortunate fact of time: my dimples aren't as well-defined as they used to be. I imagine that, before long, wrinkles will mark the spots where my dimples used to be.

I originally put the photos side by side on the fridge because I found their symmetry pleasing. Now I find them disturbing. "It seems like yesterday," my mother recently said about those pictures from the Rocky Mountains. "Where did the time go?" It's a common sentiment, the baffled refrain of millions of women who look in the mirror one day to find themselves on the other side of youth. It took me thirty-something years to understand the dismay behind that statement, thirty-something years to face my own mirror with the same mixture of shock and tumbling sadness.

It isn't necessarily a bad thing to see always in the corner of one's vision a shadow, a vague form, the ghostly image of the free-swimming medusa. Knowing that the years are not infinite, that there is indeed an end to the journey, makes me approach the days with more attention, less hurry. And while the mirror tells a story I don't quite want to hear, there is at this stage of the game a sense of contentment, of satisfaction, that I never felt in my twenties. These days, I can get from the bed out the door in just over half an hour. Most of that time is spent feeding, changing, and dressing the baby, which means I can get *myself* ready in ten minutes flat, leaving more time for the important stuff—more time, indeed, for living.

I'm *here,* I sometimes remind myself, breathing a great sigh of relief. That place I used to want so badly to be? The big event for which I spent so much time getting ready? Well, I finally made it. The big event is here and now. My train has arrived at the station, and it's a good station. There's a cozy bookstore, a cafe that serves pretty good hot chocolate, a waiting room with comfortable seats. There's great music and fine company. And occasionally, someone shows up from out of the blue, bearing a big box of Krispy Kreme doughnuts.

When Falling Is Flying

DEB NORTON

If I had to live my life again,
I'd make the same mistakes, only sooner.
TALLULAH BANKHEAD

A few years ago, when I was thirty-four years old, I found myself on my back, eyes closed, with a man standing over me telling me I had a lockbox on my throat and a monkey in my pelvis. "How did I get here?" I wondered. In my twenties, I never would have allowed myself to lie there looking foolish while an energy healer pranced around performing the hooky-spooky on me.

The man told me I had a sad, grieving lady in my calf.

"I'm going to tell her to move on," he said.

"No!" I yelled, suddenly afraid.

Where did that come from? Afraid of what?

In my twenties, I knew who I was. And because I knew who I was, I knew what I was supposed to be doing. And this was good. Here is a partial list of what I was: I was an actor, freshly and thoroughly trained and ready to enter the New York theater scene. I was quirky and hard to categorize. I knew this, because all the agents I was meeting were telling me so. I was also a smoker, like it or not, because I was very, very addicted.

But more important, I knew who I was not. This was crucial, since it kept me from wasting time, failing, or looking foolish. Here are are some of the things I was not: I was not a waiter, a writer, a teacher, or a joiner. I was not religious, either traditionally or alternatively speaking. I was not tall and thin.

So how did it happen, then, that I found myself with an energy healer, feeling quite foolish, and participating in an alternative religious activity?

As far as I could tell, I first set foot on the path that led to this strange moment when I decided I would have to quit smoking after all. My reasoning was that, as a smoker, I was setting myself up for looking foolish, and this was not okay. I was twenty-eight, living in Brooklyn, and working in Manhattan, where it had become illegal to light up in restaurants, cafes, and even bars. Neither were any of my friends allowing me to smoke in their homes. I felt transparently pathetic taking a break from a cozy dinner party, exhausting an entire package of matches trying to light my cigarette in the icy rain and then smoking through violently chattering teeth.

Ironically, quitting smoking made a complete fool out of me anyway.

There are people for whom quitting smoking is really no big deal. I congratulate them on their good brain chemicals, but ask that they kindly refrain from parading their excellent fortune in my view. Unlike them, I spent three months with no skin, and then another six carefully and painstakingly growing a new one. I lived life as an emotional sideshow, bursting into tears and bumping into walls in jittery confusion.

I dug my nails in and hung on, though, because my horror of failing outweighed my horror of looking foolish.

Quitting smoking released a mad, somewhat toxic energy in me. I couldn't sit still. I couldn't sleep. I siphoned some of it off with long workouts at my neighborhood gym, the Ninth Street Y in Brooklyn.

They had an Olympic-size swimming pool. On particularly volcanic August days, I would watch women in Speedos and goggles trotting off toward the nice cool water, and I started to really resent being limited to the inadequately air-conditioned cardio and weight rooms.

But I was not a swimmer. I had tried to learn to swim once before, at the age of six when my mother enrolled me in the Pollywog Swim Class at the Taft Recreation Center. There, I had thrashed about so wildly, gulping and spluttering every time I let go of the edge, that I incited panic in the other children. I was excused from lessons by the teacher, and never graduated to Bullfrog.

I was afraid of the water. My bones were too heavy. Becoming a swimmer at twenty-eight seemed about as likely as becoming a sportscaster.

But, God, it was hot. And, I reasoned, the Pollywog fiasco was such a long time ago, before I became a nonfailer. I called my friend Amy, who agreed to be my swim coach.

I'd meet her at the pool every Tuesday and Friday, and she'd supervise while I stood in the water, blowing bubbles and breathing. My face would heat up under the amused stares of the *real* swimmers as they slid into the pool and pushed off to cut smugly through the water, completely ungrateful for their natural relationship with this baffling element.

Then there were weeks of motoring endlessly back and forth on the kickboard. I got a lot of thinking done. I thought about how silly I must look, a grown, begoggled woman blowing bubbles and clinging to a chunk of Styrofoam. I thought about how unwelcoming the water felt, as if it knew I didn't belong there. I thought about how good things were back when I was smoking.

But my fear of failure buoyed me. I paddled doggedly on.

I never became a virtuoso swimmer—one part or another of me always seemed to be dragging toward the bottom—usually my ass. I did manage, though, to get from one end of the pool to the other, holding panic at bay, reminding myself every other stroke that drowning was not imminent, fifteen or so times at a stretch.

This was a great achievement, but it did nothing to relieve my longing for the cushiony comfort of cigarettes. I no longer spent half of the dinner party smoking out in the cold. Instead, I spent it in the bathroom, splashing water on my face in between nicotine attacks and surges of racking emotion.

I was on my way home from just such a dinner party when I was stopped by a flyer on a lightpole. It was flipping back and forth trying to free itself from a last bit of tape and it kept flashing me the word *Nicotine*. I smoothed it flat. It told me it was time to admit I was powerless over my addiction and attend a Nicotine Anonymous meeting.

My mind flashed a red stoplight. Twelve-step was very nearly an organized religion. Some of my friends had called it a cult. And I was not a joiner.

"Look!" the grown-up part of me said. "Desperate measures are needed here. You're going!" I stuffed the flyer in my pocket and dragged myself, kicking and screaming, to a meeting the very next day.

There was a woman who had gone two years without kissing her husband because, if he knew she was smoking, he'd demand that she stop. And she would rather be thought frigid than have to quit smoking. There was a man who hadn't given up smoking until the arteries in his legs had petrified, and he would never again walk without his two canes. All the other recent quitters looked just like me: dark circles ringing red-rimmed eyes, mouths tight and grim, knees jiggling, hair on end. I found it comforting to be around these people, some of whom seemed even worse off than me. In this room, I wasn't a pitiful mess, but rather courageous—heroic, even—for facing my addiction. I trembled at stories of backsliding. I cheered and choked up every time someone claimed an anniversary with that poignant mix of humility and triumph. I even prayed to my Higher Power. They all said it was the most important thing.

Praying did not come naturally. I had to fake it at first. I had done a thorough job of severing my connection to all things religious after a teenage brush with evangelical Christianity, which, instead of filling me with the love of God, had given me recurring nightmares about Satan. But eventually I did feel . . . something. It was like plugging in to a combination of electricity and mother love. It helped a little. Like water wings that boosted me just enough to keep my nose above water.

Then something so strange happened that I didn't tell anyone about it for the longest time. When it started, I was sure that it meant I'd either snapped my tether or was growing a brain tumor.

I woke up one morning and everything was different. For one thing, the slab of wretchedness that I had been dragging around in the pit of my being, was just . . . gone. For another thing, I had the distinct feeling that there was another person in bed with me, a man, compact and muscular and warm, spooning me as I lay on my side. I could feel his hand on my hip and his breath on my hair. I was surprised to find that instead of trying to bash the intruder's head in with the bedside lamp while screaming and running for the door, I just lay there feeling infinitely reassured and restful. In my mind I came to call him the spirit guy and he was just *there* with me all the time, riding the subway, eating a sandwich, swimming. At an audition, a panic attack would kick up like the puff of dust before the twister, and there he'd be, behind me, hands resting firmly on my waist, secretly, sweetly, reassuring me.

He was with me for about three months. Then he just wasn't there anymore. I didn't know what to think. Had he gone back to where he came from? Had he merged into me? And where had he come from in the first place? Had I simply manifested an imaginary friend? Had my prayers opened up a sort of portal for the spirit guy to come through?

I entered my thirties with my composure completely blown, but I was nicotine-free and knew how to swim. I still couldn't float, though. I had two speeds in the water—swimming and sinking. And as the smoke cleared after the deconstruction that was quitting smoking, I realized that I also had only two *creative* speeds—acting and sinking. It was this realization that got me three thousand miles closer to finding out about the lockbox on my throat, the monkey in my pelvis, and the lady in my leg.

I had lived in New York for six years and I had not managed to become the type of actress who made her living in edgy off-Broadway productions, on her way to landing ever-larger roles in smart and visually stunning independent films. In retrospect, I understand that for someone who didn't like to look foolish or risk failure, auditioning would have to be a tough business. Between jobs, I would lose creative momentum and begin to sink.

My acting career was somewhere between a fit and a start when my flying fireball of a friend Nancy had the idea that she and I should write some kind of performance piece together.

"I'm not a writer."

"Well, we could just do some little exercises."

"Really. I don't write. I'm a hopelessly bad writer. I get blocked just writing a note to my roommate."

"We'll just try it and see what happens." She was actually twinkling with excitement. I couldn't say no.

I showed up, a week later, at her East Side apartment with a legal pad and a pen. Nancy set a timer for six minutes, gave me a prompt, and told me to keep my pen moving.

"But . . ." I was flabbergasted. "I don't know what I want to write yet."

"That doesn't matter."

"But—"

"Go!" And she started the timer.

My thoughts trampled one another as they fled the building in a rush of abject panic.

"Keep your pen moving," she reminded me.

"But—"

"It doesn't have to make sense!"

Eight or nine prompts later, my hand was cramped all the way to the shoulder and I was soaked in flop sweat. I let out the breath I'd been storing up and flipped through pages of panicky scrawl, amazed. I'd never written that much in one sitting in my entire life.

Then Nancy chirped, "Wonderful! Now let's read them out loud!"

I made an involuntary sound somewhere between a bark and a snort. "It's just us, right?"

I read aloud the eight or nine pages of raw, gibbering garbage, confident it would shock her out of ever asking me to do this again. As I read, I noticed that, here and there, I had accidentally gotten some intriguing bits of nonsense onto the page.

When I looked up at Nancy, her eyes crinkled a merry "I told you so!"

I admitted to myself, cautiously, that I had enjoyed this . . . in the same sort of hair-raising way I enjoyed riding the decrepit wooden Cyclone at Coney Island after eating a Hebrew National hot dog at the stand across the street. Anything might happen.

Then, it struck me—no more sinking between acting jobs. Writing gave me license to create whenever I damn well felt like it. I could keep swimming!

I began to formulate a plan. I would move back to my native California. I would live in the small town of Ojai, where I had some family, and I would write. I would write a play in which I could star. I would bring this play back to New York and redeem the six uncelebrated years I had spent there.

I took stock. I was thirty-one years old and knew a great deal about acting in a play, but I didn't know much about writing one. Maybe I was risking everything on a dead end. Maybe I was courting, or even admitting, failure. Maybe my career would sputter out, for lack of nourishment, like the flame on an empty Bic.

I would get in and get out, I told myself. I just needed some time away from the rat race to write that play.

I climbed into a rickety red Audi with my computer and some clothes. Having no money or possessions was a complication that I solved by securing a small, very drafty, but not too leaky cabin at a commune. They would house and feed me in return for some chores and cooking.

The food was bland, the walk to the bathroom was treacherous in the dark, there were mice in my sock drawer, and the hippies had real boundary issues. For instance, they didn't regard my closed cabin door as a boundary. Nor did they see the "personal space" signals I was flashing, but were hugging me every other minute.

And since the commune was called Full Circle Farm, I was surprised to find that the organic garden was just a lumpy expanse of weeds and sticks. It was spring. I signed up to revive it. Writing and gardening! I would be just like Eudora Welty.

Embracing the weirdness, I plunged into the smelly, unkempt healthiness of it all. By day, I composted manure, planted seeds, and built tomato cages. At night, I wrote and indulged in my private stash of chocolate and beer.

Since I was an inexperienced gardener, it wasn't until my vegetables were nearly mature that I realized there was a sprawling gopher city hidden underneath the acre of soil that I had poured myself into. The hippies suggested I beat a drum in the garden and psychically communicate with the little bastards. I nodded politely, and then went out and set decidedly inhumane steel-jawed traps. I also tried smoke bombs and flooding. I taped coils of tubing to my exhaust pipe and pumped toxic gas into their tunnels. Someone told me they were afraid of human hair. The hippies weren't giving any up, so I went to the salon, got a big bag of hair and crammed handfuls into their passageways. Finally, I enlisted the hippies to help me dig a trench all the way around the garden. We filled the trench with broken glass, lowered in a mesh fence and filled it all in again.

Suddenly two years had passed and I hadn't finished that play.

Neither had I defeated the gophers, because as I now realize, gophers are like Afghani freedom fighters. They have a historic claim on the land, they are one with the terrain, and there are more of them than you can ever see. I gave them back their garden, finally understanding it was fallow for good reason.

I was sinking again. But now, it seemed, I was hugging the stones that drew me down.

Then my old friend Brian paid me a visit. He'd been my improv teacher in acting school. We had dated, moved to separate coasts, dated, met other people, dated, and then finally realized our true potential as friends. He made the trip from L.A. on occasion to soak up the silence of sleepy Ojai. While hiking on a remote trail in the mountains, Brian told me he had become an energy healer. He told me his spirit guides, with whom he was now in daily contact, had called him to this work.

He offered to perform a healing on me. In my twenties, I would have scorned him, but I was in my thirties now. And, since being tenderized by the hippies, I found myself scorning things far less frequently. I couldn't live among the raw idealism, the drum circling, and yes, the naked hula-hooping, and continue worrying about image control.

When we got back to my little cabin, Brian took the shimmery blue blanket from my reading chair and spread it on the floor. I lay down on the blanket and closed my eyes. There was a period of silence in which he moved around me. Through my eyelids, I felt him sweeping the air with his arms. I succeeded in breathing through a nervous giggle.

After a time, he said, "There's a chained lockbox around your larynx. It's really old and rusty."

I pictured a sort of medieval chastity belt, and suddenly felt claustrophobic.

"I'm going to take it off." His voice sounded just like it always did.

Then he found some more stuff in different parts of me, like the monkey in my pelvis. I wondered if he was coming on to me, but a pelvis-dwelling monkey didn't sound very sexy. Maybe if he'd found a bed of embers or a verdant forest or maybe a lion. At any rate, this didn't seem to be his agenda.

"Hmm. There's a sad, grieving lady in your calf. I'm going to tell her to move on."

To my surprise, my eyes teared up and I said, through a strong urge to cry, "No! Wait!"

I wondered why she was sad. I didn't want to add to her troubles.

"What if she doesn't have any place to go?" My voice cracked.

"I'll make sure she's okay," he said.

I'm losing it, I thought.

Before sending Brian back to Los Angeles, I made him dinner using local organic ingredients, because that is what we eat in Ojai and because the hippies taught me that buying organic food makes a stronger political statement than bumper stickers.

Woo-woo or not, with my voice out of jail and the lady out of my leg, I moved forward, with curious ease, into unknown territory.

I finished my play and submitted it to Theater 150, an edgy little Ojai company. It had been founded by professional actors in need of a place to stretch their muscles away from their confining Hollywood careers. There was a reading, and then a workshop production. Somewhere along the way, I managed to learn to tap dance.

In the play, Fran, living in New York, is artistically blocked, recently separated from her long-term boyfriend, and also happens to be quitting smoking. She is about as confused and lost as a person can be. Her Nicotine Anonymous sponsor tells her to get in touch with her Higher Power. Sounding familiar? Only, the woman is a painter and I changed my spirit guy into the Greek god Hermes. He enters Fran's life through the fire escape window and proceeds to enlighten, love, and lift her up. She's painting again. She's laughing again.

Early in rehearsals, my director called me, fizzing with excitement. "I was driving home from L.A., and there was this Frank Sinatra song and I swear I had a vision! You were wearing red sequins and you were tap dancing!"

"Kim, I'm an actress, and I'm starting to consider myself a writer. I can even sing a little. But I am definitely not a tap dancer."

The next day there was a strange voice on the other end of the line. "Kim tells me you need a choreographer."

I sighed. "Well, actually," I said, "I think I need an instructor."

Between rehearsals, I'd slip on my borrowed tap shoes and Laurie would drill me on flap ball changes and shuffle hop steps. Unlike swimming or writing, it came easily and naturally. And I loved it. I loved the satisfying crack of metal on the floor. I loved how my whole body jiggled when I really got going. I loved the big, arm-flapping, bouncing-off-the-furniture *foolishness* of it. The tap dancing became a key element of the play, the vehicle through which Fran regains her faith.

When it comes time for Hermes to go, Fran clings like a barnacle. Aside from being stoned in love, she wonders if the joy and freedom she feels will vanish with him. He tells her, "If fear should die, then falling is flying." She blows by this and plots to foil his escape, which of course leads to widespread disaster, his near extinction, and ultimately, despite all of her efforts at avoiding it, redemption.

On the last night of the Theater 150 production, a producer happened to be in the audience. He promptly signed us up for an L.A. run with the idea of inviting potential investors for a movie. It should have been a singularly ecstatic moment, but even as I scribbled my signature on the contract, fear began working me over.

L.A. is ambitious and cynical. L.A. is well dressed and tall and impossibly thin. I felt my play was a floppy-eared, curious puppy of indeterminate breed about to be paraded before the Westminster Kennel Club judges panel.

Before each show I hid in a corner, muttering mad entreaties to my Higher Power for the courage and conviction to go out and be the big, ridiculous, tender fool I needed to be so that the story could get told.

My worst fear was realized when *Backstage West* published a snidely scathing review. The oddly named Wenzel Jones wrote, "[The play] opens on Fran, who is paralyzed by the act of purchasing a can of corn. Paralyzed. Only the most preciously urbanized would look at this for more than ten seconds without thinking, Oh, just shut up and buy the corn."

Just shut up and buy the corn.

And it got worse from there.

I fought for my center nightly and was tap dancing just ahead of the snapping jaws of my fears when, later on in the run, the *L.A. Times* critic avenged my trampled honor by writing a love letter of a review.

The success of the play brought opportunities to teach. I was an actor, a writer, a nonsmoker, a swimmer, and I was even starting to think of myself as a tap dancer, but I was not a teacher. A teacher I was not. Why? Self-preservation!

I was especially afraid to teach teenagers. Teenagers were, by definition, cynical and rebellious and they had this *thing* about being honest. I would be the antelope and they the pack of hyenas. They would identify my weaknesses, they would take me down, and there would be a feeding frenzy.

But somewhere around the fiftieth time Hermes told me, "If fear should die, then falling is flying," I got it.

"*Flying?* Oh! I thought you said *failing!*"

I get it now. Fear is the guardian at the gate of life's goodies.

Like the lady in my leg, for instance. She was a guardian. Very sneaky of her to keep me from entering Goodyville by making me worry about her. "If you go through that gate, what will become of me?" As soon as I figure out what the monkey was up to, I'll deal with that, too.

I tell this to my students, and they look at me like they want their money back. That's okay. In the ten weeks that we're together, they will come to see fear as a big road sign that says, "This way to Goodyville!"

It took me until my late thirties to realize that I have become much more adept at negotiating with that guardian, whose job it is to say, "No! High potential for failure! Likelihood of looking foolish!" If, however, he won't negotiate in good faith, I will sneak up and knock him unconscious with a brick. Because I want in.

Crossing the Border

FLOR MORALES

as told to
Andrea N. Richesin

That's what happens to exiles; they are scattered to the four winds
and then find it extremely difficult
to get back together again.

ISABEL ALLENDE,
Paula

I was born in Puerto El Triunfo, a port city in southern El Salvador. I want to share part of my life with you. I was almost three
years old when my parents separated. My sister, Marciela, was eleven
months old and my older sister, Yeni, was five. My father was a very
jealous man. He was nearly twenty years older than my mother and
very possessive of her. When they separated, my mother never asked
him for any money to support us, or for the house her father had
given to them as a wedding gift. She just took her three little girls
away and rented a house nearby. My mother eventually married another man, named Rolando. He lived with us for over ten years and became like a father to all of us. He left my mother for another woman,
but my mother continued to work hard to support us. When she was
only fourteen years old, Yeni married her husband, Carlos. They had two
little girls and they have been happily married for twenty years now.

Even with all the hard work, my mother found it impossible to buy us a house. Finally, one day my uncle brought a truck from the United States to give to my mother. She sold the truck and bought a really old house on a lot that our mayor offered to her. She started to build a new house for us, but the house was provisional because it was necessary to finish the old house first. When I think of my father and how he lived with his new wife in the house my grandfather gave to my parents as a wedding gift, I don't understand why my mother never contacted an attorney for legal guidance. Or why she decided to let him have our house when she had three little girls and he was essentially alone. For almost ten years, we all lived with my great-great grandmother in her home right next to my father's house, which he shared with his new wife. We would occasionally ask our father for money, but soon learned he would make excuses instead of giving us any. With hard work and determination, Marciela and I finished high school. I was fifteen years old when I met my first husband during a training session for our Independence Day parade. Amilcar was a military captain and so he taught us how to march through the streets. He was twenty-one years old. A year later, we began dating. When I graduated from high school at eighteen, I married him. I knew my husband enjoyed drinking before I married him, but I had no idea to what extent he would continue with his addiction. His mother barely tolerated me and pampered and spoiled her son. When he returned from work, she would take his socks off and immediately wash them for him, chastising me for not taking better care of him! In 1994, I turned twenty and my son, Erick, was born. Amilcar began drinking heavily when I was twenty-two. I was afraid to leave my son alone with him. I no longer trusted his judgment, as he had begun drinking all the time.

I worked in a school cafeteria selling sandwiches that I had prepared to the students. My husband spent all of his salary on alcohol, but soon even his salary was not enough to support his drinking habit. I spent all of my earnings on our household necessities—electricity, groceries, all of the bills—whatever we needed. Amilcar could charge his military account at restaurants or stores, but I was never given any money. When he crashed his car in a drunk driving accident, he was forced to take the bus. My mother began telling me I was too young to have to support my husband in this way. I could find another husband who would help support me.

At this time we were living with my mother and Yeni, whose husband was away for a few weeks at a time with the mariners. One night, Amilcar tried to touch my sister in her sleep. He told her to be quiet, but she fought him off. I was so embarrassed by Amilcar's behavior I decided I had to leave him once and for all. I decided to leave Erick with my mother and visit Marciela in California in hopes of building a new life for my son and myself. Because of my husband's status as a military captain, Erick and I had a visa to go to the United States. I worked with Marciela at a cleaning company in San Rafael for five months. The second day I arrived, my sister invited me to join her at a friend's house to sell the tamales and cream cheese I had brought from El Salvador to make more money. When we went to her friend's house, I met my future husband there. Andres invited me to go dancing with him, but I said no because I was shy and a little cautious in this new country. I asked Marciela about him and she told me he was looking for a girlfriend, but he had trouble finding women who were interested because he was too serious. But I was looking for something serious. I began saving my money to bring Erick back with me and I began to slowly realize that I could build a life here in California.

When I returned five months later, Amilcar met me at the airport and asked me if I had made a lot of money. He asked me to give it all to him so we could remodel our house. Of course, I knew he wanted the money for alcohol. When I refused to give him any, we fought over custody of our son. My sister offered to send me two tickets because she wanted to get to know Erick, but when I told Amilcar, he said I couldn't take Erick away from him. I had to present a letter with permission from my husband to take Erick away, so I had an attorney forge the letter for me.

I told my mom I would finally leave Amilcar, and although she was relieved I had decided to stop wasting my life, she was also sad I would take Erick to the United States. When I returned to California, my uncle accused me of cheating on Amilcar, whom he had known in El Salvador. I told him he knew nothing about my life. Although I had a beautiful two-story home in El Salvador and a seemingly nice husband, he was a drunk and didn't give me any money. I was not happy with him and I knew he was slowly drinking himself to death. I wanted a serious relationship with someone who would love and respect me. My sister was living with our other uncle, a strict Jehovah's Witness, who decided to lock us out when we went dancing because he didn't approve of my going out as a married woman. That night, we stayed with Andres at his home and slept in his bed while he slept on the floor. Andres joked that he should have slept with me and put Marciela on the floor!

When I returned to El Salvador before my work permit expired, my friends told me that Amilcar, in a drunken rage, had called me names and accused me of having a new boyfriend. He said he wouldn't allow me to return to my new boyfriend. Amilcar went to the American Embassy to try and remove me from our visa and prevent me from leaving again. My lawyer friend assured me it would be fine because I hadn't done anything wrong and I had complied with all of the rules and returned in time back to the United States. When I returned for the third time to California, I moved in with Andres. Then I became pregnant with our son, Jonathan, and I had to return once again to El Salvador. A mutual friend told me Amilcar had threatened to kill me and my baby. My mother was frightened because he appeared to drink all of the time now. As I was returning to the United States, the immigration officer signed a paper which specified that I had only two weeks to stay in the country because I couldn't have my baby in the United States. So I took Erick back to El Salvador with me and stayed with my mother for four months. Andres sent money to us while we stayed in El Salvador because I wasn't working and was still trying to avoid Amilcar. Then, we had to make the trip back to California in time for the baby. I was scared because the immigration officer had told me I couldn't return until my baby was born. My mother was afraid our lives were in danger as Amilcar always carried a firearm on him. So I went to the Mexican Embassy to get a transmigration visa to go to Mexico. We traveled for three days by bus from San Salvador to Mexico City. My feet and legs were swollen from sitting so long on our journey. When we arrived, I called Andres and told him I had to take a plane because I was too tired to continue.

We flew to Tijuana and then we contacted a "coyote" to help us cross the border. When we made the initial contact with one, we were asked to pay him $2,500. I called Andres, who was waiting in L.A. while we stayed in a hotel in Tijuana. He said he would see me tomorrow and the coyote would meet me the next day to cross the border. On the following day, the coyote told me that Erick would have to go with another group and I would go with the coyote's group. When I refused, he said that this was my last opportunity to cross the border and this was the only way. When I called Andres to explain what had happened, he understood I couldn't turn my son over to a stranger. So I called my mother and sister in El Salvador. Yeni is very religious and she told me, "Don't leave your baby with a stranger. If you believe in God when you go to the border nothing bad will happen to you. Just relax. You should dress up and wear makeup. Act normal. Everything will be fine and I'll pray for you." The next day, I put on my makeup just as Yeni had advised me to do. Andres's friend picked us up at the hotel and dropped us off at the border patrol to check our papers. He said he would meet us at the McDonald's on the other side. I had told Erick if anyone asked him questions, to say we were going to see Mickey Mouse. When we went through passport control, I was carrying a backpack, my purse, my brave five-year-old son on my arm, and my eight-month-old son in my stomach. I was terrified. My whole life was waiting on the other side of that fence.

My new life with the love of my life and our sons. A very kind agent greeted us and asked why we were visiting the United States. I told her I was taking my son to visit Disneyland. She looked at my visa and simply said, "Enjoy your stay in the United States." We walked through and drove two hours to L.A. to meet Andres and begin our new life together.

I continued working with Marciela at the cleaning company. I was paid $60 a day, which seems a ridiculously small amount of money to afford to live in the San Francisco Bay Area, save money, and send some to my mother, but I did. Eventually, I was promoted to $80 a day because I could drive and many of the other workers who had been there for years could neither drive nor speak English. I was grateful to my boss, Mercedes, for the opportunity and for giving me a job each time I returned from El Salvador, but when another woman offered me $100 a day to work, I started working for her company. Mercedes was eventually able to match her offer, so I returned to her outfit. I started handing out my own business card to prospective clients instead of the cleaning company's cards. I worked Monday through Friday for the cleaning company and Saturday for my new clients. When I told Mercedes I had enough clients on my own to start my own business, she was angry with me for soliciting new clients, but she understood this was my chance to create my own business.

When I was pregnant with Jonathan, Amilcar began bleeding internally, the blood got in his lungs, and he died. The doctors assumed he was already damaged from fighting in the war. One of my clients explained to me that I could have applied for political asylum when I was in El Salvador since my husband was threatening me, but I didn't know support was available. I wish I had known, but no one had told me. I also didn't realize I could use my visa to get a driver's license. After Jonathan was born, temporary protected status was granted to all Salvadorans because of the earthquakes that devastated El Salvador in early 2001.

I eventually married Andres and he is now trying to legally adopt

Erick as his son. My family is thriving and my business is also growing. We recently bought our first home. We have a nice house with a backyard where my sons can play with their new dog. I discovered a literacy program and I've been working very hard to improve my English to better integrate in this country. Now all these years have passed and my father has returned to my mother asking for our old birth certificates in order to supposedly give me and my sisters an inheritance. He wants to ask for forgiveness from my mother and from us, but I believe it's too late. He should have been there when I was a little girl and I needed a father (even though I did have Rolando, my adopted father, for a few years). Now, my father would like to remarry my mother. We can't believe she's considering his offer after all this time and all her struggles. When Amilcar died, he was so angry with me that he didn't leave any inheritance money for me or Erick. As soon as I left him, Amilcar sold our house. The buyers only paid for half and agreed to pay the rest in payments, but they still haven't. A few years ago, I began the legal process to ensure that Erick obtains his inheritance to help him with his future plans.

I dream that my children will have a good education in this country. However, sometimes we read or see TV stories about Latino kids who are honor students and win academic contests but then are denied their scholarships when their legal status is discovered. They are given a deportation card, but fortunately the schools often support them and help them to obtain green cards. But sometimes they are deported anyhow. Even families applying for legal residency with kids who work hard and expect their status to change before graduation fear they won't be able to attend college. This can be very discouraging for Erick, who sees these kids working really hard and yet still not being encouraged or set up for success.

I am grateful to my mother for teaching me the value of hard work. She also taught me to believe in myself and follow my dreams. I consider myself fortunate to live in a country that values freedom. I only hope Erick will be able to fully enjoy his freedom here. My mother is sick and I send her money, but it is impossible for me to visit her now. We talk on the phone and I sent Jonathan to visit her for a few weeks. He complained of her cold baths and made her heat the water as he has become accustomed to here in California. We miss each other desperately, but at least I have my immediate family and sister close by.

Now that I'm in my thirties, I've learned to rely on myself in a way that I wasn't capable of in my twenties. I know from my experience now that, through hard work and commitment, I can succeed. In my twenties, my experiences taught me we can choose to change our lives if we're willing to take the necessary risks. Leaving El Salvador with my little son was the hardest decision I have ever had to make, but ultimately it was the best one. Erick now has a wonderful father and I have a devoted husband. I'm finally ready and able to enjoy my life with my family. As a woman in my thirties, I am confident about my decisions, and being a strong mother to two young boys has taught me a lot about myself.

Hold Your Applause, Please

KIMBERLEY ASKEW

The thing about happiness is that it doesn't help you to grow; only unhappiness does that. So I'm grateful that my bed of roses was made up equally of blossoms and thorns. I've had a privileged, creative, exciting life, and I think that the parts that were less joyous were preparing me, testing me, strengthening me.

LANA TURNER,
Lana: The Lady, the Legend, the Truth

Once, in the fifth grade, I wrote an epic-length poem about a unicorn and signed up to recite it in the annual talent show. It was another new school in another new neighborhood. We'd moved to Lubbock, Texas, from Germany when I was in the fourth grade. I'd already gone to three different schools that year. Now that I was a year older, I had some simple goals: settle down, make friends, and impress the whole school and my grandparents, visiting from California, with the sheer force of my unbridled talent.

I wore a floor-length pink dress with long lace sleeves, and my father, whose inherent creativity was generally only allowed an airing each autumn for homemade Halloween costumes and intricately decorated birthday cakes, had fashioned a wand of sorts out of tinfoil. It was my one and only prop, and it was all I needed. I was ready to shine. As I took center stage in the school cafeteria, the lights dimmed except for the one seemingly industrial-strength spotlight that shone directly on me. The room suddenly seemed too quiet. I began to recite, from memory, the first line when just as suddenly I was overcome with a bout of intense stage fright and, though I tried to control them, the tears started to flow. I kept going, sobbing through the entire performance line by line. If only I could've waved my wand and disappeared from the stage! Oh, if only I had written a shorter poem.

Afterward, in the brightly lit hallway, I shook with fresh sobs as I contemplated my failure and thought how embarrassed my family must be. To further my humiliation, the mother of the most popular girl in school was trying to comfort me. She had one arm around my shoulders; with the other she took quick, impatient drags from her ash-laden cigarette. While I strained away from her and the noxious, cloying smoke that surrounded us, she kept saying, "Honey, it happens to everyone." I just stared down at the linoleum and my shiny white Mary-Janes and suffered her attentions in silence. I've learned to treasure this recollection because it's proof of how far a person can go in life, how much they can change, and how it is actually possible to transcend even the most ridiculous childhood memories.

In retrospect, my life's philosophy just might be: it's best to make the big mistakes early on. So on the day I officially graduated from college, five months shy of my twenty-third birthday, I married the first man I'd ever slept with. It seemed to happen so fast, partly because he was anxious to begin his application for citizenship, which he could do only after we were married. Although plagued by uncertainty, I was too proud to admit that we were an impossible match. Let me explain. From our first date, we were under constant covert and overt pressure because, while he was undeniably handsome, polite, and generally soft-spoken, my boyfriend also happened to be Palestinian. I fiercely disputed anyone's reservations about our engagement, from opinionated strangers, to my parents, to coworkers who knowingly mentioned the lurid Sally Field drama *Not Without My Daughter,* while I buried my own concerns. Though we did have our tiresome culture clashes and were prone to passionate, childish arguments, I suppose it goes without saying that he wasn't anything like the person they imagined. The real problem was that I wasn't in love with him. I've always been a sucker for the underdog, so fighting the larger prejudice of popular opinion became more important than whether or not we were even compatible. In my misguided attempt to remedy social injustice, I'd managed to betray myself. To admit that my feelings for him had never amounted to more than a crush that had long since faded was something I found impossible to do until it was too late. After the ceremony, he spent almost two years trying to convince me that it could work and I spent those same two years working up the courage to bolt.

We'd moved to the San Francisco Bay Area soon after we graduated from college and I was working as an editor at a publishing company. It was a job I had long idealized and that, coupled with the camaraderie I shared with my coworkers, all of whom were about the same age as me, only helped magnify the stagnancy of my "other life." At work and with my friends I was living a vibrant, productive existence. In every way, I was becoming the person I wanted to be and it gave me the courage I needed to move on. The day I finally had the courage to break it off for good, I employed such a reservoir of strength that I actually went to bed afterward and slept for twenty-four hours straight. Once the divorce was final, I rarely spoke about the marriage except with my immediate family and one or two friends, and even then, not as often as you'd expect. In that way, I had the reticence of a disillusioned Vietnam vet like my father—this rather than, say, the bravado of a former World War II soldier like my maternal grandfather, who never stopped reliving his time in the Pacific, going so far as to force my grandmother to "vacation" in spots where years earlier he'd spent his R&R recuperating from shrapnel wounds. In fact, some of my newer friends will be quite surprised to discover that I was ever married at all. Even to me it feels like some sort of lucid dream, as if it never really happened.

Yes, it was the biggest mistake I've ever made, but it was the best thing that could've happened to me. By the time the divorce was final, I'd had quite enough of audience participation. From the ashes of my stifling marriage arose a fierce disregard for popular opinion, and more important, an intense need to nurture my own desires above all else. In the previous year I'd come to believe that I'd played my one and only hand and played it badly. Now I had the chance to ensure that regret was something I never felt again. I've sometimes wondered how much longer it would have taken me to learn that painful lesson had I been taught it any other way.

I quickly threw myself headlong into what was mostly a passionate love affair that began after a coworker accompanied me to a tattoo parlor for my first and, thus far, only tattoo. He held my hand while the artist shot painful dots of ink into my lower back. Afterward, the adrenaline pumping through my body made all the pain worth it. You could say the same about our relationship, which began soon after. We managed to survive six years of dramatic breakups, various questionable career decisions, and a chronic illness, only to sputter to a halt after a move to Los Angeles that, in my mind, was supposed to cement our commitment. This relationship, too, had its fair share of dissenters, this time for more practical reasons—my boyfriend could be excruciatingly egocentric and had a long history of depression. It didn't help that, though he was more than capable of charming whomever he chose whenever he chose, he made very little effort to win over or even tolerate those closest to me. I can't count the number of times I was subjected to the "he's not right for you" speech. But by this time, I was comfortable enough with the world having its own opinion that it had ceased to matter.

What brought and kept us together was an intense physical, emotional, and intellectual connection unlike anything I'd ever experienced. We'd talk for hours on the phone and linger over dinner at restaurants long after the other patrons had emptied the place, impatient waiters hovering, hoping for some sign that we were ready for the check.

Somehow, we never ran out of things to say to each other. His need for solitary introspection and my need for independence helped balance the zealous bent of our relationship. Moving to Los Angeles changed all that. Leading our own lives, we'd maintained a level of intensity that we couldn't sustain cohabiting in the isolation of a new, sprawling city and with the mundane day-to-day of reality television and trips to Home Depot. The six years came down to this: one night we were lying in bed and he wondered aloud how he was supposed to know whether I was the "right person" or not. I replied that if he still hadn't figured that out, I obviously was not the right person.

Despite the dissolution of my relationship, moving to Los Angeles was the best thing that could've happened to my career. In my twenties, I still had the lingering fear that I'd fall apart in the spotlight. Instead, I'd excelled at jobs that just skirted around what I really wanted to be doing. As an editor, I'd ghostwritten dry chapters on Microsoft Office and created interactive chemistry modules to accompany academic textbooks. As executive producer for an online advertising agency, I contributed business-to-business copy for websites or banner ads when I wasn't virtually shuttling documents from one person's inbox to another or laying off staff after the dot-com bubble finally burst. My salary kept growing, but it took moving to L.A. to facilitate a true career change. After almost a year of the odd freelance gig, mind-numbing temp work, several less-than-tempting job offers, and seemingly endless hours spent combing the online job sites, I landed a job that allowed me to write for a living—and about something other than computers. It was what I'd always dreamt about. Finally, I was doing what I really wanted to do, all day long.

In the meantime, I spent two years sporadically dating, but for all intents and purposes I was single. I won't deny that it was lonely at times, but it was also exhilarating. I traveled, had a romantic fling, read an entire collection of Anthony Trollope novels and then some, and cultivated new, treasured friendships. It was the first time since my sophomore year in college that I hadn't been in some sort of committed relationship. The large part of my energy was one hundred percent focused on me alone.

Although things were going really well, I still kept wishing I were somewhere else, only I couldn't decide where or even exactly why. One day I'd ponder going to grad school in Edinburgh, the next chucking it all and moving to Portland. One unusually overcast morning in early November, after almost two years in Southern California, a friend and I were sitting at a coffee shop in Beverly Hills. In typical L.A. fashion, Christmas muzak was already being piped out onto the spotless street. And I asked myself, how did I end up living in the land of bumblebee-yellow Hummers, blond highlights, and tanned hard bodies? It was seventy-two degrees outside and we were all wearing scarves. I'm an army brat, with pale skin, love handles, and literary pretensions. People like me dream about living in Paris or Prague while living in San Francisco or New York.

It was then that I recalled one of the lowest periods of living in San Francisco. My boyfriend and I were on a six-week "break" and I was fairly despondent when I made my way to the top of Nob Hill and went inside Grace Cathedral to look at a labyrinth that I'd heard about. Although I'm not religious, I am spiritual. The labyrinth and the arches, stained glass, and tapestries had the same effect on me that similar architecture and art had on countless others for centuries. Suddenly, my worries felt insignificant and I was connected to the past and the future. In that moment, in the church, I'd known that everything would be okay, better than okay. That's when it hit me: it was time to go home.

I was grateful to L.A., for just like my previous relationships, it had given me many things, not the least of which were an amplified independence, an unabashed love for pop culture, and a job I loved. Minus one boyfriend, I returned to San Francisco with all those things and more.

I may have slept with L.A., but I'd never been seduced by it. Returning to San Francisco, my first love, I remembered why I'd fallen for it in the first place. Walking home, up Taylor Street, I can stop to stand at the top of Nob Hill, directly in front of Grace Cathedral, and see down to Chinatown, North Beach, Fisherman's Wharf, and the financial district and out across the water to the Bay Bridge and Alcatraz. No matter how many times I walk that way, the view always takes my breath away. The bay window in my bedroom directly faces the trolley car line, which runs until one in the morning. Some might find the familiar clanging of the trolley bell annoying, especially late at night, but it only makes me love the city even more. I think it's because the sound, so quintessential to San Francisco, is an echo of the city's fascinating history. It also reminds me of when I was a child and how much pleasure I took in a midnight trolley ride when my family came here as tourists, seeing the lives inside the homes and apartments as a magical world we could only glimpse through lit windows. Now here I am on the other side of the window, often reading a book fireside, something I can do just about any time of the year here. Not long after moving back, I attended a reading held by a group of writers raising funds for their renowned tutorial program. The event was standing room only and it was no small venue. As I looked around the room, in an expectant hush as we awaited the first author's appearance on the stage, I realized that though I didn't recognize most of the faces in the crowd, they still felt somehow familiar. I think there's a wonderful camaraderie among San Franciscans, particularly among the writing community; our solitary pursuits bind us to one another.

Fast-forward to a night out at The Mint, a popular karaoke bar on Market Street in San Francisco. As usual, there are some serious professionals competing for stage time. I'm talking wanna-be Madonnas with the stage presence of Barbra Streisand. My "friends" have signed me up to sing a song solo and I'm furiously downing liquid courage. At some point, I decide it's getting late and I need to leave, but I'm persuaded to stay. The emcee calls out my name and my tune is queued. It's "Hopelessly Devoted to You" from the *Grease* soundtrack. It was always my dream to be Sandy, but especially the transformed Sandy of leather pants and sexy stilettos. The one who knows exactly what she wants and how to get it. Shakily, I approach the stage, hesitantly grab the mike, and stare out into a sea of upturned, expectant faces. My mouth feels dry and it takes me a moment to catch up with the lyrics that are scrolling across the monitor, but the crowd urges me on. They're clapping, cheering, and shouting my name. Almost before I know what's happened, I've channeled Olivia Newton-John and gone totally diva; the confidence, the hand gestures, the *Star Search* style. It lasted only a matter of moments, but I felt high on the triumph for hours afterwards. If only my grandparents could've seen me.

The One and Only Buddha

SAMINA ALI

When I die I shall soar with the angels,
And when I die to the angels, what I shall become,
You cannot imagine.

RUMI

Two years ago, my three-year-old son and I were standing together in the bathroom, he on a stool next to me, facing the mirror, and I turned toward him as I squeezed toothpaste onto his Elmo brush. "Mama," he said, gray eyes fixed on his own reflection. "I'm the one and only Buddha."

I stared at him in astonishment. How could he know who the Buddha is? Yet I found myself nodding and saying, "Thank you for telling me, Isham." For what else are you to say when the Buddha announces his presence?

Ishmael is my son's official name. Ishmael Ali Maxwell. A name that fully incorporates his Indian-Muslim heritage as well as his Anglo-Irish-Scottish-Welsh-German-Swedish and Native-American side. Ishmael also reflects his father's and my leanings toward the literary. Yes, "Call me Ishmael . . ." But when speaking to my family in Urdu, I say, "Ismail." Ishmael/Ismail, to me, there is only a small difference in the pronunciation. The name, the meaning, is the same.

I, too, grew up answering to two names, Samina and Zainab, a phenomenon that's not so unusual among some Indians. However, when he was two, my son decided to do away with his two names—his two identities—and announced in his best Buddha voice, "Mama, I am not Ishmael. I am not Ismail. I am Isham."

Isham, a name determined not by language or culture, but by the love that created him, mother and father, East and West, Urdu and English.

When I was pregnant with Isham, I was just finishing the first draft of my first novel. I conceived in January 1999 . . . and then panicked. As a well-programmed Muslim Indian woman, I had been imagining having a baby since I was twelve, yet, at twenty-eight, being also a well-programmed American woman, I saw my career, my novel, as my baby. It would not do to have another while I was still nurturing one! So I did the only thing I could. I called the eight-hundred number of the home pregnancy kit and told the representative that I had gotten a defective kit. I wanted my money back. The representative assured me that the kit was fully functional, then, to further press the point, added that "it wasn't too difficult to pee on a stick."

While I was haggling with her on the phone, my husband, Tim, began dialing one relative after another and gleefully announcing, "She's pregnant!" I didn't know who he was talking about. Who was pregnant?

Two hours and another kit later, I realized I was the one who was pregnant.

My pregnancy turned out to be some of the happiest months of my life. I felt a calmness I had not known before, a complete peace with my surroundings—not just with Mother Nature, whom I now knew myself to be intricately part of, but also with my husband, my agent, and, most important, my own mother, so I knew it was my baby's energy emitting from him throughout me. I felt both in command of my life, driving it forward, and, at once, possessed of an inner knowledge that all, in the end, was out of my control. What a relief to hand over my life and its greater things—like love and luck—to something larger than me.

If I dreaded delivery, it was less the fear of the physical agony than the fear of losing the awareness of being spiritually connected to the world. My son, he was like the breath within the breath, the life within the life, his great and ancient soul filling my small one with a fullness of joy I had never experienced before. How lucky I was, yet how frail this miracle of mine. For I knew from the start that there was something wrong with my pregnancy. At first, I wondered if the fetus had implanted itself incorrectly. Yet after months of nagging my OB, when he finally performed an ultrasound, there he was, my son, right where he was supposed to be, at four months no bigger than my thumb, already more of a life force than my own.

For the duration of the pregnancy, whenever I raised my fears, I was told the same thing. There was nothing wrong, everything was normal, I was just being neurotic. Throughout my twenties, when I was not just trying to figure out who I was as a person, but also as an American Muslim woman married to a white atheist after a disastrous arranged marriage to a Muslim Indian man (the subject of my novel), I did tend to be neurotic. I was well aware of this. So I told myself the doctors were right. Even if I wasn't, my baby was normal. Like that, I continued to teach through to my final trimester. During the ninth month, I hiked to the top of a mountain in the Lakes Basin Region, climbing 8,587 feet. And once I finished the draft of my novel—two months earlier than I had planned—I knew I had reached nirvana.

Then the countdown began and the car seat was installed. Days before my due date, I went to my OB a final time, this time with my husband, whom I had prepped to speak for me—"She's itching all over, she's vomiting, she's not peeing at all, isn't this unusual for a pregnant woman?"

Again, the doctor laughed it off. "By this time next week," the OB assured us, "you'll be home from the hospital with your baby, both of you healthy and happy."

By the next night I was in the NeuroICU, the intensive care unit for patients with brain trauma.

I had gone into labor the same night I'd spoken with my OB and delivered my son after twelve hours. While pushing, I had complained of severe headaches and chest pain, vision problems. For my heart pain, I was given Alka-Seltzer.

Twenty minutes after delivery, I had a seizure. And there my memory fails. What follows is what I was told by doctors, by my brothers, by my mother, and by my husband.

Eight hours after my seizure, I was finally wheeled down for a CT scan of the brain. It showed what the doctors hadn't even feared could happen: two hemorrhages, one in front, one in back. One was a subarachnoid hemorrhage, which, my younger brother, who is a resident in neurosurgery, tells me kills sixty percent of patients. That is, patients who have no other medical condition but the subarachnoid hemorrhage. I had other things going on. Liver failure. Kidney failure. Heart damage from a heart attack. Pulmonary edema. Single-digit blood platelet count. Blood that had stopped clotting. Such severe brain swelling that it wouldn't respond to medication, and the doctors were planning to drill a hole in my head to drain the excess fluid. Hundreds of strokes, that was what the doctors thought was happening in my swollen brain, a galaxy of popping and shooting blood vessels.

The neurologist told my family that if I was lucky, I would die. If not, my husband would end up being my ward.

Despite being awakened frequently, I went into a coma. When I was "awake," I am told I did not recognize anyone, not the doctors who remained vigilantly by my side, not the personal nurse assigned to monitor me around the clock, not my best friend, not my brothers, not my mother.

Tim says the first time I "woke up," he stood over me and asked how I was feeling and, in response, I said, "Who are you?"

He told me that he was my husband, and I told him that the ICU doctor who happened to be in the room at that time was my husband. For the rest of my days in the ICU, I apparently held to this conviction.

So what is it that *I* remember?

I remember Isham, shoving and winding his way out of me, and I remember thinking he had a long body. I remember the shock in finally seeing him, his face so different from what I had imagined. For nine months I had been preparing my white husband for a brown baby. Yet there he was, born with skin fairer than even my husband's, and gray-blue eyes, blond hair. I remember wanting to hold him.

Then there is darkness. And two people inhabiting this darkness.

The best way to describe the experience is by comparing it to the sensation I had after getting the epidural. I hadn't wanted it, enjoying each spike of pain that brought me closer to Isham, but the nurses insisted. Then the doctor injected it incorrectly, so it numbed only my right half. I was thrilled and, during delivery, reveled in the left half of my body, the side alive to the pain of emerging life.

Like that, in the darkness where I resided, there were two selves, and only one was "waking up" at the doctors' insistence. This self, whenever she was awake, thought of Isham, screaming that he was still inside, wanting to come out—couldn't anyone help her push? It seems the internal clock had stopped during delivery. So the one who had her eyes open, shouting for her son, was the one who was asleep.

And the one who was awake was residing in darkness. Darkness. That is what I remember. An enveloping darkness in which there are no relationships, no ties, no bonds of love, no connections, no creation, no endings, no fear. And, in this way, there is peace.

It is said that at the end of Buddha's life, when he was asked what there was to know about death, he turned over his bowl. An emptiness within an emptiness.

I was residing inside that turned-over bowl.

Coming out of it—the miracle that it was—was indeed a reincarnation, and each year, on Isham's birthday, I celebrate not only his life but my own.

Yet a month after being released from the hospital, I was still sunk in a depression that frightened even me. I kept asking myself why I had suffered so much, and still was: right-eye blindness, debilitating headaches, no depth perception, breast milk so full of toxins it had to be pumped and thrown out. Then one morning, while I was holding Isham, he reached up and touched my face. His gray-blue eyes stared into mine as though understanding something about me I didn't understand myself.

I am not alive, I realized, not even now that I've returned from the hospital. So focused had I become on what I'd been through—events I couldn't even remember!—that I had lost sight of what was before me: my son, our future together. I was going to be able to watch him grow up, me, the one who had seen the darkness inside that bowl.

Life, it is not simply to be alive, it is to be awake. That is what my son taught me. The realization was so pure, so real that it gave me the power to step outside my physical body in order to heal myself.

By coincidence, the same day Isham was born, I had been invited to a ceremony in New York, where I would have been presented with a grant I had received for my first novel. Of course, I could not attend. By the time I was released from the hospital, the check had been delivered to my home, and staring at it with my one good eye, I feared I would never write again. Three weeks later, I returned to my doctor for a checkup and confirmed this by asking him what part of the brain a writer uses in order to create. He pointed at his left brain, then the right, then the front and back. I was astonished. He said, "A writer uses all parts of the brain: memory, invention, fantasy, geometry, reason, all of it combines to produce work."

I stared down at my body, which was still swollen from excess fluids. I was unable to walk without assistance, unable to shower by myself, unable to brush my teeth. I had no short-term memory. In my mind, my Social Security number and my phone number were the same. Once, I had even mistaken Isham for a small dog.

"Will I write again?" I asked.

He shook his head no. "Most likely not. A normal brain," he explained, "has deep wrinkles in it. Your brain is so swollen right now that all the wrinkles have been wiped clean. It will take a year to a year and a half just for your brain to return to normal. Only then can we accurately say what defects you might have to live with. I say this without even including your other organs. We have to wait and see how everything heals." He then referred me to a physical therapist. I was both a mother and an infant alongside my own.

I returned to writing the same way in which I returned to health. The process lasted two and a half years. I went to the physical therapist's once, then never returned. I recognized that, like the doctor, the therapist was merely seeing my material form, not my will, my spirit, my son's challenge for me to stay awake to those things invisible, greater than me. So, while my husband went off to work and my mom watched my son, I set myself goals. Walk two steps, from the bed to the dresser. Then from the bed to the door, the bed to the bathroom, the bed to the living room. The first time I walked from my bed to the sofa, a distance of no more than forty feet, I collapsed, my head pounding in excruciating pain, and didn't get up for the rest of the day. But there eventually came a time when I was able to walk to the sofa and back again to the bed. By the time my mother returned to her own home, I was able to walk down the steep front steps of the house. The streets beyond, the San Francisco hills, loomed larger than life, taunting me, inviting. In the same way, the journey back to writing was a challenge that came from within and without. Six months after my release from the hospital, while I was still setting goals, I was asked to read with a prominent writer at a local venue. I couldn't pass it up. I took the event as a sign that I could begin writing again. The draft of the novel was complete, and I decided I would read a section from the beginning. In trying to revise a few sentences, however, I quickly discovered I had little command over language. If I thought "boat," I would write "ice skates." No matter how much I concentrated, the word *boat* wouldn't be written, nor uttered, though I was seeing the image of the boat clearly in my mind. This happened again and again, leading to such debilitating headaches that I would soon turn the computer off. Some days I worked on a single paragraph for up to six hours, then, reading it the following morning, I would see how none of it made sense and would delete it along with my efforts. It was a time of severe setbacks and minor breakthroughs, a time when only my son's face carried me through. I did end up reading with my fellow writer to a full auditorium and, two years later, I sold my novel to a major publishing house. By the time I got it back with my editor's notes, it had been two and a half years since my delivery, and like a switch being turned on, my brain began to work clearly. No more fog. No more blindness in the right eye. No more stumbling and grasping for words. By then, I was walking up Twin Peaks every day, my son strapped to my back. I felt stronger than ever. Best of all, I was discovering the magic of the world along with my son: we inspected and admired the texture of bark, examined the color of leaves, collected bugs, were in awe of the ocean, and closed our eyes against the wind. Together, we sat in the back garden, in the shade of a Japanese cherry blossom tree, and felt our connection to each other and to everything else. I became so attuned to the organic process of decay and rejuvenation that when my final visit to the neurologist revealed that I had returned to full health without any deficiencies, I was humbly relieved, though not wholly surprised. My neurologist, in delighted amazement, dubbed me "the miracle girl."

I have read that early in life, we are each presented with many paths down which to take our lives and the difficulty is to choose the path that is best suited to us. Later in life, after we have begun traversing our chosen path, the difficulty is to remain true to it, to not falter or give up, to not ditch it for another. In just two months, in late September 2005, my son will turn six and I will be smack in the middle of my thirties. With the accumulation of years and my son's development in perfect accordance to the gentle spirit I first met while pregnant, I finally feel the miracle of what has happened to me. Isham is now entering first grade and is beginning to write and read and express his views on God and friendship and the importance of remaining just and honest. He refuses to eat meat because he does not believe in killing living creatures and has, at school, turned a band of children

into vegetarians. Upon his kindergarten graduation, his teacher awarded
him a medal for being the "most compassionate child in his grade." As
I witness all this in rapt wonder, I cannot help but recognize in his tall,
lean developing body the small newborn that squeezed out of me, and
I know my continued participation in the world is nothing less than a
divine gift. For this reason, I have no doubt that I am still alive for a
purpose. The path I chose seems to have been one of learning great
strength and tender mindfulness. My lessons toward these qualities
didn't end with my recovery, however. Three months after my son was
born and while I was still severely impaired, my husband also landed
in the same neurological ward in which I had been a patient and was
diagnosed with an inoperable brain lesion right on top of the spinal
cord. My neurologist became "our" neurologist, who once joked that
Tim and I should receive a two-for-one discount from our health insurance. As much as we relied on humor to help us through, the strain
and heartache eventually became too difficult for our bond to sustain
and we divorced when Isham was three, six months after my full recovery and immediately after Tim's lesion went into remission.

Traditionally, if the twenties are for testing oneself, for education
and training, for launching a career, the thirties, especially the early
thirties, are a time for love and laughter and marriage and a slow realization of professional goals and, alongside this, self-actualization.
Or, perhaps, like my idea long ago that I couldn't be pregnant while I
was still delivering my manuscript, this, too, is a notion. That is not to
say that I don't realize that what I have gone through is unusual, and
also unusually hard and unusually terrifying. But it is to say that, like
the myriad paths available to us when we begin our journeys, so, too,
are there countless possibilities and outcomes, and I have come to understand that arriving at any single outcome is not the same as arriving at the end of the path. Indeed, there are many different kinds of
death, and many different births and rebirths. Like that, collapsing and
rebuilding, the spiritual journey, the evolution of the human mind and
soul, continues to unfold. The miracle, in the end, is in staying steady

and true to the path, no matter what it brings. It is the hardships, after all, that reveal who we truly are. Now that I am thirty-five, I feel I
have enough years behind me, enough experience, to look back on my
life and see where it has brought me. Thirty-five seems like the mountain I climbed when nine months pregnant, while the time leading to
it is the expansive valley spread out before me, its beauty and secrets
graciously offered up so that I can appreciate the entirety of this personal landscape with detached curiosity and reverent wonder.

Standing at this peak, I see exactly how I got here.

Up until my son's birth, my life was ruled by conflicting outside
forces: my conservative Muslim parents, my religion, my Indian culture, my American upbringing. I was so confused about who I was
that I gave away my power and let others decide for me. Against my
better judgment, I wound up in an arranged marriage at nineteen. In-
nocently, I hoped that by marrying a Muslim Indian man I would finally find peace. Ironically, rather than mirroring me, he revealed to
me how many American values I held, including the one that disap-
proved of my arrangement to him. I divorced him, to great family
resistance and shame, and was told by my parents to leave the state.
It was in graduate school on a different coast that I met Tim, then
moved with him to California. Now I am divorced a second time and
living on my own with my son, whom I see half the week. I am so far
removed from the submissive Muslim daughter who married at her
parents' request that my parents don't know what to make of me; I
am the first in the history of my family to venture on such an independent path. Yet what may seem to many like a series of unfortunate
events, all of which ended in the catastrophic cacophony of Tim's and
my life-threatening illnesses and eventual divorce, is the very route
that led me to my deep self-realization, which is where every path
leads. No matter the journey you chose, if you hang on, it will ultimately lead you to discovering your true nature.

So what is the path I am so definite about, now that I am in the
middle of my thirties and can count up the years like coins in a pocket

to gauge what it all amounts to? That my soul's purpose is to increase awareness of our unity, this creative force that ties us all together at the most fundamental level, and thereby help to bring about peace. I strive toward this universal goal by using the tools supplied to me by my limited identity. As a writer who fought to regain her language, I employ my words to spread my message through writing and speech. Words are propelled with breath, after all. And what is breath but spirit? Writers are inspired, moved by a higher presence, and the root word for inspire means "to breathe in."

As a woman who struggled to gain her personal freedom by leaving a traumatic arranged marriage and thereby losing her family, I speak openly about my struggles in order that others may find the courage to become bigger than the obstacles holding them back. As an American Muslim, I struggle to build understanding between the Muslim and non-Muslim communities. My first novel honestly reveals how restricted and dismal a Muslim woman's life can be when she is trapped by patriarchy and insufficient and incorrect readings and applications of Islam. In early 2004, just after the novel's release, I took the story's message to the street by forming a feminist group for Muslim American women. As our first act toward positive change, we marched into an East Coast mosque to reclaim the rights given to us by Islam but taken away by male power and ancient culture. There were only five of us, and yet we sent ripples across the world, causing more and more Muslim women to stand up for equality. This year, America's most powerful Muslim organization announced the implementation of new rules regarding women's proper and just treatment within the mosque space—a direct response to our peaceful march.

I use the media attention and university invitations I receive from both the march and the book to speak to the non-Muslim communities. In our global community, there is not much knowledge about Muslims, which gives rise to stereotypes and division and hopelessness and fear. Every day, these emotions are implemented into a system of discriminatory laws against a people who feel as victimized by the terrorists as anyone else, and who must now suffer on both ends. What is happening in the world today is no different from what happened in my family when I was growing up: a fear of outsiders has forced us to set up barriers against fellow human beings, to comply with narrow beliefs in perceived difference, to take false comfort in our apparent superiority. Rather than solve the problem, these reactions merely aggravate it. To create peace, we must accept that each of us is harmed by these vicious crimes (those committed by citizens and those committed by government) and that each of us is responsible for them as well. Only then can we create the balance this planet so desperately needs and, as one community, begin the journey toward healing.

My son's face gives me the courage to do what I must. His small, miraculous body was formed from the union between a Muslim woman and a white American man, from possibilities, from the creative force of love and oneness. As such, he demands to be raised without limitations. Even now, I feel the power of his ancient spirit filling my small one with hope, and as his mother, all I can do is teach and direct. All I must do is let him go, release and surrender. It is like the beating of the heart. I take in love, I release love. I hold fast, I let go. In leaving my body, Isham has already embarked on the path he has come here to undertake, and I love him enough to allow him to be who he must, even if it is the modern world's one and only Buddha.

In Islam, we say a small fire burns in each of our bellies, the fire of life that only Allah has the power to extinguish. When I think of Buddha turning over that bowl, I see an image of a full belly, of pregnancy, of creation and connection, the miracle of one love holding us all together.

How to Be a Seductress Without Even Knowing It

HEATHER CHAPLIN

Is that a ten-gallon hat or are you just happy to see me?
MADELINE KAHN,
Blazing Saddles

I only just realized: I am a professional seducer. Not a prostitute, or even an escort, I'm more like the women in that Woody Allen short story who are paid by the hour to lounge about discussing Kierkegaard and Heidegger with intellectually starved men.

I'm a journalist. I talk to people for a living. I pry as deeply as possible into who my subjects are in the time allowed and then capture their likeness with words. It reminds me of another Woody Allen joke, the one about the boy who cheated on his metaphysics exam by peering into the soul of the boy next to him. I've always thought this was essentially what I was paid to do. And because my career has mostly been business writing, and because men still mostly dominate the business world, my subjects have mostly been men. I've built a career peering into the soul of the man sitting next to me. And who knew, but it turns out that's a pretty seductive thing to do.

Where to start? Do I start at the beginning as David Copperfield did, or skip that crap like Holden Caulfield? Suffice it to say that I grew up in a wildly undisciplined household, the child of parents who had been set free—or at least let off their leashes—by the sexual and political revolution of the 1960s and '70s. Unfortunately, it was a little too late; they'd already had children. Nonetheless, they chased their bliss with the gusto of champion athletes competing for a spot on the Olympic team—my mother brought home strange men at a rate that made my head spin; my father, a bearded, revolution-preaching Don Juan, picked up and discarded young girlfriends with a frequency that made it impossible to keep their names straight.

My life as a writer, I see now, has been one relationship after another with extraordinary men. For a long time, I didn't understand my success. I certainly hadn't been raised to have tête-à-têtes with captains of industry. Once I expressed my bewilderment about a particular subject to a friend. She smiled, in a vaguely patronizing manner, put her hand on my knee, and said: "Don't you think it's just possible he has a teensy crush on you?" I blushed. Nausea brewed in my stomach. I told her off in no uncertain terms. I found the very thought demeaning, offensive, and repellent. "No," I explained firmly. "He *likes* me." She smirked.

It's true that the interview can be a deeply intimate experience. As a journalist, you spend many of your best hours communing deeply with people who were strangers the day before and will probably be strangers again in the future. But my friend's implication that such intimacy was not a pure meeting of the minds, but rather contained an erotic component, was both insulting and terrifying. Once, she even had the nerve to suggest that this erotic energy traveled both ways.

Somewhere in the darkness of that crumbling, overgrown, bohemian-paradise Victorian in which I grew up, I learned that sex and sexuality were far too dangerous to acknowledge, let alone play with. I watched for years as my father reeled people in, only to drop them once intimacy had been established. I saw my mother revel in her ability to make men swoon before her, only to move on while they were still staggering to their feet. It wasn't the key-swapping parties of *The Ice Storm*—my parents were far too disorganized for that kind of thing—but their shenanigans reeked of a similar desperation tangled with a confused sense of liberation. I tuned out the sexual energy that whipped around my childhood, and instead focused on what was going unsaid. When the real communication in a house takes place in unspoken dialogue, one becomes exquisitely sensitive to the unsaid. I became an expert in the art of subterranean communication. This was how I learned to navigate the world. But it turns out that there was a fatal flaw: not incorporating sex into my map of human communication made my navigational skills a little less reliable than I had realized. I've been like an explorer with a compass that's got north a few degrees to the east.

The irony is that, even as I willed away any recognition of overt sexuality, I took in every tactic these seducers used and made them my own. There is something deeply, if not inherently, manipulative in the game of seduction. It's been a tradition of femininity for thousands of years. (My father's excuse? You'll have to ask him.) Denied access to obvious avenues to power, women have long channeled their aggression, their competitiveness, and their longing for achievement through the more circuitous route of seduction (take Livia in *I, Claudius* as an extreme example). Manipulation is for people who can't, or feel they can't, approach a matter directly. Like me.

How would this possibly come in handy as a journalist? As long as men continue to discount women's intelligence and competence, to fear us as equals, seduction will always be a highly effective tool. It's not surprising woman are associated with snakes in the Bible; if we're not allowed in on our own two feet, we're going to slither in. And sometimes slithering can be easier than walking—less risky, less confrontational. Interviewing men can be as easy as taking candy from a baby. You're just a girl, how big a threat can you be? The seduction of the female journalist lies in awakening her subject to the joys of feeling close to another person, to the relief of talking. A little bit of empathy can go a long way with a man. My editors thought I was good at asking the tough questions. Really I was just good at lulling my subjects into a sense of intimacy that made them want to talk.

Now, in this, my thirty-third year, my eyes have been opened to the fact that there is actually a sexual component to all of this seducing. I know. For many women, this sounds strange: their teens and early twenties were defined by their sexual awakening. I knew those girls—the ones who exulted, without remorse, in their sexiness. In fact, they were the bane of my existence, tossing their hair and making eyes at men who fairly fell to their knees at a whiff of this blossoming sexuality. I shook my fist at a universe that had *obviously* made the cosmic miscalculation of giving such power to the wrong girls.

Me, I *talked* to men. I made them fall in love with me by sheer force of personality—or so I believed. I was shocked when a boyfriend in college said the first thing he'd noticed about me was my bosom. How dare he! It felt predatory, unpure. It was *me* he was supposed to love, not my body. That there could be a melding of the two was a concept too threatening to even contemplate. In high school, a boy—about whom I was head over heels—moved in to kiss me one night at a bar mitzvah party. I ran into the bathroom, sweating in fear, and left only when I knew my mother would be waiting for me outside in our cream-colored Chevy Nova. I walked right past the confused boy on the curb without saying a word. I refused to speak with him or go near him for months. And when he found a new girlfriend, I spent the next year pining for him. How I coveted the teenage queens' power. But I felt as capable of playing in this game as of sprouting wings and flying away. How could I compete in a sexual arena when I couldn't even see the goalposts?

But I can see it now, this so-called sexual energy. It whips around the room like an electrical wire let loose. I can hear it: the note that's been missing from my repertoire. And I find myself ducking, bobbing and weaving, and, occasionally, getting smacked upside the head as I learn to navigate around this one current of unspoken communication with which I've refused to engage. I feel like the thief in the *Pink Panther* movie, trapped in a museum vault with a big diamond and an ultra-red security system between him and it. One false move, and the whole place will be echoing with alarms and swarming with police.

Take last summer. Having just finished writing my first book, I'd flown out to California to visit friends and cool out on the beach. One night, I invited one of my favorite sources from the book to meet me for drinks. He took me to dinner and stayed with me after other friends had left us at a nearby bar. I was smoking cigarettes, which I don't usually, and he commented on it. A little tipsy, I tossed my hair—just like those girls of my youth—and said, "I just wrote a book. This week, I can do whatever I want." There was a pause, and then my favorite source leaned in toward me and said, "*Really?* Well, speaking of that, how's this husband of yours?" (When you're a journalist, sometimes people don't believe you have a family back home somewhere.) The room went dim like when you're a small child hearing a scary story; my brain turned into a din of fuzzy white noise, and hot prickles crept up my skin. I found myself hiding my face with my hands and apologizing profusely, for what I wasn't exactly sure, but unable to stop. It was the first time I'd been hit on, or aware of being hit on, in the eleven years I've been with my husband.

This week I can do whatever I want? My God, what was I thinking? I'm not doing a blame-the-victim thing. I simply realized that I had, unknowingly, been putting it out. I'd been gazing soulfully into men's eyes, egging them on to tell me more and more, to get more and more personal. And I hadn't realized that the me who was doing it was not some scowling early-twenty-something, or a sad-mouthed teenager with self-esteem a notch below sea level. It was the me of today, a thirty-three-year-old woman at her fighting weight, with clear skin, confidence that has occasionally been called arrogance, and the ironic attractiveness of a taken woman who's just being herself. "It's power," my friend said. But it didn't feel like power to me; it felt like nausea.

I've often thought it was one of life's little cruelties that women—
or so they say—hit their sexual peak in their thirties, while men hit
theirs in their teens. No doubt, I've partly been going through what
many woman my age are: the rampant insecurities of American adolescence and youth gone, we're growing comfortable in our own skin
and awakening to our own desires, sexual and otherwise. Yet I'd kept
this awakening secret even from myself. I hadn't seen that I was being
sexually alluring while being intellectually seductive. It hadn't occurred
to me I was capable of being sexually alluring. Nice work, my inner
shrink said, while crowing about what a genius you are, you've actually devoted your entire career to making men fall in love with you.
Nice one, feminist.

Okay, so maybe I have some daddy issues. But you know what, I've
been trying to see into people's souls while they weren't looking since
before I could talk. That's why I'm a writer. And reaching that level
where you are engaging soul-to-soul has given me some of the greatest
satisfaction I've known. I just didn't realize that peering into someone's eyes and asking them personal questions is very different when
you're a grown woman than when you're a young girl. In fact, I hadn't
quite realized I was a grown woman. I'd been so busy paying attention
to all the other subliminal currents in the room I'd missed the most
primal of them all, the sex current.

Now I recognize it for what it is when a subject scoots a little closer
to me; now I see the lightning bolt when I introduce myself with a big
smile and an outstretched hand. And, hardest of all to admit, I now
feel it brewing in myself after our eyes have been locked and our minds
intertwined for some period of time. I am slowly learning to sit tight
with it, forcing myself to remain conscious of what's going on, without running for the bathroom in heated fear. Sometimes I even allow
myself to relish the feeling of being wrapped, for just a moment, in
the hot tentacles of sexual chemistry.

It's not easy. I still find myself closing my eyes sometimes, or looking away, embarrassed. The nausea still returns. According to Sartre,

nausea is what happens when you look over a cliff and realize that the only thing stopping you from jumping is your own decision not to. Nausea is the terrifying, gut-wrenching realization of one's own freedom. And like guilt acting as a tip-off to the conscience that something is amiss in the soul, nausea can be a warning that there's a choice to be made, even if the implications of that choice are less than pleasing either way.

My marriage has not been easy over the last few years. Hooking up at twenty-two and finding yourself with the same man eleven years later is an odd experience on its own. You've grown; he's grown; you've changed; he's changed; you're both bored, and angry over a decade's worth of misunderstandings and mistakes. The difficulties only increase when the gender and power rules are not prescription written. In many ways, I am more traditionally masculine than my husband. In recent years, I've become the primary breadwinner, the ambitious one, the one who's learning to shine in a manner to which the world responds positively. And it's me who has consistently put the breaks on his life-long dream of parenthood—I fear being subsumed by the needs of another. I'm desperate not to lose this outside life I've finally built for myself after so many years of battling demons on a full-time basis. I've even wondered, in our worst moments, if the needs of a husband are too much for me.

This summer, I let myself engage the kind of questions you hope your partner never engages about you. Okay, I said to myself, as I was being hit on, you're nauseous, but you are a creature of free will. You can do whatever you want. Do you want to run off with this man? Tonight? Forever? I looked into his eyes, trying to peer past the blue into the nature of the man himself, and there was a disappointing thud in my chest. I was ready to let myself have whatever it was I decided I actually wanted—and I realized I didn't want this man. Not for real. Not the way I want my husband. Are you kidding? said another of my internal voices. If you had this guy's face staring back at you for the rest of your life, you'd kill yourself. I ran through a roster of all the men

I knew. And I realized there wasn't one whose face I wanted to see staring back at me for the rest my life—except my husband's.

No, this wonderful, love-affirming moment did not leave me with a pat happy ending. Just as I'd suspected as a child, there is danger in acknowledging the erotic currents of human communication. It's not deadly, but it's certainly tricky. I'm a married woman; I don't want to be attracted to other men. But I'm a married thirty-something woman who has only just learned to incorporate sexual currents into her map of the world. There's a universe of powerful experiences awaiting me should I decide to act on this realization. And I revolt in my mind at missing out on the opportunity to flex my late-blooming muscles. But I also don't want the consequences of doing so. And thus I get nauseous. Caught between what I want and what I don't want, neither feeling staying neatly on its side of the equation.

The truth is I am desperately curious about following one of my Woody Allen–style seductions to a more R-rated ending. I can't stand the fact that as a married woman who loves her husband, I gave up this option before I even knew it existed. But I can no longer hide behind the I-don't-know-what-you're-talking-about wall of the past. The nausea was the tip-off that I had choices to make, that I was living, to use another Sartre-ism, in bad faith. I was failing to take responsibility for my own desires.

I know that getting what I want circuitously holds less and less allure for me these days. Today, I want to grab what I want by the hair and wrestle it to the ground. Desires? I want everything life has to offer, good and bad. I want to have sex with a hundred different men and still come home to my husband at night; I want to travel the world without worrying who I'm leaving behind; I want to grow powerful and influential without worrying who I hurt. Instead of *what does he want,* and *how do I get him to give me what I want,* I find myself, recently, just plain wanting.

Will I get all these things? No, not if I want to maintain my marriage, not if I want to have kids, not if I want to live a thoughtful and compassionate life, which, ultimately, I do. But I rage, just like when I was a teenager, at what feels like the unfairness of the universe. I suspect it was a similarly subverted rage that led my parents into their overly sexualized lifestyle—the feeling that their lives weren't their own for the making. They believed that by disregarding the social taboos of their time, they were living freely. What do I want? I want to figure out which cliffs are worth jumping off and to have the strength of mind to do so in good faith.

My father used to say that the shortest distance between any two points is a straight line. He's a mathematician, so I'm going to assume this was one of the true things he told me. Until recently, I never even considered following a straight path from desire to fulfillment. But being just a seducer is too easy. I want to be the woman who asks the tough questions—even if it makes my job harder.

Side of the Road

DAO STROM

I'm through believing in love's holy impossible meaning
Threads of desire slung all across time
I been walking the wires of a hope that's so fine
All the other hopes they just fall to the wayside
So I'll teach my baby boy if you're gonna hang with the girls
You gotta wear your seatbelt baby and get used to the
    weight of the world . . .

DAO STROM,
"High Flyer"

I will start with the desert.

When my son was four months old, his father and I left San Francisco to move to Austin, Texas. For some reason, it felt crucial to us to get out of California on our first day of driving. We were determined to reach Needles, Arizona, by that evening. But we miscalculated how much driving and sitting a four-month-old baby could take and, sometime in the late afternoon, had to pull over on the side of I-10 on our way through the desert southeast of Bakersfield, because the baby was crying so much.

The ground was flat and sandy with shrubs growing out of it. I could find nowhere to sit down with the baby. Littered cans and bits of rubber from blown-out tires lay strewn along the shoulder of the freeway. The ground itself shook like thunder every time a semi passed, and the wind reversed itself in hard gusts—a number of semis were going by. It seemed a thankless and harsh place to stop, but it also seemed necessary. I walked away from the freeway, toward the expanse of desert, picking my way through the shrubs and across the sandy ground, holding the baby who was still crying. I was nearly in tears myself. I just wanted to get away from the ground shaking and the wind of the semis and I wanted my son to be happy. The wind blowing across his face was making him cringe and squint. I finally sat cross-legged on the ground and held my son in my lap to nurse him. In my head was the thought that this would be his first sight of the desert, even though he wouldn't likely remember it. I thought of how my first sight of the desert (on a trip to Nevada when I was in college) had awed me. A feeling both of promise and heartache was aroused in me by its vastness and barrenness. This was a romanticized view, I realize now, but I'd not had much exposure to such vistas before then. Now I thought about how my son would grow up with this—these expanses—somehow already familiar to him. I had the sensation that I would be giving my son the knowledge of both the loneliness and the beauty of certain freedoms, early. This feeling, the whole incident, felt tremendous and poignant and wrenching. It told me the truth of where I was going on this journey as a mother and as a person: that there would be unexpected stops, and that there would be walks into the desert trying to escape the shaking of the road, and that there would be, every now and again, certain lucid, unexpected moments of clarity provided by having the horizon suddenly laid out before you in all its plain forlornness.

It did not escape me, either, that my son's father waited by the truck, still close to the freeway, and that the pain and keenness I felt, I felt all on my own.

But I Am a Happy Traveler

No Tieu, no Dao. I am told this is what I used to say when I was a toddler in Pendleton, the refugee camp outside of San Diego where we stayed for a few months upon our initial entry to the States from Vietnam in 1975. The older little girls would chase me around wanting to hug and play with me. They would call out my name, "Tieu-Dao, Tieu-Dao," and I would yell back at them my perhaps (as I see it now) precognizant self-denial, *No Tieu, no Dao!*

I have heard this story more than once. I am hearing it again now at my cousin's engagement ceremony in San Diego, where I have flown in for the weekend before Christmas with my son, Lincoln, now just shy of four, for a brief visit with my mother, brother, and sister. My brother lives in San Diego and my sister is currently stationed here, as she is in the navy. My mother has driven down from her home in the Central Valley to meet us. For this short trip I have even purchased a push-up bra, which my mother had told me I would need, as it is the proper kind of bra to wear under an *ao dai*—a traditional Vietnamese dress. Our visit is happening to coincide with a cousin's engagement ceremony, and my mother has suggested we attend (we truthfully might not have, had it not been convenient) and that she and my sister and I all wear *ao dai*s for the occasion, for the fun of it. It is well known to us all that this will be a rare spectacle, the three of us in traditional Vietnamese dress, and together.

The couple telling me the "no Tieu, no Dao" story this time are a Vietnamese doctor and his wife whose daughters my sister and I used to play with. I only vaguely remember having visited this family. This half of my history is often a blur to me, for there were always so many relatives on my mother's side—some blood kin, some simply old close friends—and their lives always seemed very different from ours. While they lived in suburban and urban parts of California, and appeared to have stayed connected with the larger Vietnamese-American community, we grew up in El Dorado County somewhat as anomalies in a mostly white, rural setting. Consequently, I grew up identifying more with the redneck-tinged, ex-hippie, mountain-life culture of northern California small towns than with any apparent aspects of Vietnamese-American culture. The doctor and his wife are telling me the "no Tieu, no Dao" story in Vietnamese, which I don't understand, but I know which story it is when I hear them say my name and when I hear the "no Tieu, no Dao" part followed by their laughter. They are looking at me fondly, so I laugh and smile, too. I am allowing myself to be remembered, I think, as I try to beam innocent positive energy into the exchange. Several hours later, in line to get to the food tables after the engagement ceremony, the Vietnamese doctor comes up to me again and says with surprise, in English, "You don't speak Vietnamese." No I don't, I admit. He says he hadn't realized this before when earlier he told me the story. So he tells it again. "You no like to be hug so much so you run away. 'No Tieu, no Dao!' you say." He smiles and laughs again and pats me on the shoulder.

If there is something like a code to one's destiny in a name, I would like to consider what mine might be. My mother named me Tieu-Dao, she says, because at the time her life had a lot of complexity and tragedy in it—her first husband had just been killed, her own activities as a journalist were causing her to be harassed by the corrupt South Vietnamese government, and, of course, there was a war on. So she named me Tieu-Dao with the hope that this would free me of similar burdens in my own life.

Tieu-Dao is an unusual name in the Vietnamese language. It is derived from the Chinese and its meaning has connections to Taoism. It is a name most Vietnamese people would be fearful of giving to a child, especially to a girl, my mother has told me, for they would worry a name like this might cause the child to leave home or be fated to live an unconventional life. It is also a name understood only, really, by artistic or more educated Vietnamese, my mother has also told me; more ordinary people (these terms are frank, though they seem derisive when she uses them) only hear the common words the name sounds like: *tieu* sounds like the Vietnamese word for "pepper," and *dao* (actually pronounced *yow* or *zow*) sounds like the word for "knife." This explains why my older cousins, the times we would see them, jokingly called me Pepper-knife. The more poetic (and intended) translation of my name, I am told, is "happy traveling" or "happy traveler." In one dictionary I find it translated as "at leisure," in another "wanderlust." I know all about these philosophies and in theory have long admired them and wished to adhere to them for myself. In practice, however, the process of moving around and meeting every new rise in the road with grace has proven to be at times not exactly easy, not exactly like water rolling off a duck's back.

I go by Dao now, with the hard *d* sound; I have for as long as I can remember. Sometimes I think of that passage in *East of Eden* by John Steinbeck where he talks about people who've adopted alterations of the names they were born with, as if it were, for whatever reasons they deemed crucial, also in their destinies to change, or at least somehow alter, their destinies. Sometimes I wonder which part of the phrase "happy traveling" I may be trying to alter, or remove.

What Is Contained

My first year of motherhood in the Lone Star State, where we knew almost no one went something like this:

A drab gray apartment complex in a not-so-great neighborhood, the only place we can really afford. My partner (we never technically married) is gone most of the day, from seven to seven, working. In the heat of our first Texas summer, I try to keep myself and the baby entertained by spending hours in the park and in places like Target, where I've recently discovered the convenience of shopping carts and mega-merchandising layouts. There is something about timing our outings, I've learned—get out of the house early enough to beat the heat and back in time to coordinate the baby's nap. During Lincoln's naptimes, I try to write. I am interrupted frequently by his wakings, though. He is a light sleeper, a big cryer. When I hear him, I run back to the bedroom to lie with him and nurse him to sleep again, all the while composing sentences in my head that I will try to remember but often forget by the time I get back to the computer.

I watch college kids in the swimming pool visible out our patio door. They splash and wrestle and make out together, bobbing around the pool in animal-shaped floaties. The whole spectacle is slightly repulsive and perplexing to me in my current frame of mind; it is also purely biological and not cute or sexy, as I see it. Motherhood has made me wholly unsentimental about the rites of romance. Feelings of excitement are stirred in me lately only by things like that poignancy I felt in the desert, and by reading about things like archaeoastronomy and the sense a subject like that gives me of the spiritual texture of the world. But most of all by the love and connection I feel to my son— by the thought of huge intangible patterns hovering patiently over the mundanity of our lives, waiting to be uncovered and to unfold. Motherhood was not an accident for me, no matter what the circumstances looked like; it was something I arrived at with a sense of knowing. For months before becoming pregnant, before even meeting my son's father, I had gone about my life in San Francisco with a portentous feeling looming over me: I had even thought it could be a premonition of death. And it *was* a death of a sort, I suppose.

These are the parts about becoming a mother that they—other women, books, our own mothers—do not tell you about. At least this was so in my experience. Though I do realize there are other ways to interpret the experience of adjusting to new roles.

On a visit to my parents' house shortly after my son's birth, a neighbor who is an old family friend and also a religious man, came by to see the baby. At one point he laid his hand on my shoulder in a confidential manner and said, "I believe becoming a parent is the event that truly marks one's entry into the human race. Welcome."

There are other kinds of changes. A former lover, whom I'd long held out the hope of one day having more of a relationship with, sends a letter from a point of transition in Lebanon, Missouri—I've not heard from him in years—and I write back about how I now live in Texas and have a baby, live with someone but am not married. There is a feeling of both satisfaction and resignation in writing this information to this particular person.

Motherhood is a form of isolation no one talks about, I think. You inhabit the same spaces for so much time and tend to the earthiest details of life with such a sense of necessity that you come through it all feeling both incredibly wizened and fragile; everything is sharper, every interaction on the outside holds heightened import suddenly; and you realize how amazingly capable and needy, both, a woman can be, should she choose to follow one direction over the other. This is the journey mothers take, I think, sequestered alone at home with their babies and seemingly going nowhere, the real strangeness and depth of their endeavors largely unbeknownst, even to themselves. The outside world is not the realm of the stay-at-home mother. The outside world pretty much disregards her, in fact, wanting only to view her as inexhaustibly good-natured and desireless, self-sacrificing and tireless. When I am out there I often feel as if I'm in disguise. I stand and wave at the passengers on the miniature train that goes by in the park; I take my son's wrist in my hand and make him wave, too, letting on to no one the deception I feel is inherent in a gesture like this. I am just another young mother in the park waving at the train with her toddler and we are all the same. It occurs to me that perhaps this is how adults are meant to go about in the world, defined each by their most apparent roles. I don't know if I can bear that, if it's true.

Marriage ensures privacy of the soul. I read that Virginia Woolf once said or wrote something to this effect. I will consider my own isolation as a time in which to make myself sharp, then, and to hone my visions. There's a phrase Joseph Campbell uses, too, about finding a way to live within society that yet allows one to "incubate your destiny." Hoping my destiny involves getting a book published, I throw every spare ounce of energy I have into my writing. Before having a child, I had been more reluctant and sardonic about the idea of trying to make a living as an artist—it had seemed indulgent, so I was lazy about it. But now it seems necessary.

And when I can no longer eke paragraphs of fiction out of myself, then I pick up my guitar and try to find songs or bits of songs. There are so many voices wanting to be aired and so many stories asking to be told, so much in me that seems not to want to be contained.

The Dress, the Container

An *ao dai* is a two-piece outfit made of silk: a long-sleeved shirtlike dress with small snap buttons all the way up the neck, falling over a matching pair of wide-legged trousers. The dress is very fitted around the arms and neck and torso, very loose and elegantly flowing around the hips and legs. There are side slits that bare just a tiny glimpse of skin above the waistband of the pants, if you raise your arms high enough. Perhaps Vietnamese women in *ao dai*s traditionally never raised their arms very high, though, more likely kept them close to their sides, I think. When my sister flips the skirt of her dress up and jokingly sticks out her hip, one of our male cousins exclaims, "Wow, I never see Vietnamese girl do like that before!" and laughs. My sister has the body and the charm to pull off a gesture like this—she laughs at herself, almost embarrassed but self-knowing.

As we are finishing getting ready at my aunt's house, one of my older female cousins pushes a bracelet on me. I try to refuse it. It is a light, gaudy silver thing, and it is not so much that I don't like its style as I feel reluctant about accepting gifts from them for some reason. I know that my sister feels the same, though she has somehow managed to successfully decline the jewelry they've pushed on her. "For you," my cousin says to me, clicking the bracelet into place on my wrist. Her tone strikes me as being strange, and with a kind of insipid deliberateness, the same tone she would've used to proffer gifts like this to me when I was ten, when I would've eagerly accepted them, probably. Now I am almost offended by this in a way I can't quite grasp. Another female cousin, the one who currently has a seven-month-old baby, asks with aggressive incredulity why my husband is not with me. They do not, it seems, know all the technicalities of my situation (probably my mother doesn't mention to her sisters that I neglected a few of the customary steps). It is their brother's engagement ceremony we are attending.

We pile into cars to drive to where the ceremony will take place. Here, my sister and I and several other girls in *ao dais* are given trays of food to carry down the sidewalk toward the bride-to-be's parents' house, passing other faux-Spanish-style suburban homes with adobe fronts and curved red roof shingles, squat decorative palms on lawns, other desert plants in beds lined with white pebbles. We are reenacting the traditional practice of the groom-to-be's family bringing gifts to the bride-to-be's family, or some mutation of a few traditions, I am not sure; maybe this represents something about dowry, I think. A big crowd of relatives and family friends moves loosely down the sidewalk along with us, a group of eight girls carrying trays of food, each tray draped over by a red cloth. My son, wearing his backpack, trudging along between my brother and my mother, has an amused, happy expression on his face. I can tell the procession is fun for him and that he is aware it is something special. It would be safe to say we've not been a part of very many processions in his life so far.

The ceremony takes place in the living room of the bride-to-be's family home. People are crowded together all the way up the stairs and down the hall and around the perimeters of the room, in the front entranceway as well. My sister and I put our trays of food down on the long dining table at the far end of the living room, as do the other girls. The bride-to-be comes down the stairs to stand between her mother and father in the center of the living room, and the father speaks into a microphone. My cousin and his parents also stand in the center of the room, though most of the focus appears to be on the bride-to-be. In Vietnamese, introductions between the two families are made, family members around the room are pointed out, and after each name there is a round of applause. This goes on for some time. There is also a part of the ceremony in which earrings are put on the bride-to-be's ears—they are a gift from someone important— and the mother and soon-to-be mother-in-law each tackle an earlobe. I spot my son lying on the floor across the room, amid the feet of other guests, playing with an unattached microphone he has somehow gotten ahold of. Since he is clear on the other side of the room there is no hope of my reaching him and correcting his behavior, I realize. I try to signal to my brother, but Lincoln won't stay with him, and presently is crossing the room to be next to me, leaving the micro- phone on the carpet. He then lies on the floor next to my feet and starts making loud, bored noises. He rolls around, playing with pieces of paper confetti he has gotten from somewhere. When I kneel beside him to try to tell him to quiet down, he gets up and throws his arms around my neck and begins energetically kissing my face. Already, the elderly Vietnamese woman who is standing on my other side, and who is not from our relatives' side of the gathering, has looked my way a couple of times with disdain. She has clucked her tongue and shook her head at Lincoln's lying on the floor, gesturing that he should be standing. Now, in the fervor of his hugging me, I realize the side snap buttons of my dress have begun to come undone. My sister, noticing this, kneels beside me to help rebutton them; a couple girls nearby us also notice and are laughing sympathetically. "This dress," I whisper to my sister, "this dress does not want to stay on me." It oc- curs to me it is possible, quite possible, that the accessories women wear might very well have lives, energies, of their own—they may know upon whom their powers of beautifying and refinement will better work. In order to distract him I now let Lincoln take the bracelet from my wrist. He lies down on the floor again and places it in his mouth. At seeing this, the elderly woman next to me glares and hisses in Lincoln's direction, then crosses herself.

Now the Book Is on the Table

It isn't long after the engagement ceremony visit to San Diego that I move into my own apartment and begin sharing custody of my son with his father. This will launch me into yet another stage of development and adjusting to new roles, redefining myself and my many and varied concepts of what it means to be a woman, a mother, a lover; also, what it means to share or not share the privacy of my soul, as I see it. And it seems I may've arrived at the conclusion that I want to try to be my own guardian of those spaces.

In this time, and for many months before, I have given a lot of thought to what separation means and to what the distinction is or can be, if there is one, between severing ties and altering them.

I have even entertained the theory that there are two kinds of people in the world: those who must at points move on because they fear they will lose or damage something if they don't; and those who stay because to love for them means to persevere and to hold on. Both, in truth, are attempts at preserving something. I do believe this, though what that something is, I think, is never the same from person to person or even explicable, for the most part.

I have been both of these kinds of people at various points in my life, I might say, though maybe I've been the former more often than the latter. Ideally, I like to think, a balance would be struck.

My mother was one of many who left Vietnam after 1975, while many others stayed. People left out of fear of what would happen if they stayed, or in hopes of a different kind of life, or in pursuit of those they loved who had gone; and people stayed out of loyalty to the homeland, or because they did not want a different life, or because they had faith in things working out for them where they were. And there are many other reasons—too many to list, I know. I also know it's too simplistic, and inappropriate, of me to draw conclusions or make analogies between this and my own situations, so I present this here only as an equation of a sort, or a backdrop, against which I've tried to arrange the puzzle pieces of my own life thus far.

I also see: I may have fulfilled the potential fears the name Tieu-Dao would hold for the kinds of parents who wouldn't give that name to their daughters—I have opted to live far from my mother and other family members, I have shied away from the conventional dictates of matrimony and family.

But I am a happy traveler.

No Tieu, no Dao.

Also on that visit to California, the weekend before Christmas, was when I spotted my book in a bookstore for the first time. My first novel. My brother, sister, Lincoln, and I were roaming about in a Borders with other Christmas shoppers when I noticed it lying on the New Paperbacks table. I pointed it out to Lincoln, and he recognized it immediately.

"Hey, we have that book," he said.

How I See It

IVY MEEROPOL

Experience teaches that
silence terrifies people the most.
BOB DYLAN,
from liner notes of
Bringing It All Back Home

My grandparents were only in their thirties when they died. Yet even as I approached that so-called milestone of adulthood, they still appeared old in a way that made it impossible for me to recognize them as young. It was easy to be thrown off. In photos from the last years of their lives, my grandmother was old-ladyish in her frumpy coat with the fur collar and fussy hat, while my grandfather's boyish face and physique were obscured by a pencil-thin mustache and dark suit. This was the 1950s, too, when thirty really was *old* and you had children, a career, and a home or else your family was concerned. Their names didn't help either: Ethel and Julius Rosenberg. Old-fashioned names, historic names. But ultimately it was the photos that confused me. In most of the photos from those final years (set in quite somber settings, there they are handcuffed in a paddy wagon or blinking and simply trying to brave the onslaught of klieg lights outside a federal courthouse) they look grown up in a way that only people who have been put on trial for their lives could be. In the time it took to arrest, try, and convict them (two years), all signs of youth had fled from their eyes. What remained were two people facing their own terrible mortality by the time they were thirty-two and thirty-five.

As it turned out, I was thirty-two when I began making what would become *Heir to an Execution,* a personal documentary that examines how the executions of my grandparents created a complicated legacy for their families. The experience of making the film changed my life, not simply because I discovered truths about my family but because I discovered abilities that had long been lying dormant in me. But at thirty, I was debating whether to adopt two cats and move in with my boyfriend. I wasn't sure where my nascent "career" as a screenwriter/journalist/copywriter and general creative odd-jobber was going at all. I was foundering, surprised to find myself older yet more confused and unsure of myself. Only five years before, I'd been a cocky twenty-five-year-old working for a congressman on Capitol Hill.

My father was recently asked in an interview how he felt when I'd approached him about making a documentary of our family. The question drew an uncharacteristically curt response from my typically effusive dad. He told the reporter, "If she had asked me at twenty-five, she would have done it without me." Aside from waitressing, working on Capitol Hill for a U.S. congressman was my first job out of college, and I'd already been there three years. I'd envisioned spending a year or two at the most before taking off to be a Writer. I was writing up a storm as a legislative aide and speechwriter, but I was also beginning to feel the need to express myself. Ever since I was a kid, I'd thought it was a writer's life for me, not knowing what that really meant. Every time I went home for a holiday, there was a reminder of that plan.

I had written and illustrated a timeline of my life when I was eight years old, and it was still hanging on a wall in my parents' kitchen. It recounted highlights from those early years—my first solid food, my first trip to a local amusement park, my brother's adoption. Then I went on to predict my future. At twelve, I wrote, I would have brown hair. It's important to note that my best friend Amy had brown hair. At eighteen I would study writing in college and, unable to imagine myself any older than twenty-two, I ended the story envisioning myself writing children's books for insatiable kid readers like myself.

As it turned out, my projected timeline was off by a decade. It took much longer than I'd anticipated to find a way to communicate what was roiling around in my own mind. My twenties would only lay the groundwork for what became the most ambitious and productive time of my life.

Despite the occasional pang of regret over a dream deferred, I loved my job on the Hill. I loved the way my shoes echoed in the great marble hallways, how the raised letters on my gold-embossed business card felt, and, most important, I loved the challenge of taking a problem in our district and seeking a legislative solution. I was idealistic, full of outrage, sniffing out injustice everywhere. I visited schools and wrote speeches with lines like "It's not that a good teacher is hard to find, it's that a good teacher is hard to pay!" I believed that what I was doing was more important than the short stories I'd labored over in college. In Washington, I cultivated a rigid sense of right and wrong. I would seethe at the sight of Orrin Hatch and chase after Pat Schroeder like a crazed fan. I cried when the first President Bush vetoed a civil rights bill I'd worked on.

For the most part being "a granddaughter of the Rosenbergs" didn't particularly weigh on me. I'd grown accustomed during high school to living a kind of dual life, keeping essential information to myself. As I grew older, the legacy I'd inherited would occasionally collide with my life and provoke such a confluence of sadness and anger that I would struggle with the need to express it, to somehow make it my story, too. Once I accompanied the congressman on a trip to the district where he was to address a group of retirees. I'd penned the speech and was milling around in the crowd as my boss took the podium. When a tiny elderly woman tried to read the heat-curled nametag on my jacket, she gasped as I unrolled it for her. "Are you?" she asked me. I knew instantly what she meant. "Yes," I whispered to her, "I am." She shrieked and before I knew it, all eyes were on me as a curious crowd gathered. The woman who'd discovered my identity hugged me and sobbed, "I was there. I loved them. I tried to save them." Of course she'd never met my grandparents, but she, like many others of her generation and background, had suffered along with them. It shook me that as their granddaughter I could have that effect on people when I myself felt so disconnected from them and the story.

I continued to work in politics, but after the excitement of Clinton's election died down, I began to feel restless. I was itching to write something, not an op-ed piece but a story with characters and drama. An unusual case had come across my desk. James Stanley was a constituent of ours who'd been used as a guinea pig in the military experiments with LSD during the 1950s. He'd approached my boss after losing a long legal battle that culminated with a Supreme Court ruling against him in a 5–4 decision. We were his court of last resort. The story he told affected me deeply. The country he served and dedicated his life to had betrayed and treated him horribly. And so he fought back, quietly inching his way through the courts until he reached the highest one. His last chance at justice was with us. We introduced a private bill (meaning it concerned only him). It was called, For the Relief of James Stanley.

I obsessed over this man's life and his story. It wasn't just the fight to compensate him that I relished, it was my role as the storyteller. When I wrote appeals to other members of Congress to support the bill, or drafted the testimony for my boss to read at the hearings, I went into detail about how Stanley was tortured and confused by his own actions, how he beat up his wife and wouldn't remember in the morning. I told how he hallucinated while teaching and when he looked out at the class, saw his own image sitting at every desk. I, in turn, saw his story played out in images in my mind's eye. Eventually, the bill became law and a check was cut, but it didn't end there for me. When I called Stanley to tell him the good news, he was his usual reserved self. He thanked me for all of my hard work and said, "You know, all I ever really wanted was an apology." That one sentence, delivered with such devastating resignation, made me see him in another light, see his decades-long battle more clearly than I had. I'd been so focused on compensation, as if money could make up for lost years and an entire belief system destroyed. How can a piece of legislation capture that? I now understand what I couldn't see then, that I was angry about what happened to Stanley in the same way I was angry about what happened to my grandparents. Both stories represented an abuse of power by our government, yet in my immaturity it was all about James Stanley, a man to whom I had no other connection. What had happened to my own family was still too close to see.

I began to imagine Stanley's story on the big screen. Richard Attenborough's film *Cry Freedom* had affected me profoundly when I was a freshman in college. I was well aware of apartheid, but that film allowed me to feel the struggle of black and white South Africans deeply. It put a human face on an issue I knew only through the debate over sanctions. I walked out of the theater crying with outrage but also thrilled by the possibilities of cinema. You can tell a story, I thought, and change the world. I remember thinking then, in my naïve, eighteen-year-old mind, that I wanted to make people cry that way over what had happened to my grandparents. I didn't know yet that the story I would tell was about what had happened to my father and uncle and to all of us living with this history.

While working in D.C., I accompanied my father to a conference that the Center for the Study of Intelligence, the academic arm of the CIA, was holding in Washington. With much fanfare, the government had recently released the Venona documents, so-called decrypted KGB cables, indicating that my grandfather Julius had been a spy. I grew up, just as my father had, believing in the total innocence of my grandparents. They said so in their letters, they said so through their

lawyer and throughout the trial, and they said so even as they were being led to the electric chair. One of the people appearing at this conference was Robert Lamphere, the FBI agent who had handled much
of their case. Because the Venona documents stated that Ethel wasn't
an espionage agent, Lamphere was forced to address the question of
her innocence. He hemmed and hawed but essentially admitted the
government had a weak case against her and that he had recom-
mended a lesser sentence than death.

My father had vainly attempted to be recognized from the floor
and was surprised when at the very end of the day the modera-
tor suddenly called on him in the audience. "I understand Michael
Meeropol is here and would like to say something." Unprepared,
he fumbled with the papers in his lap. Giving up on the speech, my
father stood up, and in a shaking voice, demanded that Lamphere
explain why he had not tried to save his mother's life. It upset me
to see my father so undone. I could feel the effect he had on the
room. This was the first sign of emotion at an otherwise cold and
analytical meeting. When my father sat down, flushed and wild-eyed,
I saw for the first time the human face of our family history. It
sounds odd because I'd lived with that face my whole life but not like
this. In my father's eyes was the truth as I saw it. When a photographer approached us later and asked my father if he would pose for
a photo with Lamphere, he refused and, referring to Lamphere,
growled, "He's got blood on his hands." I knew then what I know
now—that all of the FBI, CIA, or KGB documents in the world can't
come close to telling the story the way I, and my family, see it.

I decided my next project had to finally be a screenplay about the
young soldier tested with LSD. But the decision that changed my life
most dramatically was a move to Cape Cod, where my parents had
just bought a house. For the first time, I was to take myself seriously
as a writer. I needed a fresh start and I found one in that empty house,
the flat winter sky and vast expanse of ocean. For six weeks I was a her-
mit, until I met the man who would become my husband. My work

probably suffered as we navigated the passionate and volatile advent of our relationship, but two months stretched into eight as I became part of a community that included artists, writers, farmers, and teachers. I became the fiction editor and a contributor to a local art magazine. I fell in love with the Cape and with the guy.

As much as I loved the Cape, I knew that when autumn approached I'd have to head to the big city and enter the fray. I wanted to be published and produced. New York was also where my husband-to-be lived. I was turning thirty and living in Brooklyn in a ridiculously small room in a shared apartment. I'd finished the LSD script and was peddling it around town while burning through a ten-thousand-dollar inheritance that had arrived just in time. Over the next couple of years I cobbled together a meager living as a reader for film companies and a freelance writer at magazines and websites. I wrote and pitched articles, getting my foot in the door, and then wasn't convinced I wanted to be there. With a friend I adapted a novel for the screen. What I really wanted was an all-consuming project, one that I lived and breathed.

I was also becoming increasingly attracted to and repelled by the story of my grandparents. I wanted to know more about them. Not what they may or may not have done in terms of passing secrets to the Soviet Union, but who they were, as lovers, friends, and parents. As I approached the age they were when they faced the electric chair, something began to take shape in me, some bit of bravery and the confidence that comes from having an inkling of who you really are.

When I was younger and thought fleetingly about a Rosenberg project of my own, I'd focused on setting the story straight, making people cry, provoking outrage, or changing the public's view of my grandparents. When I was about thirty I began to toy with the idea of doing a fictionalized version (à la Doctorow), writing a screenplay or even a long essay—something that would work out and express my own feelings about our history. But none of those felt right. I soon found that, instead of presuming to tell the world something new, what was driving me was the need to find answers to my own particular questions. The desire to know more seemed to be coming from a primordial part of me.

As the fiftieth anniversary of my grandparents' executions (even now it seems an impossible thing to say, "my grandparents' executions") approached in 2003, I knew the public eye would soon swivel our way again. But it was that number, fifty, that struck me, not so much as a great milestone to capitalize on but as a real deadline. The people I needed to talk to, whose stories and memories I increasingly craved, were getting old, very old. Fifty years later meant they were in their eighties, nineties, and more. I wanted to sit across from them and feel closer to my own family. It began to feel like a real duty for me to capture them on film. And it was urgent; as I write this in 2004, already four people I interviewed are gone.

Still, I'd never made a film, so why a documentary? I can see now that I've always sought meaning in the Rosenbergs' story through images. If I understood anything about it, it was visually. And for me the visual was visceral. As a kid, I studied the round, pale moon face of my grandmother thinking, like a mantra, "This is my dad's mother, this is my grandmother." I copied the Picasso drawing of them in my own six-year-old hand. I watched a 1978 documentary when I was ten years old called *The Unquiet Death of Ethel and Julius Rosenberg.* Watching that film's footage of my grandparents, stone-faced, in and out of the paddy wagon, and then my father and uncle, little boys in matching wool coats in and out of Sing Sing Prison, I experienced for the first time the physical sensation of my heart breaking. Those images were so evocative; they held so much mystery yet also the promise of truth. I wanted to use them in a way that made sense of the story to me. I was realizing at thirty-two that I needed to look hard at them, and at all of us. I was their age and I was ready to face them as peers. I never decided to become a documentary filmmaker; it was this story that chose the medium for me. So now I'm a filmmaker and a writer, and surprised to find that those labels don't matter much anymore. I used to want them so badly but would feel such a liar if I ventured to use them. And now, as they say, I've arrived. But where did I arrive? It certainly wasn't my appearance on the *Today Show* where they sprayed my face with foundation, teased my hair, and asked me uninformed questions. Nor, though it sure felt so at the time, was it my film's invitation to the Sundance Film Festival. Even the HBO premiere and all of the trappings, exciting as they were, didn't alter my DNA. All of the attention and accolades, even criticism, have made me a real part of a film community, but it's still not what's changed me inside. That, I know now, comes from having created something inextricable from my self. I know now that my feelings of disconnect from Ethel and Julius Rosenberg were also a disconnection from myself.

There's footage I found, some of which I use in the film, where I, as a ten-year-old, point to photos of the Rosenbergs and tell the camera that they are my grandparents. I also interview my father and uncle, asking, "What's this about the atom bomb?" My young self looks curious, interested, but wholly at home with the proclamation that they are my grandparents. Maybe it's that self that I've returned to, the one with no fear of asking the questions, the one that can look at all of it through my own eyes and say, here is the story.

Milk Dress:
A Nursing Song

ERIN CRESSIDA WILSON

Any woman knows the remedy for grief is being
needed: duty. bugles and we'll climb out of
exhaustion every time, bare the nipple or tuck in
the sheet, heat milk and hum at bedside.

RITA DOVE,
"Mother Love"

A boy," I cried. Leaned over, doubled over. I wept as if they had just told me, "You have black lung." But the news was "a boy." A snapshot of the evidence. The doctor wrote "penis" on the sonogram. Said I could embarrass him in years to come. Put it in the album. But I was crushed.

My dream of pink girls. My dream of girlhood. My dream of femininity, prissiness, lace dolls, crayons and purple drapes and flowers was gone. The childhood I had never had.

Raised by a feminist, such a feminist she didn't even call herself a feminist. Who never taught me to wash a dish, bake a cake, stir a stew, plant bulbs or calla lilies. A sexy professor whose pastimes were love, erotics, English as a Second Language, and fierce autonomy. She served TV dinners and never mended the curtains—they still have safety pins in their hems forty years later. And my father? He was a charming loner who lived inside books. Who woke up every morning at five A.M. to write. I'd pad behind him in my nightgown and sit down to move my fingers on the pretend typewriter keys that he had carved into the wood of my desk, so I could be just like him.

Instead of food, I grew up eating words and definitions, dictionaries and books of etymology for dinner. My fantasies were not of weddings or men in shining armor, but of independence and a bed made especially for writing in all day long.

As an adult, I ended up with two left hands in the kitchen and became confused by a needle and thread. It would be through my daughter that I would repair my feminist and bookaholic upbringing.

I would teach her not just what my mother had taught me, but what she had not: to be a hostess, a glitter girl, a wife, and a cream puff. Together, my daughter and I would learn to make cupcakes and conquer the world. But, instead, the sonogram showed a penis. With testicles formed already in utero.

Nine point nine," the nurses exclaimed as my boy screamed out of my C-sectioned stomach, the doctor's hands pulling him out without any grace. John watched from the top of the tent as I asked, "Will I vomit?" And the anesthesiologist said, "I know the theme of this one." "Will I throw up? I feel nauseated," I said over and over again. And out of desperation, I grabbed the nurse's arm, caressing the dark hairs that ran to her shoulders. The last touch I would have before I was forever changed by the sight of his mouth, his eyes, the sound of his cry.

They stuck oxygen on my face as I continued with the "Will I vomit/I feel faint" litany. I cried through the mask as John held his dangling body up for me to behold. His very long limbs, and yes, his testicles. His face, like a girl's. Squinty eyes that had a good look at me. And rosebud lips. A tiny nose. And from then on, everything up to that point in my life was utterly insignificant.

Wheeling him in his plastic see-through bed down the halls of the hospital, I wear bare feet.

They say, "Don't you have slippers?"

But I don't care, I want hospital all over me. I want to gush blood on their floor. I want to pee for the first time, shit for the first time, as a mother. Feel the whole thing. With him in my arms. All night long.

My roommate says, "Don't take this wrong . . ."

"Yes?" I ask.

"He has the most beautiful cry."

And I agree.

I will hold his mouth up to my ear and let him scream his 9.9 out of 10 voice into me.

We couldn't name him. I wouldn't settle on anything. Twenty years of naming fictional characters, and I was incapable of naming my own flesh and blood. Until forced to sign papers for the birth certificate and proof of fatherhood. Liam was his name, because of his legs. He had Liam legs. Enormous mitts and fingers with the sweetest nails.

(Later, I remembered, trying to keep it in my mind for the rest of my life, the first real tear that fell down his cheek. The first tooth that cut through his swollen gums. And good-bye to that toothless mouth that opened wide with the sadness and joy of life.)

He spits up milk. Runs down his cheek. And onto my blouses that now smell rotten. My tits have worry lines. I've got nipples for days. And then the breast pump from hell.

Pull at me like a handle. I'm fat and now I can't imagine anything but a boy. Not a girl. But a boy. And though we will cut his tongue, untie it from his rosebud lips, we will not cut his penis. Keeping its integrity, I feel blessed and relieved that now I don't have to confront a woman. That I don't have to be the mother to a daughter. That I don't have to stand up and live this feminist, postfeminist dream. That I can live ensconced in men and boys. And remain the one girl in the house. Writing erotica and R-rated films.

He will be our little boy, with a widow's peak and pudgy feet. I shall feed his weeping into my ear and let him grow up to be a thug, a street fighter, a lawyer, a failure, an actor, a dropout, a genius. He may, and is allowed to, scratch my face off, begging for food.

He sings nursing songs. And then he farts. A word I could not actually bring myself to say until now. Shits up his back. Like Grey Poupon mustard.

This is the way you write when you're nursing. No time for sentences. Just shorthand in hieroglyphics. "That's a good boy. That's a good boy. It's okay, it's okay, it's okay." And then, "I love you."

His breath rolls across my face. And I write with my eyes along his flesh. Because I don't have time, because I only speak in baby talk, because I am embroidered with his feedings. No procrastination. No capital letters. The logarithms of motherhood. And I realize, this is what I was meant to be. Twenty years of writing was only practice to do that thing that everybody I went to school with did right away. Now they are having midlife crises. And I am forty, finally doing what I was born to do. By making rice cereal and wiping it off his fingers and taking the boiled carrot off the top of his eyelids from where he smeared it, by picking up his shirt the moment it drops to the floor, by telling the story of the caterpillar who ate the apple and imitating the quack of a duck, I become the bunny I was meant to be.

I learn how to walk and talk like a woman. Other women finally speak to me with more than furtive glances. And I learn to write like a woman, with no punctuation and no pause. Because now I have no time.

Now I can repeat myself, introduce the theme halfway through, or even too late, establish who I am after I dive into the wrack of emotions. I can skip all the introductions, just full speed ahead, get it out, before he wakes from his nap.

And so many times, long ago, in the million years before the six months that have just passed since his birth, I had to write or fuck in an attempt to have a baby. And all along, all I had to do was say, "This time, don't pull out."

I've been wasting my time fucking without conception, writing without sperm. Now, in my new incarnation, I'd like to set up arts and crafts tables, knit in my spare time, and have infinite patience.

His ear is a tiny fossil. I look into his past as he drinks and laughs for hours. I watch as his two small layers of eyelashes form on his lids. And the day he stuck out his tongue for the first time.

My heart is already broken by the boy who will become a man, who will step into the shoes I give him and walk out our front door. I kiss his feet and mourn the moment it will become inappropriate. I want to wrap his toes in dough and eat them as hors d'oeuvres, fry up his fat knees for supper. The smell of the back of his neck and the sweet milk breath with the white on his tongue that we wash away with a silver spoon full of boiled water every night.

He is, at first, no more than half a centimeter from my body at all times. Because his tiny intestines need my warmth.

Besides, all the books say he still thinks he's inside of me.

He falls asleep with his hand and mouth open. And I am rolling in motherhood. Drowning in milk. And the wiggle of his mouth: the way he latches on in one fell swoop.

He is a bomber, a peacekeeper, a hippie, an economist. He will hate his parents for being hippies, he will spray paint the peace sign on his bare chest, he will wear the tie-dyed onesie my shrink gave him, look at the Diane Arbus print given to him by Stephen. "Because," as he wrote on the card, "you will not be born once, but reborn every-day of your life."

I tell myself, he is not the center of the universe, but then he just plain is. I want to play washing machine with him when he is six months old in the YMCA pool, teach him to skate with his father on the long river in Ottawa. I'll draw his face on napkins. I cannot be healthy about this. My body is his to graze upon.

And all the sadness of the first miscarriage, and the fantasies of that little girl who would ride shotgun with me, are swept away. At three months, the sonogram guy was very silent.

"What's the matter?" I asked, as his expression became grave. I thought we were happy. I thought we were looking at my three-month-old fetus.

"What's the matter?"

He tells me he is not allowed to speak to me. Only the doctor can. He puts me into an empty room and makes me wait. And I do for five seconds, but then I tear down the hall, taking the doctor out of a meeting. I cry before she tells me the news of the dead fetus inside of me. And by the way, you'll need an abortion to get it out. They put me in yet another room. Shut the door so the other pregnant women won't hear my grief. Two months later I'm buying my first package of diapers at Walgreens in San Francisco. But they are for my father.

There was a girl I went to school with buying a pregnancy test. She is in front of me in the line at Walgreens in San Francisco. It is two months after my miscarriage. I stop her outside in the parking lot.

And after a few seconds, she recognizes me. We never really liked each other, so why did I stop to talk to her? Because, I think, it's not eighth grade anymore. Surely we can speak with civility to each other. She tells me about the three children she has at home and seems distracted in a deeply fulfilled way. She steps up into her SUV: the traveling hutch for her offspring. But not before telling me she "worked for a few years" and then had her first child. And then I realize she is one of them. One of those girls I went to school with who "worked for a few years" and then had her first child.

I step into my parents' Toyota, with a trunk full of adult diapers, lotions, and Chucks in case the diaper doesn't catch all of my dad's pee. I want to throw myself off the Golden Gate Bridge. I am nursing the dying and not the living. I am thirty-nine years old, with a movie, twenty plays, and a professorship under my belt, some ex-lovers and "experiences," and on my second miscarriage, downing progesterone and fucking for three minutes flat, trying to get pregnant. Until one day, rather quickly really, I do. But I refuse to believe it as I spend my first trimester on Amtrak, commuting every week, back and forth between my musical in New York City and my teaching job in Providence, Rhode Island.

Me and a bunch of businessmen on the Acela Express. I am trying to be macho, even with his little embryo inside of me, waiting to be sonogrammed and marked "Boy" and "Penis" for life.

And finally, milk teeth and the bumblebee outfit. The name of the book is simply *Duck,* and it is made entirely of cloth. The trail of dried salt down his cheek—evidence of more naughty crying. An enlarged lower lip that signals, "I shall now cry bloody murder."

Pads soaked in milk, placed inside my brassieres. And now I am a size 40E. I've got spit-up down the back of my dress. And bras that are just for nursing, not for taking off.

And then there is my hairdresser who tells me I'm the most unlikely person in the world to be a mother. But he doesn't know a fucking thing. Is this very different from the girl who posed naked with her girlfriend for her book of erotica? From the woman who wrote a film about submission and spanking? From the person who refused to ever get married? She is a world apart from this, and exactly the same, submitting and turning inside her body to give away.

I'm no longer sure where to place the question marks. I embrace the dangling participle and spell check. I am in a hurry for anything that is not the quiet focus of watching his eyes light up, his crooked smile, his arms outstretched at a plate of cake, his first everythings. The evolution and maturation and gestation of this baby that was carved with the gentle knives of my womb and the gift of sperm. And I have stayed home for two decades, nursing plays, papers, laptops, unfinished novels. But none of them woke up every morning and looked at me with a twinkle and a half smile. He is my rose cheek. My family. He is why I am a woman.

To All the Men
I've Loved Before

AMANDA EYRE WARD

And keep my image, there without me,
By telling later loves about me.

DOROTHY PARKER,
"But Not Forgotten"

Dear D,

Is it just me, or does every thirty-something feel like writing letters to ex-lovers? You speed on through sexy eighteen and contemplative twenty-five like a freight train, making all sorts of pronouncements— *I don't believe in marriage,* or *fudge and cigarettes seem like a good lunch to me,* or *pass the baby oil . . . I'll never regret this deep, dark tan*—and then you hit thirty.

All of a sudden you're sitting on an airplane with a baby wrapped around you like a monkey, and instead of admiring glances, you're getting glared at, or worse, ignored. You're invisible! How the hell did that happen, I ask you? And so instead of dumping the baby and the diaper bag in baggage claim and catching the next flight solo to Rio, you decide, now that the child is finally, finally asleep (his sweet body sprawled across the middle seat) to write to the men of your youth.

You want to reflect on how you got to where you are. To remind yourself that you were a sexpot once, despite what that smug businessman in the window seat might think. I'll have a Bud Light with my peanuts! I was a wild child! You know what I mean, D?

Maybe it's just me.

Regardless, D, I've made a list of men on my airplane napkin, and you're at the very top. Though you were in diapers when we loved each other, you're in your thirties now, too. I wonder where you are. Maybe Rio, in a thong. Maybe on a flight to Boston, typing furiously into a BlackBerry and trying to ignore the wacky lady in the aisle seat and her jam-covered child.

It could have been one of those storybook romances, D. "We met in preschool," we'd tell the guests at our wedding, and I would chuckle and add, "We finger painted in the nude." This is true—do you remember? Although I believe this sort of behavior is illegal now or at least frowned upon, Mrs. Castiglia used to cover the walls with paper, strip us naked, and hand out the finger paints. Later, she would dump us all in one big bubble bath. It could have been so sweet, a lifelong romance. But in late October, your father was transferred to Chicago.

And there it ends for us, D.

Best,

Amanda

Dear F,

Next on the napkin is you, F. I think your name was Frank? Maybe Fred. You had the blond, swoopy hair, you had the lacrosse stick. And when your voice finally changed, it had a seductive quality. But screaming "*AMANDA WARD, FLAT AS A BOARD!*" in the middle school hallway didn't turn me on. Sorry, pal.

Amanda

Dear J,

I still feel like a jerk about you. You were kind to me, and I didn't understand that. You were the most amazing-looking man. (Perhaps you still are, though most high school football stars have gone bald by now.) You found me right after my braces came off, when the Sun-In highlights were just beginning to turn my hair orange. You bought me perfume, and told me I smelled like heaven. Sometimes, in a drugstore, I'll pull the top off a bottle of Stetson for Men and sniff. Just to remember.

We went to the senior prom, though I was a freshman. My parents were in the middle of their divorce, and we had lost our house. We were living with friends. My mom, working for the first time in fifteen years, bought me a pale peach dress with folds like a scalloped shell. She helped me primp for the prom, wincing slightly when I got going with the Aqua Net.

My mother hadn't planned on being a divorcée, but she was moving toward independence with grace. Still, I remembered her stunned look as you arrived in a tuxedo with a paint-splattered cummerbund. When you picked up the wrist bouquet between your thumb and forefinger, I think my mother was surprised to be the one holding the empty plastic box. We drove away in your Pinto. I tried not to think about my mother, doing the crossword puzzle in someone's guest room. I drank three Bartles & Jaymes wine coolers, trying to sweeten my kiss.

We were fine without my dad. We moved into a small yellow house next door to a drug dealer. My mother's caddy from the golf club lived down the street. We were so happy, but we also had to say that we were so happy, whether or not it was true.

I spent afternoons at your house. I quit the cheerleading squad. We watched television, and you lay next to me and you were so warm. One day, my father called and told me he was getting married. He didn't make sense, really, but made me promise to tell my sisters and my mother that he was blissfully engaged. Wasn't I happy for him? he wanted to know. Yes, I told him, I was very happy for him. He told me that he would take us to Playland on Wednesday, but then he never came.

I made lunch for you every day, packing it in a little brown bag with a love note. I wanted to take care of someone. I packed you the Ho-Ho's and Ding Dongs my mother had bought for my youngest sister to eat when she came home from school and was alone.

The holidays without my father were strange. We didn't know where he was. We didn't want to know. We missed the way the Christmas tree lit up the grand house that was no longer ours. My mother's new job paid for presents, and her department store credit cards—not yet canceled—paid for more.

My youngest sister still believed in Santa Claus. On Christmas Eve, we watched a cold night outside. It was warm in our weird house. Cars idled in front of our driveway, waiting to meet with the drug dealer. We decorated the tree with ornaments from our old life.

There was a knock at our door. My mother went quickly, peering out the peephole. She stood back from the door, flushed with pleasure. She unlocked the chain, and then the door. It was wonderful to see her smile.

You walked in, dressed as Santa Claus. I don't know where you got the beard, or the fuzzy red outfit. You reached into an old pillowcase and pulled out presents, badly wrapped.

Things happen. I went to boarding school. You are happily married to a librarian. It took me until my thirties to realize I needed a man like you.

My mother kept smiling that lonely Christmas, and my sister ran into the kitchen, returning with the plate she had arranged for Santa Claus: cookies and celery sticks. You bit into a cookie and said, "Deeeelicious!"

For that, I will always love you.

Amanda

Hey, Skateboarder,

We smooched during spring break while I was staying with my Nana and Papa. I dressed (as my father put it) like a hooker. You dressed in Jams with no T-shirt. I asked to wear your Star of David necklace and you gave it to me. You said I was only dating you to shock my Catholic grandparents. In the end, I have to admit, you were right.

Yours sincerely,

Amanda

Dear Clam Man,

I got arrested for you. You were doing whip-its from a can of Reddi-wip at the Edgartown Cumberland Farms. I spoke up in your defense and landed in the Martha's Vineyard jail. (There is one! Which many tourists might not know.) My cellmate had put her husband's face in a fan.

But the problems started earlier. I was working at Murdick's Fudge, and you were frying clams. One day, we went for a bike ride along the beach. You rode ahead of me, and I watched your skinny legs pumping. I could smell the ocean and feel the sun on my shoulders. But something happened; I lost my balance. I fell, twisting my knee.

I didn't cry out. Instead, I watched you, and waited to see how long it would take you to turn around, to notice I was no longer following. I sat in the sand and watched as you rode away. You never peered over your shoulder, never looked for me.

All the best,

Amanda

Dear R,

When we broke up for the tenth or eleventh time, I went into therapy. I had hit a point where everything seemed gray, and so I made an appointment. While our college classmates played Frisbee outside, I spent afternoons on a pleather couch, talking with a woman who wore Birkenstock sandals. Her hair was reddish, and cut in an unflattering pageboy. She was one smart cookie.

Therapy taught me some very important things. For one, I learned not to make decisions in the middle of the night. "No matter how important it seems at two A.M.," the therapist told me, "it can wait until morning." Truly, words to live by.

Another thing she taught me was that my gut instinct was not always on the money, especially when I was drunk. She told me to keep a journal, noting what I wanted to do in a given situation, and what a normal person would do. "Just be aware," she said, "of what a normal person would do." For example, *I want to call R at four in the morning to see if he still loves me. A normal person would have some chamomile tea and go to sleep.*

Most important, the therapist taught me the lasagna trick. If I had something wonderful to come home to, she suggested, maybe I wouldn't stay out too late and end up with the wrong men. She told me to try a scented candle in my dorm room, or bubble bath. As it turned out, a scented candle wouldn't bring me home from the bars. But a big, cheesy lasagna would. Having a delicious lasagna in my mini-fridge saved me from many a late-night mistake.

I told my therapist that I wanted to learn to trust you again, R. I brought you in to meet her. You sat on the pleather couch and explained sincerely why you had cheated on me and why you couldn't seem to tell the truth.

At our next meeting, my therapist pushed her reddish hair behind her ears nervously. She told me that she couldn't, in good faith, help me learn to trust you. She told me that trusting you, R, seemed like a bad idea.

I stomped out of her office and never saw her again. I went to your room, and asked you to forgive me. We got back together for the thirteenth time.

Clearly, I should have stayed on the pleather couch.

Thanks for the memories,

Amanda

Hi Ski Champ,

I remember the first time I saw you, leaning against the wall in a University of Montana hallway. We had just heard a hilarious writer read from his work, and I was thrilled with words. We went to a party at someone's house. Red wine in paper cups, and a melting Vienetta ice cream roll. You were haughty, which I appreciated.

I would drive to your house after my classes and we'd watch old movies. We were going to go through every Oscar winner. I think we made it to 1950, *All About Eve.*

One time, I was talking, and you said, "Can you just be quiet? You can be very annoying." This was the point I realized our relationship might not work for the long haul. I was still in my twenties, however, and didn't dump you. I waited, held on to our crummy union with desperation.

Yes, I got your e-mail. But you know what? I read it in the middle of the night. I was awake because I had just nursed my baby son. My son had fallen back to sleep, and there was snow on the trees outside my window. In the bedroom was my husband, the kindest man I know.

I deleted your e-mail, that electronic invitation. The last time I'd seen you, we'd fought in Glacier National Park. We had been camping, with plenty of chocolate for you and wine for me. You had gone into one of those quiet moods, when you were irritated by everything I said and did. (Like the time I used your kitchen sponge to clean up my new kitten's spilled litter. Or the time I read *The New Yorker* while you packed up our whole campsite and didn't even offer to help. I was engrossed! And you could have asked for help. Jeez.)

This time, I think I wasn't paddling enough, or trying enough, or something. We fought, and we reached the shore, and I told you to leave me alone and you did. You drove away in your weird little van and I sat in the canoe by the parking lot and the rain fell down.

A few months later, I was in the middle of another party at another person's house. The door opened and a man walked in. I didn't know then that he was the love of my life. But I did know his smile made something in me ease. I walked right up to him, and tried to think of something to say.

As for you, you left me in a canoe in the rain, and thank God.

Bye,

Amanda

Dear M,

We met at a geology party. (I was a creative writing student, and was crashing.) I remember the door opening, and you walked in, tall and blond. You looked twelve and twenty-six at the same time. I was wearing a green sundress with a wool sweater and snow-covered Timberland boots. You had a goatee and ocean-blue eyes.

I was used to lots of drama. I craved it. We went on a date and I drank Scotch. We went on more dates. Each time, you would drive me home in your red Toyota truck and drop me off without asking to come in. My friends thought this was suspicious.

One night, you said you would call and did not. My friends assured me it was over. When you called, a few days later, you said that you'd been fishing. I got angry. The next night, you didn't come to the bar where I had been expecting you. You explained you had been study-ing. I didn't believe you. I ate lasagna.

On my birthday, you caught a fish and cooked it for me. You didn't buy me a present. I broke up with you. I just didn't understand a straightforward, absentminded man. I didn't understand the joy that runs through you when you open yourself up to love.

A side note: you are still not the best gift-giver. Last year, you gave me ski goggles and swimming goggles. I was perplexed. "I'm not trying to *say* anything," you explained. "I just thought you needed goggles."

We had known each other about a month when, late one night, you sat beside me and took my face in your hands. I'll never forget your offer: *Let me bring you peace.*

We moved in together a few weeks later. We shared a happy apartment in Missoula. It was filled with books and rocks. When you were accepted into the Ph.D. program at the University of Texas, you asked me to come along by making a Texas-themed dinner and writing "Will you join me?" on a postcard of an armadillo. When you got a job on Cape Cod, you called home with pride, and I said yes.

You're the last name on my napkin, M. You still drive the red truck, but it has a baby seat now. You're likely on your way to pick us up at the airport, where we'll be landing soon.

I know this is a special time in my life. I know I have to savor it, taste every minute. When we get home, we'll go to the playground, and our son will climb to the top of the slide. He'll hesitate, afraid of what lies ahead. But you will crouch at the bottom, your thirty-two-year-old knees creaking. You'll open your arms.

He will make a wonderful sound, something like, "Whooooah, Dada!" Then he'll launch himself forward, eyes open. He'll pick up speed on the way down. His mouth tightens. He doesn't have to worry. You'll catch him.

And then you'll turn to me, my love. We never thought we'd be here, in a playground on a Saturday night. We're not twenty anymore, and we can't quit our jobs or sleep all day. (Or all night, for that matter.) You can't fish whenever you want, and my *New Yorker*s pile up on the bedside table, waiting to be read.

The businessman in the window seat sees a harried mother, but in your eyes, I'm still a crazy novelist; a girl with big dreams and Timberland boots. And that means a lot to me, as we move into our middle age. I know you're a sunburned grad student who sleeps in a sleeping bag unrolled on a mattress, no matter how fine our cotton sheets.

This feels like a confusing time to me: we're changing from being someone's children to someone's mom and dad. From making pronouncements to making real decisions. I'm glad you're along with me for this ride.

Remember our small backyard with two bushy trees in Texas? I had lived in Greece, and one night as we sat outside under the moon, I told you that I missed Greek tavernas. They have little lights hanging above the tables, I told you, and I loved that. We talked about where we'd go in the world and what we'd do.

A few weeks later, when I returned home after a weekend away, you led me outside by the hand. You had cut away the low branches of the trees, and strung lights. You had put a table and two chairs under the lights. It was a magical place, my taverna in Texas.

Your mind, your zaniness, your kindness—you fill me with wonder. And now you're waiting for me in the airport. Lucky me.

Yours,
Amanda

Single, Mother

JENNIFER BAUMGARDNER

I laughed as I said it
This is my situation
It's not pictures or privilege
It's just self-preservation

AMY RAY,
"Reunion"

I wonder what Mary thought when she found out she was pregnant when she didn't expect to be. Did she weigh her options? Did she even want to be with Joseph? I have spent years thinking about how no woman knows what she'll do with an unintended pregnancy until it happens, but I always used that line to describe women who get abortions, when they thought they never would. Who thought they'd get abortions, but don't. What about deciding to bring a baby into the world when you pretty much know you don't want to be with the child's father? Perhaps you've gleaned that my interest is not purely academic. You are right.

Jesus only lived to be thirty-three. I once dated someone who thought there was significance in being that age because of Christ. Maybe there is something to it, some subconscious sense that your life should get meaningful that year, because the Christmas that I was thirty-three,

I felt desperate for something to give. The kind of desperation I had felt when I was thirteen and needed to get my braces off and grow the hell up. It was twenty years later and, with itchy discomfort, I was feeling like a child again. I had just broken up with my sexy but troubled boyfriend (thus not in a relationship), was still in my East Village studio, still writing my bisexuality book, still in credit-card debt— *still still still*. Back in Fargo that typically freezing December, I felt like my skin was too tight. I didn't want to face the thirty-third time I would be bounding down the stairs to open my stocking from Santa, having known that Santa was dad since roughly 1976. By December 30, I couldn't take being in my childhood home for a second longer. I abruptly changed my ticket, flew back to New York City on New Year's Eve, took a taxi to the ex-boyfriend's apartment, drank champagne, had sex, and released the tension. *Happy New Year!*

I found out that I was pregnant in a Dallas Hilton at one A.M., February 6, 2004. Earlier, I was speaking at Southern Methodist University with my writing partner, Amy, the third and final lecture in a three-day Texas lecture trip. We normally talk about politics and young people, how we grew up with feminism "in the water" and while that might not make us label ourselves as feminists, we are very likely to enact feminist lives. Really commonsensical, accessible—even mainstream, I'd say—stuff. But that night, for some reason, the event's sponsor had asked us to address porn. Thus, the title of our talk was "Live Nude Girls: Pornography, Sex Work, and Critiquing a Culture That Hurts Women."

As my crystal-clear memory of this talk's title perhaps conveys, I fear being reduced to a cliché of radical feminism—despite the fact that I host women who come to New York to get later-term abortions, have had girlfriends, and wrote about my STD for *Glamour*. I generally feel I'm a "normal" person who happens to be a feminist. Most likely I focus on the fact that I'm from Fargo, North Dakota, confirmed Lutheran, somewhat happily bourgeois, et cetera, because I have seen how easily one can be marginalized when working in alternative or social justice movements and then, you know, no one invites you any-where nice because they are afraid you're going to scream about fac-tory farming. For me, at least, going to the margins was something I had to do as a younger feminist, but to stay there would just be admitting I couldn't handle the rest of the world.

A childhood friend, Dan, who is now a lawyer in a big firm, walked in as I was addressing how I came to a personal understanding of porn. I was making the point that by having girlfriends and later boyfriends who watched porn, I found an entry point for the medium: *Oh, you can be the viewer, not just the person who is humiliated and excluded by porn.* During the Q and A, a woman who identified herself as bisexual and pagan aligned herself with me. After this talk, I was feeling every bit the weirdo as Dan and I hugged and then drove to his condo, where his hetero wife and probably not Wiccan one-year-old daughter were waiting to dine with us.

His wife is a stay-at-home mom, and I sometimes think that we are misunderstanding each other, that she feels as if the fact that she has a brain and extra-domestic ambitions isn't visible to me, and I fear she also assumes that I am this work-driven, abortion-promoting pervert. So when she asked me if I thought I would ever have kids, I saw my opportunity to overcompensate. "Yes! In fact, I might be pregnant now," I blurted, then continued, "and if I am, I'd have the baby."

It rang out a bit too loud. My period was due about then, and true, I hadn't gotten it yet that day, but there was little reason to make the grand statement. I immediately felt foolish. It seemed both out of nowhere and Big News.

Dan and I kept talking and his wife retired to put her baby to bed. As I was leaving, several glasses of wine later, she asked me, "Did you mean that about maybe being pregnant?" "I don't know *why* I said that," I sputtered, "but, I mean, I guess I *could* be pregnant. I'm, like, a day late." "Oh, well, I have a pregnancy test upstairs," she said. We stared at each other. "Take it, if you want it."

I tore the wrapper off at the hotel, ran into the marble bathroom, and peed on the stick. As I was waiting I remember wishing "I hope it's positive." That was weird, because I don't remember consciously hoping to have a baby prior to that moment. Within seconds it changed to the two horizontal lines configuration that means pregnant.

I hopped up and strode around the room, giddy and kind of scared. I felt I should call someone, but who? It was one thirty A.M. Texas time. Amy was asleep down the hall and we had to get up at five for our early-morning flight back to New York. My parents. It seemed not quite the right time. Besides, despite my excitement, I was still thinking I might have an abortion. Thinking this in only the most superficial way, as if I had to cloak myself in "almost" having an abortion because of my commitment to abortion rights and the fact of my asinine relationship. I hadn't yet figured out that it's dread about the two lines on the pregnancy test that necessitates an abortion, not glee.

It crossed my mind to call my ex-boyfriend, Grant*, but in the same way that it crossed my mind to call my parents. I also felt . . . like the pregnancy was just for me. And scared that going through with it implied one of two scary futures—single mom or life with Grant. If I tell Grant, I thought, *then I'm saying he is in this with me.* I wasn't ready for that commitment yet, so I called Kim, the wife of the friend, the acquaintance who gave me the test. It was nearly two in the morning.

"Hello?"

"Hi Kim. It's Jennifer. Dan just dropped me off and I took the pregnancy test and it's positive, so . . ." I paused—what to say next? "So I was wondering if you knew the rate of false positives?"

She said that the false negative was sort of an issue but her understanding was if it was two lines, "you're definitely pregnant." I hung up feeling oddly elated again—this bubbling, growing feeling of "Oh my gosh, I might have a baby" that I didn't quite know how to read.

As the days passed and I told people that I was pregnant, my in-

---

* His name is not Grant, but he hates that I write about him and thus I feel I must use a fake name. He was Grant in two other published pieces. And he is known as Greg in another piece.

ability to openly transmit that pure happiness continued. Because I worked assertively to make abortion available—sitting on the board of an abortion fund, hosting women at my apartment, writing about *Roe v. Wade*—it surprised me that I had no instinct to get one in the case of this accidental pregnancy. I revealed my pregnancy to my father, a doctor, by calling to ask for medical advice: "It says not to take these vitamins if you're pregnant—and I'm pregnant, it turns out—so do you think I should take the vitamins?" You'd think the pregnancy was *not* the point of the call. Finally, I called my mother. I laid down the spiel I'd been telling everyone.

"I'm pregnant. My instinct is to have the baby but I'm considering abortion." My mother immediately cut through that fog. "Jennifer, I need to know, am I going to be a grandma or am I supporting you through an abortion?"

I paused. "You are going to be a grandma."

Six months later, I was in my fifth month of pregnancy—in that little window after the vomiting but before every shirt I fit into had a stain down the front—when it dawned on me that I couldn't live with the baby's father, as I now called my ex-boyfriend. I didn't live with Grant as it was, so this realization didn't require us dismantling our bookshelves, arguing about whose copy of *Franny and Zooey* it was. Grant and I had been lovers for a year in a relationship that had sex and passion but no comfort or support. When I finally confronted how much time I spent explaining Grant to others, we broke up. But because of the sex and passion (and his seemingly good-faith effort to reform), I slept with him on the sly. Still "broken up," we enjoyed romantic dinners, but no public social engagement—for five months until the fateful New Year's Eve.

When I realized that Grant and I were never going to be partners, despite the fact that we would be parents—weird how those two words have the exact same letters—I felt both relief and terror. Relief that I wasn't stuck in a relationship that felt off except when in bed or watching *The Sopranos* together, but terror that I was alone—and possibly alone and raising a baby when I have problems paying the bills as it is. The awareness came slowly, of course, as all of the problems we had prepregnancy remained stubbornly unchanged, even as I grew rotund with dark brown nipples and the fullest head of hair I have ever had. Grant, meanwhile, grew, too. He grew increasingly anxious about how the impending child would affect his lifestyle. *Would he still get to practice with his band? The baby would cry all of the time and he would have to take him to the bathroom in public till the kid was about five!* He seemed unable to connect to the exciting part: there was going to be a baby soon! He could help name it! The baby would have chubby knees and smile when we nuzzled its tummy! It was no use, all of my cheers provoked the same nauseated scowl. Grant, given his commitment to rock 'n' roll, was not eager to be an adult, to ratchet up a generation the way you must when you procreate. By contrast, from the moment I first sensed Skuli was in me, I felt connected to him. If anything, I was fearful that something might happen to take this pregnancy—so accidental, almost stumbled upon, perhaps undeserved—away from me.

The night my son was born, I lay shocked on the hospital bed. The birth in a sentence: terrifying, intense, unfamiliar yucky sensations, unbelievable pain, impossible pushing, and then over. They brought my son to me. He was wrapped like a burrito in a hospital issue blanket, his head round and purple. He opened his mouth and a bubble came out, as if he had swallowed ivory liquid on his way out of my body. "This wasn't exactly what I had in mind," I thought, as the nurses alarmedly rushed him down to the neonatal ICU to deal with his "wet lung" and Grant rushed after them. I lay there thinking, "I don't feel that deep reservoir of maternal love, that connection I have never had. Hmmmm . . ." while my sister's husband ran to McDonald's to get me a shake. When Grant came back a half-hour later, he was in tears because his little baby had squeezed his finger in his tiny, tiny fist. "He knew who I was," Grant said, looking at me with red-rimmed eyes. "You can tell already that our son will never give anyone a moment's trouble. You can tell he's going to be the best kid." And that was it really. In a second, Grant's fears about himself were overwhelmed by his love for this squishy, pimply seven-and-a-half-pound person.

I spent the night alone without Grant or Skuli. Odd as it may sound, it was better that Grant left the hospital after I got settled in my room. We had been through this big event, putatively together, but it didn't really feel that way. It felt like I had just run a triathalon and Grant had been there, but not really going through it—just a by-stander, trying to help but accidentally saying scary things to me, like telling me to push when I wasn't fully dilated—he retained next to nothing from the natural childbirth class—and standing on my IV. Grant and I looked at each other, searching for crumbs of connection, before he left, but there was no shared emotion; the fact that neither of us preferred to be together at that moment speaking volumes about the relationship.

Was it Woody Allen who used to live not with, but across the park from, Mia Farrow? Or was it Katharine Hepburn who advocated living across the hall from Spencer Tracy? Grant and I have taken it a bit further—we live across the Williamsburg Bridge from each other. Grant's split-second transformation from resentful aging rocker to passionate father is one I'm grateful for. And my journey from shell-shocked birthing machine to reasonably happy mother is a relief, too. But Grant and I, well, after a few months of living together in order to care for Skuli, we began caring for him from separate homes.

Grant and I are actually doing pretty well as separate parents. He takes Skuli nearly every day after work and two or three times a week for an overnight at his place. We do early-morning handoffs at the L train. He has his own daddy setup: crib, changing station, exersaucer, bottles, food, and baby tub. He has to be as active a parent, a Mr. Mom, as I am, because when Skuli is at his place, there is no one else but Grant to take care of him. Occasionally that means Grant calls me sobbing at eleven P.M. because Skuli won't go to bed, but generally, he just deals. We both occasionally feel alone and overburdened, but not as often as we are thrilled by the daily adventure of Skuli. I see a very positive side of this arrangement for both of us. I don't have to be the martyr-mom, doing all of the baby maintenance (remembering to get food and diapers, making doctors' appointments) while he gets to be fun dad who swoops in just to play. We both have to do both, and when one of us is not on Skuli duty, that person is free as a bird. The feminist in me really likes this part of the arrangement.

Because Grant is so involved with our son, I can't say that I'm a single mother. I'm single, and a mother. The single part is the next Rubicon I must cross. Such a dilemma. I can imagine the headline in a women's magazine: "Baby Daddy Isn't the One? How Yummy Mummies Find Love." Or I imagine the personal ad: "blond, blue-eyed, 34. Gave birth in October. Just getting body back . . ." I look to celebrities as a model, since they always seem to be leaving their baby's dads two days after giving birth. *What would Uma do?* I often think.

So far, Ethan Hawke has become my fake boyfriend. He's perfect because there is no real chance that I could actually date him, so I can pine without having to be mad at myself for not asking him out. (Carpe diem, as they say in *Dead Poets Society*. "I *would* carpe," I respond, "but I don't have his number.") I think, in my fantasy life, that we are well suited. We are the same age, we both have young kids and, I would assume, a huge desire not to fuck them up. He obviously likes tall blondes. He's especially perfect because he's not here, so I can practice having feelings without really dealing with moving on yet. I imagine that we would talk theater and film, gossip and eat at fun restaurants in New York. We'd read each others' writing and bitch about publishing and critics. I'd attend the Oscars. I also fantasize that Grant has met someone. For some reason she is twenty-five and named Stacey. In my fantasy, she is good with Skuli, but not too good. Eventually, they have a child together of their own and Skuli has a sibling. Grant often says to Skuli that perhaps he'll impregnate another woman who hates him so Skuli can have a little sister or brother.

My friend Marianne and I commiserate about our relationships. At our most negative we boil it down to this: in the ones in which we are comfortable, we are stifled. The ones that are challenging are also lonely and devastating to our self-esteem. Many couples scare me ("I don't want *that* relationship") and others make me envious, such as my friend whose baby-daddy always seems happy to see her friends and stay home with their son. My friend whose playwright husband toasted her gorgeously at her thirtieth birthday. That couple that laughs all the time. My sister's husband, who knows how to fix the computer and makes homemade pasta. When I complain to the playwright friend, she points out that I have Skuli. It's true. I no longer can believe that pregnancy is random. It couldn't have been another baby; I couldn't have waited to find a partner for his parent. It had to be Skuli.

It's funny, too, because it was my mother who, again, helped me see the light about my relationship to Skuli. After the birth, the hospital kept him in the NICU for several days where he was covered in tubes and sensors, surrounded by sirens and beeps: an oral-gastric tube was plunged down his throat and sucked fluid (which interfered with his lung capacity), an oxygen mask was taped over his nose, his little arm was in a splint with a catheter administering IV antibiotics, and his foot had to be pricked regularly to test for sepsis. Even though Skuli was two or three times the size of the other babies in the ward— they were all premature and he was full-term—he looked utterly pathetic, like Keanu Reeves when he finds himself in the goo of the *Matrix*. Every few minutes he sucked vigorously on his O-G tube like a teenager enjoying a malted milk at Schrafft's, suckling that was supposed to be happening on my newly huge breasts. I began to cry. My mother stood by me as I stared at my alien baby. She looked at me for a moment.

"I'm in love with him already," she said, breathless with delight, and it wasn't until I heard those words that I realized I was, too.

Plus One, Plus Two, Plus Three

LOUISE JARVIS FLYNN

Star-far from the person right next to me, but
closer to me than my bones you
you are there.

FRANZ WRIGHT,
"Flight"

Somewhere below Fourteenth Street, sometime after midnight, I found myself at another party I had no business attending. I was wearing the blue dress my mother bought for me even though she thought it showed too much, clung too much; but I was young and this was New York and she was, during her visit anyway, caught up in the magnanimous, invincible spirit of the city at that time. The party was in the apartment of a celebrity money manager, who would later go to jail for bilking his star clientele out of millions, but I didn't know whose home it was, and it hardly mattered because at that point in life I often went to places where I knew no one and left knowing no one new. I was my boyfriend's Plus One on the invitation list, a crowd filler, the nameless date who got to come along with the Name. I had a typical Plus One job, the lowest-level magazine writer and, like most Plus Ones, I used only my first name when introducing myself because a last name seemed to imply a level of relevance I could not even pretend to deserve. I was the girl who happily reintroduced herself to the same people who nodded and stared over her shoulder. I didn't appear to notice or care. I had no shame. As a Plus One, shame, like pride, got in the way of enjoying all the excellent freebies. So, I was a Plus One on this night in my slightly slutty dress, and as such kept to my rightful orbit, circling among my own kind, nibbling wasabi peas and sipping cocktails, while waiting for a Name person to do something extraordinary or embarrassing that I could tell my friends about the next day.

At this particular gathering, movie stars chatted freely in their constellations, having left their personal minders back at the hotel. I leaned into a corner, listing from the booze, and tried to read all the lips, but it was like sitting in the back row of a theater watching an American movie dubbed in Japanese. My boyfriend was talking to someone who had no interest in talking to me because I was, after all, a Plus One with small breasts and cheap shoes, so I went to the kitchen to fix myself another drink. I was picking used lime nubs off the counter and dropping them into my gin and tonic, which I then stirred with my index finger, when Leonardo DiCaprio walked into the kitchen with a blazing white cockatoo perched on his shoulder. He stood beside my bare arm and poured himself a drink. I considered my options: I could ignore him. I could say hello. I could ask if there were any more limes in the place. Instead, I turned to him and said, "Can I touch your bird?"

That was the line. Punch line, starting line, pickup line, either way the line was meant to fit into a story, *an anecdote*—everybody had a good celebrity anecdote. Mine would be the kind of tale that young women, especially those who justify their humiliating mistakes as "life experience," secretly hope for: one that involved a jet bound for Fez, a case of Cristal, and the magazine plebe in the cheap, blistering slingbacks getting sold for seven camels to a publishing scion with a heart of gold. Or something equally over the top. Of course, the line went nowhere then, though I recognize it now as the end of one story, *one anecdote,* and the beginning of another. Only this one I didn't have the imagination to dream up.

Leo did not let me touch the bird, which was not his in any case. I somehow got home, a walk-up in Brooklyn, where I resumed waiting for the inexplicable thing that would signal my future had begun. (Should have known it would not involve exotic pets.) I was twenty-five and quietly outraged that my life was ticking by at such a slow and unremarkable clip. I felt like Rip Van Winkle's much younger girlfriend, waiting anxiously for his eyelids to twitch and pop open. A couple more years passed, in which time I got a nominally better apartment and exponentially better accessories, but the nagging expectation that something more should be happening never dimmed. Nothing was enough. It didn't help that the city around me was showing the age we were living in. All that glittered was plastic. Fast money and Lucite celebrity supplanted the asphalt romanticism, the inevitable surprise, the improbable optimism that attracted me to New York in the first place. The publicists had run off the poets. When the tech stocks tanked, the hors d'oeuvre trays got a little lighter and I drank cheaper wine, but nothing else changed, or so I thought.

Turns out, I wasn't paying careful enough attention.

I hadn't noticed, for example, that I'd missed family holidays and memorial services and birthdays, that I'd lost touch with faraway friends, that I was too self-absorbed or neurotic or broke to own a pet, even. I didn't notice I was getting, ever so slightly, *older.* Age was still relative; I was younger than my boyfriend and all his friends and most of my editors. I couldn't possibly be held accountable for my missteps, my flakiness, my inertia. Around that time, I read in a women's magazine that forty was the new thirty. This came as a great relief because I certainly didn't feel ready for thirty, either. If I could have kids in my forties, and was going to live well into my eighties, then why not extend the heat-seeking, tolerant twenties an extra ten years? What was the point of the thirties anyway?

As far as I could tell, the only thing that distinguished one decade from the next was an increased earning potential that translated into better digs and hair colorists. The thirties brought more professional credibility and a nice maturing of bone structure, better posture, and novel vacations. Women in their thirties actually used the gym memberships they started in their twenties. But their daily life, inner life, even romantic life seemed to me no different from mine. I believed there were two kinds of women in their thirties: those who looked and acted twentyish, and those poor souls with kids and husbands who seemed much, much older, like forty-five or something. For the longest time I thought I knew, without a doubt, which group had it right. By then my boyfriend had crossed the Rubicon of forty without so much as a scratch on his fully inflated bachelor survival suit, which he showed no interest in taking off. It occurred to me that I did not want to be the female version of him in twelve years. I did not want my thirties to be a continuation of my twenties, and my forties to be a bitter reckoning of the thirties I never had. There was not all the time in the world to do all the things I wanted to do, never mind all the things I feigned ambivalence about, like marriage and children. I saw myself tumbling down the river of cocktails, inane social encounters—*Can I touch your bird?*—and pop culture debris, and it was, frankly, horrifying. Thirty dangled straight ahead, a shiny lure drawing me close. I suspected there would be a trade-off for taking it; there always was.

By the end of my twenties, I was a lean and efficient self-creation. I wasn't writing what I'd set out to write and I wasn't living a particularly sustainable existence, but I made enough money to cover rent and my social life and this, it seemed to me, was enough. Though, a catalogue of my possessions during this time probably reveals something closer to the truth: I owned a small sofa. I owned some fancy Le Creuset pots. I owned an extraordinary photograph of a Tennessee hill bisected by an electrical cable that I bought at a Chelsea gallery. One side of the landscape was green, fenced in by barbed wire, and it led the eye up to a distant grove of trees. The other side of the landscape was straw yellow, dead but wide open and interrupted by a ribbon of asphalt road. Those were my major possessions, and all of them were for some life other than the one I was leading. The sofa was my attempt at a home that felt cozy and complete; the pots were for some future in which there would always be someone to cook for; the photograph was about choices I would face, or had already made.

In other words, it was all about family.

I'd spent a lot of time and money putting myself many hundreds of miles and experiences away from my family and East Tennessee, where I grew up. The best way to describe why I did this is to borrow a term from my grandmother's maid: "journey proud." It's the feeling you get when you're looking forward to a big trip, a trip you've planned in such detail that you can already picture yourself in the place, and you can hardly wait to live in that perfect, anticipated memory. A good portion of my adolescence and twenties was consumed by being journey proud for my future life, which, as I imagined it, played out in New York City, where I worked as a writer with smart and witty friends and a terrific boyfriend, who could fade in and out of the picture as circumstances required. And, for the most part, I had that.

The problem with being journey proud is that the real destination, never mind the trip itself, rarely lives up to the imaginings. As far as I know, there's no special Southern term for that deflated feeling of dashed expectations, but it's not disappointment or melancholy or winsomeness, though it encompasses all those. Whatever it's called, I experienced it in my late twenties as a kind of homesickness. I didn't miss the snug nucleus of family or quiet small-town life. There was no bittersweet pull of nostalgia. What I missed was the thing only family can provide, the sturdy, reassuring comfort of roots, however twisted they may be. Still, I wasn't sure how to go about creating new roots for myself. I had gathered that this wasn't something one did alone or with any kind of premeditated design. It was grounding I was looking for, not the madcap opposite, but I didn't see any reason why that wouldn't be just as hard to find.

Since my twenties were about subtractions, discarding the old family roles, the rusty friendships, the outdated interests and styles, I figured the next decade would be about additions. I started dating a guy who grew bearded irises and brewed his own beer. A guy who wrote lovely sentences about horrible life events. A guy whose eyes didn't flash with fear when he talked about marriage. A really good, kind, funny man. It sounds delusionally retro on the page this way, but the fact is we fell in love quickly and happily and without hesitation. Within a few months I was carting off those few possessions of mine to a tiny seaside town north of Boston, where this fella had a house. The new math was so easy: one plus one.

Of course, I worried it was too easy.

Nothing good could come from something so easy. I was both suspicious and intrigued by this new idea of permanence, the unnerving directness of this love, so I devised a way to diffuse it by commuting between my two cities, my two lives. The weekends were spent blissfully with my fella in a town I wanted very much to like (but didn't), while the week days were spent in New York, a city I loved, working on what I tried to enjoy (but didn't). On the morning of September 11, I was slipping on my shoes to go to my editing job when the friend whose spare room I was renting shouted for me from the living room. We saw the whole thing on television, even though the chalky, acrid smell was already drifting through our windows. We listened to the radio for instructions that came too late in the day to give any reassurance. We watched the empty buses go down Eighth Avenue to pick up bodies that weren't there. We tried to get through to our friends and family but the phone lines were mostly jammed. We counted the paper flyers and candle shrines going up overnight.

When the terrible thing happens, you take hold of whatever roots you've still got. In that moment, your real life, not the imagined future life or the reimagined past, but the real warts-and-all present immediately snaps into place. My real life was straddling two towns and two lives, but the choice between the two disappeared that day. I wanted to be with *him,* anywhere he was. The idea of life without him was an option I couldn't even consider. Before, place had always trumped people, family. Now, I was willing to leave everything for one person and this vague notion of laying down roots. When the trains started running again he came to fetch me, to take me away for a second time, for good. I remember thinking, "This is either the true beginning of adulthood or the end of self-reliance." And I was numb.

Boston is a city of fetishized practicalities: one must have a car, a mortgage, and a pair of warm, waterproof shoes. If Boston is the nanny, New York is the ADD child, albeit the child who grows up to pay the nanny's 401k. Boston is a city where pedestrians have the right of way and dinner parties break up at the sensible hour of eleven. One would think it was just the place I was looking for in my scramble for security. After all, the roots that sprawl beneath the Boston metro area can't be shaken by an earthquake. Neither, as it turns out, are they easily tapped by interlopers.

I arrived there a decade too early, or a lifetime too late, to properly appreciate my Boston bedroom town, and so I spent the last year of my twenties feeling very much out of place and out of time. Soon it was just the two of us in our little house near the seawall. We were shut-ins by the gray beach, unmarried and childless writers in a tiny town of stroller traffic and commuter trains. We could not connect our lives to others. We did not fit in. I wondered if this new loneliness I felt was the trade-off I had feared. The answer is, yes, it was. And in the grand scheme of things, I think I got a bargain.

At least we were unified outcasts, and this bond made those first months of transition easier. We talked about getting married. We agreed that we already felt married. We were an Us, an Us apart from Them, Them being family and old friends, and our former lives. Our couple-dom was snug and smug and all-encompassing, and who knows how long we would have hibernated there if it hadn't been for the news that my father was very sick. The news intruded on us so suddenly, like a flash flood, that I reacted with a kind of soul-searching panic—*Where am I? What am I doing?*—reaching out blindly for the friends and family I'd neglected, hoping they would be there still. And they were, of course. They were always there.

My twenties had started with one parent having cancer, so there was a hideous symmetry to the decade ending with another parent fighting the disease. When my mother was diagnosed with breast cancer, I was in college but living in Aspen for the spring term, working at a magazine for class credit. I had cut off all my hair and dyed what remained a winter-squash orange. I wore small John Lennon reading glasses, and I was dating the town handyman, who also ran the radio station and played the French horn. I did not go home when my mother called with the news. Instead, I learned to fly-fish and write restaurant captions and appreciate Mahler, which the handyman played for me in the empty concert hall that smelled of lemon oil.

I did not go home even for her surgery. I was twenty-one and my mother said she'd be fine and there was nothing I could do, and family stressed me out anyway. My older sister, Ann, came to live with my mom. Ann changed her lymph node drains and brought her the little lunches with folded napkins that mom brought to us when we were sick as children. Ann researched our mother's treatment options with her clear, dry attorney's eye, and she set up the appointments at a major cancer center for a second opinion. As for herself, Ann would say, "I'm keeping it in the road."

I was terribly busy being twenty-one, completely ill prepared to do what my older sister did so capably, steering one-handed through that sad and frightening time, keeping tabs with the tight, forced smile. I suppose the guilt of that memory is why, at twenty-nine, I was obsessed with doing all that I could to save my father. Even if that meant getting swept out of blissful coupledom by the tides of modern medicine— *Who's the best surgeon? Where to go? What are the odds? What are the stats? What are his chances?*

What were my chances?

Everything else in my life was submerged by fears of his death, and I didn't even realize it. I didn't look up. I couldn't see exactly what had happened.

Here's what happened: When doctors have bad news to report, they take you into a little room with Holiday Inn lobby furniture. You sit down and they sit down and everyone's knees are bunched together and there is a will on the face of the teller and the listener, both hoping the little room is big enough to contain everything that might happen there. Dr. D'Amico is a graceful reed of a man, a surgeon with pianist fingers and a mellifluous voice and very poor eye contact. It was lung cancer, he said, and I nodded as if I already knew. "Does *he* know?" I asked. I'm not sure why this was so important to me right then. Of all the things I needed to ask, why that? I suppose I thought the news itself might kill him. "Who will tell him?" I wanted to know. I certainly couldn't, but I hated the idea of a stranger telling him when he was alone. I would tell him. I could do that, at least. Ann would have done that. "He knows. They always know," said the doctor. "I don't know how, but they're never surprised."

I went to the recovery room and he knew, just as Dr. D'Amico said he would. He looked so old and tired just then, his eyes gluey from the anesthesia. I knew he knew because when he saw me he gave me the tight smile, an apologetic smile like the one he used when talking about my mother after they got divorced. That tight, sad-eyed smile. And I saw something else in that smile, too, the purity of parenthood.

I realized he was thinking of me, that he was worried about me, sorry for me that he had cancer. That was the most heartbreaking of all.

I cried on the airplane and I cried at baggage claim and I cried at the curb as I waited for my fella, Sean, to pick me up, all without making a sound. The tears just poured out and I made no attempt to stop them. I felt everything at once and remembered everything all too vividly: my anger toward my father for leaving us, the times I didn't call, the times I didn't go home, the times I could have sworn he cared far more about himself than his children. And then the newest memories flickered past: my father, the sick man in the thin gown with the tight, sad smile, consoling me. His hand in mine. His eyes cloudy and bewildered and afraid.

What I remember next is Sean making me scrambled eggs and giving me a Xanax I had left over from September 12. He knew I wasn't myself, that I needed a primal sort of rest. He didn't try to fix it or cheer me up or hunker down in the misery with me. He was steady and calm because he knew I wasn't. He knew what I needed: to switch off all the thoughts, the old and the new memories, the good and the bad. And in that moment, I saw that he knew me better than anyone ever had. He stretched out beside me in bed, and I slept until the next day, straight through sixteen hours. Each time I think about that forced sleep, I'm reminded of how the choices we make end up feeling inevitable and the risks we take often yield unexpected blessings.

Then, of course, there's the fact that roots, however fresh or ancient, are sturdy things. We got married later that year. My father, a straw hat protecting his radiated scalp from the South Carolina sun, walked me down the aisle in front of our family beach house. A few months later, I turned thirty, and soon wondered what it would be like to go from Plus Two to Plus Three. I found that what they say about getting married also applies to having children: when you know, you know; when you're ready, you will.

Age isn't something you earn—everyone gets the same annual allotment, they hope—but I did feel that my thirtieth birthday was somehow achieved rather than given. It was the first one that felt like the tipping point of adulthood. I realize every year after that is accompanied by a certain amount of anguish for lost time, just as every year prior brought impatience for real life to begin. But at thirty the scale is in perfect balance. For a moment anyway, there is comfort in numbers.

ABOUT THE CONTRIBUTORS

 SAMINA ALI was born in Hyderabad, India, and raised both there and in the United States. Her debut Novel, *Madras on Rainy Days* (Farrar, Straus & Giroux), chronicles a young Muslim-American woman's journey to freedom and was awarded the Prix Premier Roman Etranger 2005 Award (Best First Novel in Translation of the Year) by France, and was also chosen as the finalist for both the PEN/Hemingway Award in Fiction as well as the California Book Reviewers Award. *Poets & Writers* named *Madras* as one of the Top 5 Best Debut Novels of the Year. The novel has been translated into many different languages and released around the world. Samina is the recipient of the Rona Jaffe Foundation and Barbara Deming Memorial awards for fiction. She has written for publications as diverse as *Self* and *Child* magazines, the *New York Times,* and the *San Francisco Chronicle*. She resides in California with her son. Visit her online at www.saminaali.com.

KIMBERLEY ASKEW is a writer and avid blogger. She covers haute couture and the latest trends in pop culture for the Fashion Institute of Design & Merchandising. Her short stories have appeared in *SOMA Literary Review* and *Urge Magazine*. Askew's book reviews have appeared in *Elle* and been excerpted in the *New York Times*. After a three-year exile in Los Angeles, she returned to San Francisco, where she maintains two personal blogs, KimSaid.com and RomancingTheTome.blogspot.com, a commentary on literary adaptations.

JULIANNA BAGGOTT is the author of four novels, including bestseller *Girl Talk* and *Which Brings Me to You: A Novel in Confessions* cowritten with Steve Almond (April 2006), as well as a book of poems, *This Country of Mothers,* and a series of novels for younger readers, The Anybodies—www.theanybodies.com. Her work has appeared in such publications as *Best American Poetry, Glamour,* and *TriQuarterly,* as well as been read on *Here and Now* and *Talk of the Nation.* She teaches in the creative writing program at Florida State University. Julianna lives in Tallahassee with her husband, David G. W. Scott, and their three kids. Her website is www.juliannabaggott.com.

JENNIFER BAUMGARDNER is a Fargo-bred writer and activist living in New York City with her son, Skuli. She is the coauthor, with Amy Richards, of *Manifesta: Young Women, Feminism, and the Future* (Farrar, Straus & Giroux, 2000) and *Grassroots: A Field Guide to Feminist Activism* (Farrar, Straus & Giroux, 2005). Baumgardner writes for numerous venues including *Glamour, The Nation, Ms., Harper's,* and NPR's *All Things Considered.* In 2003, she created the I Had an Abortion project to reduce stigma around the procedure and, for that campaign, produced the film *Speak Out: I Had an Abortion* (with the director Gillian Aldrich). Her book on bisexuality, *Look Both Ways: Girls and Sex,* is due out in late 2006.

LILY BURANA is the author of two books: a memoir, *Strip City: A Stripper's Farewell Journey Across America,* and *Try,* a novel. Her journalism and criticism have appeared in the *Washington Post,* the *New York Times, GQ, Details, The Village Voice, Entertainment Weekly,* and many other publications. Visit her website at www.lilyburana.com.

VERONICA CHAMBERS is the author of the critically acclaimed memoir *Mama's Girl.* She has also written five books for children, most recently *Celia Cruz, Queen of Salsa,* and several books for adults, including a new novel, *Miss Black America.* She has contributed to several anthologies, including the best-selling *Bitch in the House,* edited by Cathi Hanauer. She has written and edited for national magazines for more than twelve years, including *Premiere,* the *New York Times Magazine,* and *Newsweek.* Veronica has been the recipient of several awards, such as the Hodder Fellowship for emerging novelists at Princeton University and a National Endowment for the Arts fiction award. She was born in Panama and grew up in Brooklyn. Veronica has written several episodes for UPN's hit show *Girlfriends.* She currently divides her time between Los Angeles and Tokyo. She is married to Jason Clampet, an architecture and travel writer. Her website is www.veronicachambers.com.

HEATHER CHAPLIN is the author of *Smartbomb: The Quest for Art, Entertainment and Big Bucks in the Global Videogame Industry,* an investigation of the business of the modern videogame industry and the culture it's created. Heather has been a business and culture writer for ten years, writing "The Reluctant Capitalist" column for

Salon.com, and the media critic column for *American Demographics.* Before leaving to write *Smartbomb,* she was a senior writer for *Fortune Small Business,* and is currently working on a book about American entrepreneurship. She continues to write about fashion, videogames, culture, and business from her home in Brooklyn, where she lives with her husband and two dogs. Heather's book website is www.smartbomb.us.

MEGHAN DAUM is the author of the popular essay collection *My Misspent Youth* and the critically acclaimed novel *The Quality of Life Report,* which was a *New York Times* notable book in 2003. Her articles and essays have appeared in numerous publications, including *The New Yorker, Harper's, GQ, Vogue, New York, Black Book,* the *Los Angeles Times* and the *New York Times Book Review.* She has contributed to NPR's *Morning Edition* and *This American Life,* and has been a visiting artist at the California Institute of the Arts. She lives in Los Angeles. Her website is www.meghandaum.com.

TANYA DONELLY is a founding member of three seminal recording groups, Throwing Muses, the Breeders, and Belly. The latter earned a Grammy nomination, a gold record, and the coveted front cover of *Rolling Stone* magazine. Living in the Boston area since the release of her first solo album, *Lovesongs for Underdogs,* Tanya and her husband, Dean Fisher, have raised their daughter, Gracie, now five. Tanya continues to tour internationally and release albums, the last two of which were *Beautysleep* and *Whiskey Tango Ghosts.* Visit her online at www.tanyadonelly.com.

ERIN ERGENBRIGHT is the coauthor of *The Ex-Boyfriend Cookbook,* with Thisbe Nissen. She is codirector of the Loggernaut reading series, and her writing has appeared or is forthcoming in *The Believer, Tin House, After: Parenting Fiction from America's Top Writers* (Overlook Press), *Colorado Review, Indiana Review,* the *Oregonian,* the *Portland Tribune,* and elsewhere. She lives in Portland, Oregon. Her website is www.erinergenbright.com.

LOUISE JARVIS FLYNN'S nonfiction has appeared in *Travel and Leisure, Elle, Glamour, Self, Marie Claire, Redbook,* and the *New York Times Book Review,* among other national publications. She lives with her husband, Sean Flynn, and son, Calvin, in Durham, North Carolina, where she is at work on a novel.

AYUN HALLIDAY is the sole staff member of the quarterly zine *The East Village Inky* and the author of *Job Hopper, No Touch Monkey!* and *The Big Rumpus: A Mother's Tale from the Trenches.* She is *Bust* magazine's Mother Superior columnist and also contributes to NPR, *Hipmama, Bitch, Utne,* and more anthologies than you can shake a stick at without dangling a participle. Ayun and her well-documented husband and children live in Brooklyn, where she's allegedly "hard at work" on *Dirty Sugar Cookies,* a food memoir to be published in the spring of 2006. Dare to be heinie and visit www.ayunhalliday.com.

HEATHER JUERGENSEN produced, cowrote, and starred in the hit indie film *Kissing Jessica Stein.* An accomplished writer, she has written screenplays or teleplays for Miramax, Warner Bros., ABC, VH-1, and CBS among others. Her work has been honored at the Chicago International Film

Festival, the Miami International Film Festival, and the Indie Spirit Awards. Her acting credits range from the dark independent character drama *Red Roses and Petrol* starring Malcolm McDowell to the family comedy *Haunted Mansion* starring Eddie Murphy. Most recently she wrote, directed, and starred in the short film *The Suzy Prophecy,* currently playing at film festivals. She lives in Los Angeles with her husband and two dogs. Visit her website at www.heatherjuergensen.com.

CARLA KIHLSTEDT, violinist, vocalist, and composer, studied violin at the Peabody Institute and the Oberlin Conservatory. She is a founding member of the groups Sleepytime Gorilla Museum, Tin Hat Trio, and 2 Foot Yard. She has performed in numerous contemporary music series, including New York's Music at the Anthology, and has written music for the Bang on a Can All-Stars. She has worked with John Zorn, Fred Frith, and with the ROVA Saxophone Quartet, and has contributed to recordings of Tom Waits, Ben Goldberg, and Mr. Bungle. Carla's band websites, which share equal billing in her life, include www. 2footyard.com, www.tinhat.org, and www.sleepytimegorillamuseum.com.

LAILA LALAMI was born in Rabat and educated in Morocco, Britain, and the United States. Her work has appeared in *Mizna, The Baltimore Review, First Intensity,* the *Los Angeles Times,* the *Los Angeles Review,* the *Independent,* and elsewhere. Her debut book of fiction, *Hope and Other Dangerous Pursuits,* was published by Algonquin Books in October 2005. She is also the editor of the popular literary blog Moorishgirl.com. She lives in Portland, Oregon. Her website is www.lailalalami.com.

IVY MEEROPOL is a writer and filmmaker. She directed and produced the film *Heir to an Execution* and has written for such publications as the *New York Times* and *O, The Oprah Magazine.* Ivy's screenplays include, with Mark Campbell, an adaptation of Dawn Powell's *The Happy Island* and, with Allison Anders, *Against the Wind.* Her six-part documentary series, *The Hill,* premieres in the fall of 2006. She lives in Brooklyn, New York, with her husband and son.

FLOR MORALES is a native of El Salvador. She immigrated to San Francisco in 1998. Flor joined the Marin Literacy Program in 2002. She runs her own housecleaning business and lives in northern California with her husband and two sons, Erick, twelve, and Jonathan, six.

DEB NORTON is a playwright, actress, and teacher. At American Conservatory Theater in San Francisco, she played roles in *1918, Babylon Gardens, Twelfth Night,* and more. She also spent several seasons with San Francisco's Encore Theater Company. Then after a six-year stint in New York City, where she was the unrivaled queen of off-off-off-off Broadway, she began writing to keep herself creatively alive. Recently she authored and starred in her first full-length play, *The Whole Banana,* in Los Angeles, where she garnered rave reviews and a movie option. Deb now lives, writes, and gardens in the mountains of Ojai, California. Her website is www.officialdebnorton.com.

MICHELLE RICHMOND is the author of the novels *Dream of the Blue Room* and *Ocean Beach* (forthcoming). Her collection of linked stories, *The Girl in the Fall-Away Dress,* follows four sisters as they leave their Gulf Coast childhood behind and venture into the world. Her stories, essays, and travel writing have appeared in many magazines and anthologies, including Salon.com, *Playboy, Glimmer Train,* and others. She lives with her husband and son in San Francisco, where she teaches creative writing and edits the online literary journal *Fiction Attic.* Michelle's personal website iswww.michelle richmond.com.

MARISA DE LOS SANTOS has published poems in many literary magazines, including *Poetry, The Antioch Review, Southwest Review,* and *Prairie Schooner,* and her collection *From the Bones Out* (University of South Carolina Press) appeared in the James Dickey Contemporary Poetry Series in 2000. Her first novel, *Love Walked In,* was published by Dutton in December 2005. The novel's foreign rights have been sold in eight countries and film rights were sold to Paramount Pictures. Marisa lives in Wilmington, Delaware, with her husband, David Teague, and their two young children. She's working on a second novel.

TANYA SHAFFER is the author of the book *Somebody's Heart Is Burning: A Woman Wanderer in Africa,* which was selected as one of the *San Francisco Chronicle*'s Best Books of 2003. She is an award-winning playwright and solo performer whose plays *Brigadista* and *Baby Taj* and solo shows *Miss America's Daughters* and *Let My Enemy Live Long!* (winner of a Bay Area Theatre Critics Circle Award for solo performance) have toured more than forty cities in the United States and Canada. Her stories have appeared on Salon.com and in numerous anthologies, as well as being translated into Italian and read on Australian National Radio. Visit her online at www .tanyashaffer.com.

DAO STROM is the author of *Grass Roof, Tin Roof.* She was born in Vietnam and grew up in northern California. She is a graduate of the Iowa Writers Workshop and has been the recipient of an NEA grant and a James Michener Fellowship, among other awards. Dao is also a singer-songwriter who released her debut album, *Send Me Home,* last year. Her second novel, *The Gentle Order of Girls and Boys,* is forthcoming from Counterpoint Press. Dao lives in Austin, Texas, with her son, Lincoln. Her website is www.daostrom.com.

AMANDA EYRE WARD is a novelist and short-story writer. Her first novel, *Sleep Toward Heaven,* was optioned by Sandra Bullock and Fortis Films. Her second novel, *How to Be Lost,* was optioned by Frank von Zerneck Films. *How to Be Lost* was released in paperback by Ballantine Books in October 2005. Amanda's short story "Motherhood and Terrorism" is included in the anthology *Stumbling and Raging: More Politically Inspired Fiction,* (MacAdam/Cage, January 2006). Amanda lives with her family on Cape Cod, Massachusetts. Visit her website at www.amandaward.com.

ASHLEY WARLICK is the author of three novels, *The Distance from the Heart of Things, The Summer After June,* and *Seek the Living.* She teaches in the M.F.A. Program at Queens University in Charlotte, North Carolina. She is at work on a new novel based on the life of M. F. K. Fisher. Ashley's website is www.ashley warlick.com.

JENNIFER WEINER made her debut with *Good in Bed,* the first of four novels that include *In Her Shoes,* now a major motion picture starring Cameron Diaz, Toni Collette, and Shirley MacLaine; *Little Earthquakes*; and *Goodnight Nobody.* She graduated from Princeton University and worked as a columnist for the *Philadelphia Inquirer.* Her work has also appeared in *Seventeen, Redbook, TV Guide, YM,* and Salon.com. She lives in Philadelphia with her husband and their daughter. Visit her online at www.jennifer weiner.com.

ERIN CRESSIDA WILSON is a writer and professor in the Program in Literary Arts at Brown University. She won the 2003 Independent Spirit Award for her screenplay, *Secretary,* starring James Spader and Maggie Gyllenhaal. She also wrote the film *Fur,* starring Nicole Kidman and Robert Downey Jr., directed by Steven Shainberg. Her twenty plays have been produced regionally, off-Broadway, and abroad. She coauthored *The Erotica Project* with Lillian Ann Slugocki, produced at Joe's Pub and published by Cleis Press. She is a graduate of Smith College.

SARA WOSTER has exhibited her painting and animation in New York, Japan, London, and Amsterdam and was the cofounder of the Brooklyn gallery Aaron America. She also creates quilts and T-shirts that are so overpriced that her psarents ask her if she's kidding when she tells them how much they sell for. Her first novel, *Survival Skills,* has been optioned for a movie while her second book, a love letter to her grandmother titled *My Grandma Is Insane in Her Head,* is just getting started. She breaks up the monotony of living in New York with frequent trips to the Midwest. Visit her online at www.sarawoster.com.

ACKNOWLEDGMENTS

I owe a great debt of gratitude to Julianna Baggott for encouraging me from the beginning. You are a wondrous force and I thank you. My eternal love and respect to my dear friend and coconspirator Kimberley Askew. Your constant assurance and steadfast support have seen me through so much. My sister-in-law, Ginette Warwick King, also proved a faithful editor, offering notes and advice. I would like to thank my family, Richesin, Burlingame, and Warwick among them, for whom I have the utmost love and devotion.

I have been very fortunate to have a remarkable agent to see me through this process, who, as she put it, "does not give up very easily." Thank you, Jennifer Carlson, for your enormous support and guidance. My thanks to Rolph Blythe and Henry Dunow as well. Sara Carder, my brilliant editor, believed in the book and made every effort to create the best collection possible. She proved an invaluable resource for me and shepherded the work so carefully. Thank you for the extended deadlines, especially during my pregnancy. My thanks to Kat Kimball for helping us get it all together. A big thank-you to Laurin Lucaire and Amanda Dewey for designing our gorgeous May Queen cover and book, respectively. I would also like to express my gratitude to my husband, Joel Warwick, who offered delicious dinners and editorial guidance during many late-night hours, and daughter, Lily, for their on-going love and support. You are home to me.

Thank you also to the many women whose writing was submitted for publication but could not be included.

Finally, for their beautiful words, enthusiasm, and willingness to share their private selves and lives, I thank the contributors who created *The May Queen*. It has been my great pleasure and privilege to work with and come to know this incredible group of women.

CREDITS AND PERMISSIONS

PHOTOS

Samina Ali: by Suzette Stephens

Kimberley Askew: by Chris Askew

Julianna Baggott: by David G. W. Scott

Jennifer Baumgardner: © Ali Price

Lily Burana: © Chris Carroll

Veronica Chambers: © Anna Williams

Heather Chaplin: © June Chaplin

Meghan Daum: © Alix Lambert

Tanya Donelly: © Dana Tynan

Erin Ergenbright: © Robert M. Reynolds

Louise Jarvis Flynn: Ron Pruitt

Ayun Halliday: © DA Photography

Heather Juergensen: © Vincent Versace

Carla Kihlstedt: © Merri Cyr

Laila Lalami: by Alexander Year

Ivy Meeropol: by Thomas Ambrose

Flor Morales: by Andrea N. Richesin

Deb Norton: © Salena Dews

Andrea Richesin: © Joel Warwick

Michelle Richmond: © Misty Richmond

Marisa de los Santos: © Luigi Ciufetelli

Tanya Shaffer: © Vincent Versace

Dao Strom: © Denise Prince Martin

Amanda Eyre Ward: © John Foley

Ashley Warlick: © Piper Warlick

Jennifer Weiner: © Andrea Cipriani

Erin Cressida Wilson: by John Mackenzie

Sara Woster: by Kate Engelbrecht

ABOUT THE EDITOR

 ANDREA N. RICHESIN grew up in a hamlet in the foothills of eastern Tennessee. She has worked in book and magazine publishing and advertising with Rapid Science Publishers in London, at *Red Herring* and *Edutopia* magazines, and McCann-Erickson in San Francisco. She lives in northern California with her husband, Joel Warwick, and their daughter, Lily. Visit her online at www.themayqueenbook.com.